T0354864

God reminded us that we will have troubles in our lives. Yet it is difficult to know how to use all the brokenness from those troubles to become better. Paula leads her readers through a course of Bible stories and scripture, helping them better understand their own stories and truths about who they are in Christ. The workbook format provides daily lessons for reflection and direction. Paula's own journey through a broken marriage creates vulnerability and believability in this course!

Debbie Laaser, MA, LMFT,
author of Shattered Vows and
From Trauma to Transformation

People recovering and moving beyond a painful past need a compassionate voice and gentle guidance for the journey. Beautifully Broken provides a biblically based and Christ-centered road map to help individuals or groups on a journey of healing and hope.

Jennifer Ellers, MA,
Christian counselor, life coach, and author

In Beautifully Broken, Paula writes from her own experience, her heart, and years of supporting broken people. The book is strongly biblically based and provides a faith-based foundation for the healing journey. Essential topics, such as facing difficult truths about one's own family dysfunction, shame, and finding one's personal identity in the power and safety of God, are addressed. Thank you, Paula, for giving a hurting world a biblically based foundation for finding hope and healing in the present as well as keeping us grounded in scripture as our healing journey continues.

Tim Barber, MA, MDiv, DMin

Beautifully Broken

from broken past to golden path

PAULA FRENCH

WESTBOW
PRESS®
A DIVISION OF THOMAS NELSON
& ZONDERVAN

WestBow Press books may be ordered through booksellers or by contacting:

WestBow Press
A Division of Thomas Nelson & Zondervan
1663 Liberty Drive
Bloomington, IN 47403
www.westbowpress.com
844-714-3454

ISBN: 978-1-6642-8988-8 (sc)
ISBN: 978-1-6642-8989-5 (hc)
ISBN: 978-1-6642-8990-1 (e)

Library of Congress Control Number: 2023911270

Print information available on the last page.

WestBow Press rev. date: 07/12/2023

This book is respectfully dedicated to the many volunteers of the Center for Women's Ministries who offer hope and healing to the hurting. Your devotion to help women heal their past and your determination to be excellent counselors is inspiring. God uses you in amazing ways to bring women from being broken to more valuable than gold.

Contents

Acknowledgments...ix

Introduction...xi

Chapter 1   Let's Get Started! 1

Chapter 2   No One Wants to Hear Their Family Was
             Dysfunctional 25

Chapter 3   Instructions for Proper Attachment............................. 51

Chapter 4   Ain't It a Shame! 82

Chapter 5   No Suffering for Me, Please............................111

Chapter 6   Let the Healing Flow!................................. 143

Chapter 7   Living in the Truth....................................174

Chapter 8   Making All Things New Ain't Easy 201

Chapter 9   Forgiveness 237

Chapter 10   Finding Purpose 270

Conclusion.. 307

Appendix A Group Leader Notes 309

Appendix B Agreements...319

Notes 321

Acknowledgments

Thank you to WestBow Press for accepting this project and publishing this book. Thank you also to Stanley Robertson, who met with me every month for a year, giving me wisdom and accountability in writing nearly every chapter. I am also very grateful for Jared Austin, whose knowledge and edits accelerated the writing process by weeks and made the manuscript so much better. Thank you.

Thank you, Deb Laaser and Jennifer Ellers, for your support for this book and for me. You each were an important part of my own healing, and I respect you both so much! I deeply appreciate your endorsement. Thank you also to Dr. Tim Barber, someone I admire greatly and whose work I highly respect.

My most heartfelt thanks go to my girls, who have listened to my frustrations and doubts and have been my biggest cheerleaders. You are each intelligent, honest, and wise in different and complementary ways, and I couldn't live without your feedback and friendship. I love you so much; you are the reason this dream has finally been accomplished.

Lastly and most importantly, I thank God, who is my faithful covering. You did not ask me to write this book, but You allowed me and helped me push through. I would ask for Your blessing and Your healing on every person who reads this, every group that journeys through it, and every center that adopts it—for Your glory.

Introduction

Welcome to this ten-week experience of making peace with your past. I am glad you have decided to take time to evaluate your life—where you have been, where you are now, and where you are heading. Many people live their entire lives going down whatever road is before them, never knowing where it will lead them. They cannot tell you how they got to where they are now, and they certainly do not know how to successfully get to the end. Many of us can see behind us the brokenness from the choices we have made and choices that were made for us. Thankfully, our lives are not seen by God as blocked and broken roadways but carefully designed spans of time lovingly planned from birth to death by a sovereign God and Heavenly Father—a more perfect Father than any of us here could have known. And while He is indeed the sovereign designer of our lives, He is also a Father so loving; His desire is simply for us to know Him. He will not force us down a specific path. Yet there is no halt or turn, no shock or surprise on our journey He is not aware of. There is no event or circumstance He is not already there waiting for us to choose the direction that leads toward Him. There is also no part of the path we have already traveled He cannot heal and redeem.

Many of us are unaware how the path behind us has led to where we are today. Perhaps we are so busy with today's decisions we have never taken the time to look back. Perhaps we are too afraid to look back or have determined never to do so. Others may have already spent countless hours, weeks, or even years seeking help for the consequences of the past. I do not believe those efforts were in vain. Some healing requires more time and many more steps. Thank God for the healing you have already received! One thing I know for sure is God does not do a halfway job at anything. He left no detail undone in creating this incredible world or our incredible minds and bodies. Our minds and bodies have been studied for centuries, and we are still learning how they work! Jesus did not halfway bring Lazarus back from the dead (John 11:1–44), nor did He halfway heal the blind man (John 9:1–11). Whatever healing He has begun in you, He will continue to completion. There is no brokenness He will not make whole, as long as we continue following the path and choosing His leading at every turn.

It is true that some healing will be completed to perfection when life here is over. But consider the apostle Paul begged God three times to remove an infirmity he struggled with, and did he receive healing? God's answer to him was sufficient grace and strength in his weakness (2 Corinthians 12:8–11). While Paul's earthly healing was different from what he had asked for, there surely must have been a tremendous healing. He no longer felt like a victim of this infirmity. He no longer let it hold him back. He no longer felt defeated because of it. In fact, he was able to boast about how God's strength was there for him. He boasted about it gladly, and he delighted in this weakness that in effect made him stronger than without it! Only someone who is on the path daily with an affliction given to God at every turn can understand this kind of healing. Whatever path has led you here, I assure you there is healing for you.

When my marriage ended after thirty-nine years, I was completely crushed and heartbroken. I felt betrayed and abandoned by God, not only because I had tried to live a God-honoring life and had prayed earnestly and desperately for God to save my marriage but also because He knew this was going to happen. I remember sitting in my red chair weeping bitter, angry tears while crying out, "You *knew* this was going to happen! You *knew* when we said our vows this was going to happen! And you *knew* every anniversary we celebrated how many we had left! *Why did you let me fall so in love if you knew I was going to lose him after all this time?*"

In his book *The Red Sea Rules*, Robert Morgan shares ten "rules," or principles, God showed him in Exodus 14 for how to handle life's difficulties and times of crisis. Red Sea Rule number 1 says, "Realize that God means for you to be where you are."[1] This was difficult for me to understand in my time of crisis. It felt cruel and uncaring. Life always feels cruel and uncaring when things don't go our way. But everything that happens in this life, whether by human choice or natural causes, happens because God either allows it or causes it. And whether it is by God's permissive will or His design, whatever you are facing on life's pathway is an opportunity for you to head in the direction of the One who knows the way forward. He means for you to be where you are, and I believe He means for you to be here, beginning this journey of healing your past.

In the Japanese culture, there is an artform known as *kintsugi*. Historians attribute its beginnings to a fifteenth-century shogun who, being displeased with an unsightly repair, was searching for a more aesthetically pleasing way to mend a precious piece of pottery. Instead of trying to hide the cracks of the broken piece, an artisan decided to highlight them using a lacquer or epoxy dusted with gold. The result was more beautiful than the original yet still honored the imperfect history of the piece.[2] Kintsugi is a perfect metaphor for the brokenness of our pasts, our journey of healing, and the beautiful result only God can achieve. We are not denying the mistakes or experiences of the past; we are inviting our masterful Creator to make something beautiful of all the pieces.

In these ten weeks, I encourage you to participate as part of a group. Certainly, God can heal someone working through this alone, but group interaction offers great value. Groups can make us feel either safe or exposed. If you are one who tends to isolate, know you will gain much insight from choosing to stretch yourself and be vulnerable before others. Speaking aloud helps process our thoughts, affirms truths, and allows others to speak into any faulty thinking. On the other hand, there can also be safety in numbers. It can be comforting to discover others have similar woundings and experiences. In addition, group experiences allow us to give and receive emotional support, empathy, recognition, and affirmation for circumstances not in our control or grace for mistakes we have made. Overall, there is a bonding that occurs when we are accepted for who we are, no matter what we've been through or what we've done.

Being part of a group is also a responsibility. You are committing to other people's processes—to be there for them as part of their healing journey. And you are trusting them to do the same for you. The most foundational aspect of any relationship is trust. Especially where damaged emotions are concerned, trustworthiness is essential for healing to occur. Healing in a group is no different. To build trust among the group members, certain agreements must be followed. There will be an agreement you will be asked to make with yourself and an agreement between the members of the group.

This book is arranged in a ten-week format. Your group leader may certainly choose to spread the material out longer than ten weeks, but it is not advised to spend fewer than ten weeks. Each week will provide five daily reading assignments for you to think about and answer. Each daily assignment will begin with one or more scripture passages for you to read along with a discussion that follows about the passage that will tie into that day's lesson. This will help ground you in the truths you are learning. There will also be a suggestion of prayer. These are prompts for you to pray on your own. I encourage you to pray them in your own words, making them personal between you and God. The next section will be the teaching portion of the day, followed by questions for you to answer. I encourage you to highlight concepts or sentences in the daily lessons and record in the margins any thoughts you have. Your group will discuss each day's lesson along with the questions at each day's end. This is where you will benefit from sharing your answers with each other. You will, no doubt, receive valuable feedback as well as find you are not alone in your opinions and experiences.

The most important part of every session will be the time you spend in prayer individually and as a group. God is the great Creator and the great Healer. He made you and has been with you on every step of your journey. He alone knows what healing you need. And He is trustworthy! Inviting Him to continue to lead you is the first step toward complete healing. And it is a correct turn on the path! Congratulations! And welcome!

Chapter 1

Let's Get Started!

Day 1

Read: 1 Peter 5:7

In this instructional book by Peter to scattered new believers, Peter knows these new Christians are facing difficult circumstances. They are under harsh Roman rule, and some are being unfairly and severely persecuted. Yet he continues to give them instructions on how to live, despite being persecuted.

This week, we will venture down the path of difficulty, much like these early believers. We will begin to look at times where life did not go so well for us. Perhaps these are times you are experiencing right now. We will also look at how we handle these circumstances—what behaviors we use to cope when life feels out of control for us. Finally, we will compare this to the abundant life Christ promised and invite Him into this path of healing on which we are about to travel.

Throughout this process and all along this journey, Peter's words to us will be valuable at every turn. There may be uncomfortable moments or times of fear or doubt. But we can be assured God is traveling with us every step of the way. His loving compassion is surrounding us. Whatever you are feeling now, as we begin, and at every turn, "Cast all your anxiety on Him, because He cares for you"!

Prayer for Today

Thank God for His compassion toward you in times of trouble. Thank Him for receiving the cares you lay on Him, and ask Him to remind you He is there waiting to take them.

What Brought You Here?

Many of us go through our lives maintaining the status quo in our relationships, our jobs, our health, our finances, and the everyday working of our families. Day after day, week after week, month after month, things keep working, until they don't. There's a rift in the marriage or an accident, we lose our jobs, we receive a cancer diagnosis, we can no longer pay our bills, our aging parents need twenty-four-hour care, or a host of other roadblocks cause life as normal to screech to a halt. Suddenly, life as we know it is no longer working for us.

At first, we may try to handle the changes or the crisis as best we can, putting one foot in front of the other to make it through the day. Eventually, no matter how hard we try, we realize we are struggling to manage. We may be flooded with emotions, becoming angry and lashing out at people we love, or we may be spending most of the day crying or barely getting out of bed. Perhaps we are forgetting important appointments or are having difficulty concentrating at work. Maybe we are drinking or eating too much or not enough. We may be isolating from normal activities or people, including God. We may be finding no matter how long or how often or how earnestly we pray, God seems nowhere, so eventually we may pull away and quit praying altogether, doubting He cares about what we are going through.

For others, there may be no crisis, but life just seems to stop working. There is no joy or passion, and it feels like we are going through the motions year after year with no end in sight. It is typically at these places in life, whether experiencing a crisis or feeling stuck, when we begin to think about getting help from a counselor, pastor, support group, or trusted friend. Perhaps someone who cares about you has suggested one of those options or has told you about this study. In the space below, write your honest feelings about where your life is now.

What brought you here?

_____

_____

_____

_____

What is working well in your life right now?

_____

_____

_____

_____

What is not working in your life right now, or how are you stuck?

_____

_____

_____

_____

Recall your memory verse for the week, 1 Peter 5:7. "Cast all your anxiety on Him because He cares for you." Although seeing in writing what is not working in your life right now might bring up some uncomfortable emotions, you can give those anxieties to Jesus. You are courageous to begin this journey, and healing awaits. Just remember you probably had the same problems yesterday. The difference is now they are on paper before you. That is the first step toward healing. Acknowledging the issue is a big step you can feel good about. Tell God you are counting on His care for you.

Day 2

Read: Job 1:13–19

Few of us can relate to the intense and prolonged suffering of Job. But perhaps we can understand his concern for his children. There is nothing I love more than when my girls' families are all together having fun. To be sure, I like being there as well, but even if I'm not, there is something that makes me happy knowing they are choosing to be together. Job's adult children were accustomed to partying together too. Job surely felt blessed to have his children living near him. The news he received while they were all together was devastating. But notice he receives a second round of bad news before the first messenger is done delivering the first bad news! And this happens four times in the same conversation! How can he bear to hear all this tragic news? And we learn later his suffering is not over yet! Losing home, livelihood, health, and family seems unbearable. It helps put our times of suffering in perspective. Perhaps some of you have suffered almost as extensively as Job. Many more of us have not suffered as severely. Yet suffering is relative.

We know from the prologue to this story in the Bible that God thought highly of Job. While God did protect Job from death, He allowed Job to handle his crises however he saw fit. Job mourned and wept and used many ways to cope, including prayer, questioning, and the support and help of friends. He plummeted to the depths of despair, even wishing to die! Yet in the end, he proved courageous and victorious in his struggle. We each have different tolerances for pain, different thresholds of suffering, and different capacities for bearing up under stress. One person might be able to handle well what might cause another person to feel hopeless and depressed. Many factors affect how well we manage life. Yet what seems to be an important factor is a person's own evaluation for how manageable or hopeless life is.

Prayer for Today

Thank God for His presence in your life during times of suffering. Thank Him that He understands suffering, and ask Him to teach you new truths as you examine your suffering.

How Do You Cope?

Trudi and Kate were both young moms who lost their husbands to cancer. Kate was an attorney, and with her husband's substantial life insurance policy, she had no fears about the financial future of her family. Additionally, her parents, sister, and brother all lived in town and were happy to help with the children when necessary.

Trudi, previously a stay-at-home mom, was eventually forced to go to work as her husband's insurance barely covered his medical expenses. Her family was several hours away, which left her to find professional childcare.

Both grieving moms had every reason to feel despondent in the face of such circumstances. And one might argue Trudi even more so as her resources appeared less than Kate's. Neither woman, however, was despondent. While Kate's resources of financial security and nearby family support were more concrete, Trudi's resources of self-worth and emotional maturity allowed her to manage her difficult circumstances with grace and courage. Both women experienced a life-changing event no one would blame them for calling unbearable. Yet both women were able to draw on resources and life skills that would aid them in managing their difficult life paths.

Now consider a third case, Victoria, who was also a stay-at-home mom and widow from the death of her husband, Rick. Nervous about relying on less income, she decided to work part-time, which also served to keep her mind from focusing on her grief. Her sister's family lived in the same school district, so carpooling and afterschool care were not problems. Victoria's part-time job soon became a full-time position with occasional travel, which she liked because it gave her more money, and the excitement of travel kept her from incessantly thinking about Rick. Since taking the full-time position, her exposure to community events led her to volunteer to chair two large charity fundraisers, one in the spring and one in the fall. When her sister pointed out she had gone from a stay-at-home mom to barely seeing the kids because of her work, Victoria hired a live-in nanny to avoid her sister's criticism.

All three women handled stressful situations the best they could. Each also may face difficulties in the future because of their initial loss. One, however, has a higher risk for those difficulties because of the unhealthy way she dealt with her grief. Victoria thought keeping herself busy and away from the house helped her in her grief because she thought less about losing her husband. Her way of coping with her problem of missing Rick was to work and work more. What she thought was dealing with her grief was, in fact, ignoring it. Throwing herself into her work and out of her house also left her children alone to grieve their father. In a sense, they had lost both parents. By not dealing with such a huge loss in a healthy way, what issues might Victoria also face in the future?

_____

_____

_____

_____

Before we criticize Victoria for how she dealt with her loss, this is not a study of what not to do after the death of a spouse. Rather, the point of the exercise is to recognize Victoria was indeed coping the best way she could at that time, and she was taking steps to carry her life forward instead of allowing herself to wallow in self-pity and become depressed.

When Victoria first entered counseling, she was seeking help to deal with her oldest son, now sixteen, who was failing classes in school and spending time with "the wrong crowd." In time, she realized her coping had left big holes in her parenting, which was now showing consequences in her son's behavior. She moved her mother in with them from out of state to help with the children, let the nanny go, resigned from all her outside volunteer positions, and built a home office where she could occasionally work from home. Having her family closer and spending time with them allowed them all to grieve their incredible loss together, which helped her son's behavior as well.

In discussing how she chose to cope with her loss, Victoria admitted she had lost her father in a work-related accident when she was in elementary school. She remembered her mother stayed in bed for what seemed like years while Victoria's older sisters took care of the home. When her own husband died, she had new compassion for her mother's loss but determined she would not lock herself away from her children in depression like her mother had done. Sadly, doing the opposite of what her mother did produced similar results. Both choices were unhealthy ways to cope with similar loss, although both women did the best they could at the time.

Coping can be defined as a response to stressful life events and daily hassles that attempt to diminish the accompanying physical, emotional, or psychological burden. In other words, whatever we do to relieve the burden stress brings upon us is coping.[1] These relief responses may have varying degrees of effectiveness. Some may be effective in the short term but ineffective in the long term, or they may be effective or ineffective in both the short and long terms. We can also differentiate between problem-focused coping and emotion-focused coping.[2] For example, problem-focused coping would be making changes to better deal with stressful life events such as changing jobs to be closer to aging parents. Emotion-focused coping would be marrying immediately after a divorce just to provide a father figure in the home before proper growth of the relationship or allowing the children to grieve.

In Victoria's case, can you see her actions may have begun as problem-focused coping because she was solving the problem of needing supplemental finances since her husband's death? Unfortunately, her efforts for emotion-focused coping were misguided, rooted in issues of the past, and proved ineffective to her healing. In addition, they brought with them more problems.

We can name almost as many coping strategies to deal with life as there are people. Some strategies may be healthy and effective for one person, but the same behavior may be unhealthy or ineffective for someone else. For example, we might label the following behaviors as completely healthy: prayer, faith, counseling, medical help, or relying on previously successful strategies. But what happens when any of these are relied on to the exclusion of anything else and permitted to become the sole focus of one's life?

Consider also the woman who saw her doctor for headaches following an auto accident. After many tests concluded no brain trauma or serious head injury, she began to fixate on what the tests may have missed and developed anxiety over this, seeing her doctor again and again for a myriad of different symptoms. This continued for years with no medical diagnosis. Seeking medical help seemed like a healthy thing to do, but for her, it became unhealthy.

Or consider the young pastor who received a diagnosis of treatable cancer. He refused further treatment, saying he chose instead to rely solely on his faith as the tumor grew and grew. While his choice can be controversial in religious circles, the simple facts might suggest while relying solely on faith could certainly be effective in one person's case, relying only on one possible solution, in his case, was not.

The lesson here is we cannot list coping strategies or behaviors as only healthy or unhealthy by themselves. They must be viewed in terms of whether they prove effective in each case. We must ask whether they alleviate the stress and trauma or they add to it by creating additional problems.

How many other coping strategies can you name for difficult or unbearable circumstances?

_____

_____

_____

_____

Recall Trudi and Kate were both able to effectively deal with their loss, while Victoria spent several years ineffectively dealing with a similar loss. Earlier we said that *one person might be able to handle well what might cause another person to feel hopeless and depressed. Many factors affect how well we manage life. Yet what seems to be an important factor is a person's own evaluation for how manageable or hopeless life is.* Victoria's past included an experience that negatively affected her choices in the present. Her family of origin played a significant role in her thinking and her choices, as no doubt did Trudi and Kate's as well. We are not privy to family-of-origin factors for Trudi and Kate as they only attended grief support groups, whereas Victoria received individual counseling where her past was discussed. It would be helpful to know whether factors, such as effective parental modeling, strong family support, or other strengths, affected Trudi and Kate's self-worth or their ability to cope. Often our coping mechanisms and skills may come from family behaviors, patterns, and teachings. These may include both effective and ineffective ways of coping. Many people rely on faith and prayer in difficult times. Others may have a strong sense of competence or perseverance. Still others may turn to diversions, such as shopping, eating, drinking, drugs, denial, or ignoring to get through tough times.

By now you may be thinking about a difficult situation you have dealt with in your own life and evaluating how you handled it. Remember many factors affect how well we manage life, of which our family of origin is only one, albeit a powerful one. As we begin to think about these difficult times in life, let's agree not to compare our difficulties or our coping behaviors and to deal with ourselves and others as Christ would, without judgment or criticism. Remember these beautiful words from Romans 8:1: "There is therefore now, no condemnation for those who are in Christ Jesus." Whatever we have been through or whatever we did to cope does not need to define us, nor do we need to feel condemned or shame over it. There is healing. Like Victoria, you can always choose a different path!

Part of healing requires us to acknowledge our stories. We cannot heal that which we continue to bury or never talk about. Perhaps there is more than one time where life became difficult or felt unmanageable. Perhaps your entire life has felt unmanageable. That's OK. You have done the best you could and are here now to find healing.

We will go into more detail later in the book about why it is necessary to talk about our stories, but for now, write what you can. Write what you feel comfortable sharing.

Tell about a time when you felt your life became unmanageable or extremely difficult to deal with.

_____

_____

_____

_____

What behaviors did you use to cope with that difficult situation?

_____

_____

_____

_____

Which behaviors were beneficial to your healing, and which were not? Did any result in more problems? Explain.

_____

_____

_____

_____

Day 3

Read: Genesis 12:10–13, Genesis 26:1–9, and Genesis 27:19–29

Often when we look at how we deal with a crisis or a difficult situation, we can recall times in our upbringing where our parents, and maybe even our grandparents, coped in similar ways. In our scripture readings today, we look at portions of the stories of Abraham, Isaac, and Jacob, God's chosen forefathers of the people through whom God would send the long-awaited Messiah. God would bless them down through the generations, not because they were perfectly obedient men (clearly, they were not) but because God made a promise, and He always keeps His promises. But other things, besides blessings, would also pass from one generation to the next.

During a time of famine, Abraham took his wife and fled to Egypt, where he became fearful for his life. He plotted to lie and present Sara as his sister instead of his wife. His plan worked for a while as Pharaoh took Sarai into his harem and treated Abraham well for her sake.

Later we see the exact same scene played out with his son, Isaac, who also feared for his life during a famine and used his wife, Rebekah, as his sister. Our third reading shows Isaac's son, Jacob, also devising a deceitful plan to lie to his dying father, pretending to be his older brother so he would receive the paternal blessing reserved for firstborn sons. In times of stress and fear, this family did whatever it took to control outcomes in their favor. They coped by using deceit, lying, and manipulation.

We are not discussing all the cultural and spiritual lessons of these stories, of which there are many. We are, however, pointing out one pattern of lying, deceit, and manipulation this family used when things got hard, instead of facing the situation head-on with truth and honesty. This way of coping was not something that was *taught* from generation to generation but rather *caught*.

Prayer for Today

Thank God for the scriptures and all the stories in the Bible from which we can learn so much. Ask Him to open your mind throughout these ten weeks to family patterns and dynamics He wants to heal and cycles He may want to break.

Your Family Portrait

In the field of psychology, when families are studied, researchers and counselors often use a genogram. A genogram is like a family tree, but one that can be used to show relationships, strengths, vulnerabilities, traits, and other information that might reveal patterns between generations.[3] If we were to imagine Jacob's genogram as a study for how his family handled difficult times (like famine and the near death of a parent), we could see a pattern of lying passed on from generation to generation. A simple genogram for Jacob might look something like this:

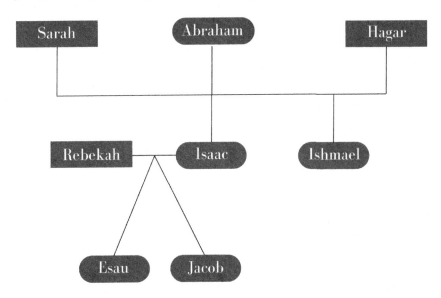

So much can be done with this simple genogram. We could use it to show strained or favored relationships or in our case behavioral patterns within the family and between generations. If we added a jagged line to identify the deceitful behavior between family members, Jacob's genogram would look like this:

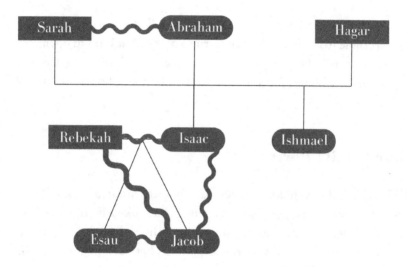

Using Jacob's simple genogram as an example, *draw a diagram of your family of origin*. You may include your grandparents if you like. You may also include your spouse(s) and your children, especially if they are grown. Use a rectangle for male family members and a circle for female members. If you did not grow up in your parents' home, please still include them, but also include whoever your parental figures were. This may be grandparents, aunts or uncles, a step or foster family, or perhaps your parental figures in an orphanage. Include the people you consider your family of origin. Your genogram will make sense to you.

Yesterday we talked about coping behaviors you may have used during a difficult time in your life. Perhaps you became depressed and shut down or isolated, or maybe you used emotional eating or drinking or another substance. You may have worked harder or more hours or tried to sleep away the pain or trouble. Perhaps you used denial to shove down your emotions and carried on as though nothing were happening. Or you may have wisely used healthy behaviors of coping. Whatever coping behaviors you used during stressful times, think about who those behaviors may have affected. Did your children suffer because they were not getting the parent they were used to or should have had? Did your relationship with your parents or in-laws suffer because of your behavior? Were you and your spouse able to make the adjustments necessary to get through the trying time?

Much like we did the red squiggly line for the deceit and lying on Jacob's genogram, *go back and draw a similar line between you and anyone in your family your behavior may have affected.*

Now think about the family you had growing up. Try to recall a time then when life was difficult. Perhaps a parent was hospitalized or injured. Maybe there was a serious illness, a death in the family, a job loss, or an addiction or legal issue. Did you notice any behaviors that were likely coping behaviors your parents or grandparents used?

Make a list of any behaviors you believe your parents or grandparents may have used to cope with difficult times and who may have been affected by their behavior.

_____

_____

_____

_____

Now go back to your genogram and draw another squiggly line between your parents' or grandparents' behavior and family members who may have been affected by the way they coped with difficult events.

You may or may not see similar or identical ways of coping between family members. Like our earlier story of Victoria, sometimes family members, hurt by how a parent coped, determine never to do the same thing. A parent who abuses alcohol or becomes an alcoholic may have a child who vows never to drink a drop of alcohol but may turn to out-of-control eating, spending, rage, or depression. The behaviors may be the same, or they may be completely different, but the coping strategies may still be unhealthy. They will remain unhealthy and can pass from generation to generation until they are acknowledged, they are evaluated, and the work to change is done.

Did you notice any *patterns* of coping behaviors in your family of origin? If so, what did you notice? What, if anything, surprised you?

_____

_____

_____

_____

Day 4

Read: John 10:9–10

Abundant life! The very thought of it brings images of overflowing bank accounts, blissful relationships, vacation homes, good weather, and convertible sports cars! Of course, those images are not what Jesus had in mind when He made this statement. In this chapter of John, Jesus refers to Himself as the door through whom we enter to find safety and freedom within the secure confines of the sheepfold. He also refers to Himself as the shepherd who cares for the sheep, watching over them and protecting them. Imagine the life sheep would have if left alone in the wild where predators and thieves would steal, kill, and destroy. They would be never resting, always hiding, fearful, and vulnerable. And that's if they weren't mauled and killed! Now compare that to the life the sheep have whose shepherd is Jesus. Because this strong, attentive shepherd would lay down his own life to protect his sheep, these sheep freely enjoy the lush green pastures without a care in the world. They thrive in living to the fullest!

This is not always the life we feel we are living, but it is the life Christ intends for us: safety, freedom, and thriving. That is abundant life. It does not mean the absence of predators or situations that seek to destroy us. It means resting safely in the care of the good shepherd, knowing He is strong and attentive and will protect and provide in the midst of trouble. Sometimes I picture myself as the sheep who has wandered to the far end of the sheepfold, hidden behind the rocks. I have wandered beyond being able to hear the Shepherd's soft, gentle voice, and I begin to think I am lost and He is no longer speaking. But the truth is I am still within the safety of the sheepfold. And He knows exactly where I am. His watchful eye saw me move farther and farther away. And He is still speaking. I need only to move closer to hear Him.

Prayer for Today

Thank God for His watchful care and protection as our
good shepherd. Acknowledge any times you may not have
thought of Him as good or protective. Ask Him to show
you throughout this study what it means to have abundant
life.

This Is Abundant Life?

There are times in our lives when we question God's goodness. There
are times we doubt, or at least wonder about, His protection. And there
are certainly times we would say the life we are living is anything but
abundant! Isaiah 55:8–9 says,

> "For my thoughts are not your thoughts, neither are your
> ways my ways," declares the Lord. "As the heavens are
> higher than the earth, so are my ways higher than your
> ways and my thoughts than your thoughts."

We cannot possibly know how God thinks or why God does what He
does. His thoughts and actions are different from ours. In fact, so different
are our thoughts and actions from His that the difference is as huge as
the distance between heaven and earth! That is light-years apart. I try to
remember it is a good thing I cannot completely figure God out. If He
were someone I could completely understand and figure out and know
what and why He was going to do something, if my small mind could
know that, He wouldn't be an all-wise or powerful God. Truly His ways
and thoughts are not our own. That is why God gives us His Word and
the gift of prayer. Scripture is full of truths and promises we can stand on
when life gets tough. There is the communion we can have with Him
during those times where we can come to know Him and His love for us.

Jesus's own words in John 10 were, "I have come that they might have life
and have it abundantly." No matter what life throws at us, His will is for
abundant life. That is something to stand on. That is a promise to count on.

Having read today's scripture discussion about abundant life, how has your definition of abundant life changed?

_____

_____

_____

_____

Would you say you were living the abundant life right now? Why or why not?

_____

_____

_____

_____

What would be different if yours was an abundant life?

_____

_____

_____

_____

Day 5

Read: Matthew 6:9–10

At a recent conference, I attended an early session to hear a pastor speak on "the good news."[3] I had always thought of the good news as being the Gospel, the story of Christ dying for my sins—the news I am supposed to proclaim so people will believe and we can all make it into God's kingdom for eternity. Instead, this pastor suggested a different take on the good news based on the prayer Jesus taught His disciples in Matthew 6.

He suggested we are all little kingdoms walking around possessing and protecting those things under our own dominion. There are kingdoms of our private possessions, our families (and there are often various "rulers" there), and kingdoms of cultures, cities, countries, and so on. These kingdoms do not always operate smoothly. In fact, our earthly kingdoms right now are a big mess!

But there is also a heavenly kingdom where God is in charge. What He says goes, and His will is always done without hesitation or question. The saints and angels are constantly doing His bidding, and it is splendid! But God's kingdom is also here, around us now! God's kingdom entered this world when Immanuel (God with us), Jesus, "the kingdom-bearer" [4] came to earth, and when we accept Him as Savior, the Spirit enables us to spread His kingdom here on earth. May your kingdom come here on this earth and your will be done here just like it is done in heaven. So God's celestial kingdom is actually down here every time we repay good for evil, every time we sacrifice financially so others can hear, every time a husband or wife humbles themselves before God to save their marriage, or every other time God's will is done. Every time we act in Christlike ways and bring His kingdom to earth, the kingdom of God breaks into all the messed-up kingdoms here in our messed-up world. That is the good news! It includes the good news of the cross, yes. But not just so we will all go to heaven someday. The good news, including the cross, is God's plan to restore and renew and set all things right again—back to His will being done everywhere, all day, and every day for eternity. His kingdom restored. And He will not bend my will just so I can be part of it. He allows me dominion over my own kingdom, though He waits for me to turn over my reign on every given issue.

Prayer for Today

Thank God for His plan to restore and renew all things and for inviting you to be part of that. Thank Him for His patience in your life and His sacrifice to reconcile humankind back to Himself. Ask Him to help you in these ten weeks to turn over to Him the reign of your kingdom for His healing.

Healing for Your Kingdom

Remember earlier in this chapter when we talked about God not doing halfway healing? We can be sure as God's plan unfolds to restore and renew all things there will be no halfway job here either. In the next ten weeks, there will no doubt be some deep places of pain and hurt from the past God wants to heal. There will be parts of your "kingdom" we will talk about (family relationships, events, patterns, dysfunctions, choices, etc.) that may be difficult to talk about. And you always have a choice. Sometimes the places that need healing the most are the hardest to talk about. God wants to heal every part of your kingdom. He wants nothing left untouched. That is not to say you will be perfect at the end of these ten weeks or even perfectly healed. For some of you, healing will be a process. His ways are not our ways, remember? But He will take charge of every part of your kingdom you are willing to give Him dominion over, and He will begin to do a healing work in you and bring you to a place of abundant life. So when it gets tough or there is a part of your kingdom you would rather keep closed off, consider giving Him dominion over it, knowing His plan is to restore and renew all things.

I had the great joy and incredible challenge of caring for my ninety-four-year-old dad the last year of his life. He was in a wheelchair and suffered moderate dementia that worsened as the months went on. My dad was an artistic genius, but humble, almost self-deprecating about it. He had a great sense of humor and used it to engage and endear everyone who ever met him. His proudest accomplishment (other than his family, for which he gave all credit to our mother) was being a United States marine. My dad served in WWII at Pearl Harbor, something we are all extremely proud of. But like many servicemen, Dad wasn't one to talk about things that happened during his time in the military. We all knew there were things that happened he carried shame and guilt about.

Occasionally Dad's mind would be clear and we would sit at the table and discuss scripture or spiritual questions he had, while he drew a random landscape, animal, or character on the back of a paper plate. I so treasured these times with my dad. I didn't know how long he would live, and I wanted him to feel completely empty of anything he wanted to say about his life. I felt so honored and blessed to have this time with him, and sometimes the floor around my table felt like holy ground. One day he was especially reminiscent and told me the Jeep story we were all aware of. I always thought it was probably his most shameful moment in life.

Being military police officer meant my dad had his own issued Jeep and regular hours he worked. One night when he was off duty, he and a couple of his buddies went into town to meet some girls. At some point, there was an accident that rolled the Jeep and critically injured a girl who had left the bar with them. There was an investigation and a court-martial that resulted in my dad facing only minimal punishment. Still, the proud image of a United States marine and one of a court-martial are two images that do not belong in the same story, and my dad was always ashamed it ever happened.

But what he hated worse came out that day at the table in a moment of precious healing. "You know," he said, choking up, "I tried to go back and see that girl in the hospital, and they never let me. The worst part is

I know she had a severe head injury, but I don't even know to this day if she lived or died."

There was nothing I could say to my dad that would change what happened or erase the shame he felt. So I sat silently and held his hand. He then began to talk in vague, stitched-together sentences of other battle scars he kept hidden for over seventy years, maneuvers he went on and things he had witnessed. He was openly crying now, and most of what he was saying I couldn't understand.

When he was done, he looked up at me like someone begging for mercy and said, "We all just did what we were told."

I shook my head, looked at my sweet dad, and whispered, "You were a good marine. And you know what, Dad? You were really just a kid."

My dad broke. His shoulders immediately slumped, and his chest heaved as he sobbed. I went over and hugged the twenty-year-old marine inside him who had carried such a heavy load all these years.

After a few minutes, he sat up straighter, wiped his eyes, looked right at me, and said, "Thank you for saying that, pal."

We smiled, I did a quick two-finger salute, and said, "Thank you for serving." It was the last serious conversation I had with my dad.

God's kingdom came down that day. His will for perfect healing was done on earth, just as it is always done in heaven. But it would have never happened if my dad didn't have the courage to finally talk about those things. There were many other things he talked about with me and my sisters during those months—things that required courage and things for which I believe he received healing. He talked about growing up with an alcoholic father and all the events in his life related to that. It takes courage to talk about things in our lives that seem shameful.

We won't have questions in our lesson today. I hope you will take some extra time to think about the things we have discussed this week. Think about how you have coped when life became difficult. Think about your family and your genogram and what living an abundant life would look like.

I encourage you in these next weeks to be courageous. Your heart knows what healing it needs. And God knows what healing you need. Let God guide your heart and be courageous.

I have had this beautiful passage of scripture on the back of my Bible for years. It is such a comforting promise to my heart. Perhaps you have it written somewhere yourself. If not, write it or type it out and keep it in a place you can read it often. What beautiful words! What blessed assurance!

But now, this is what the Lord says --
He who created you... He who formed you: "Do not
fear, for I have redeemed you; I have summoned
you by name; you are mine. When you pass through
the waters, I will be with you; and when you pass
through the rivers, they will not sweep over you.
When you walk through the fire, you will not be
burned; the flames will not set you ablaze. For I am
the Lord your God, the Holy One of Israel, your
Savior...
Since you are precious and honored in my sight,
and because I love you.

Isaiah 43:1-4

Chapter 2

No One Wants to Hear Their Family Was Dysfunctional

Day 1

Read: Genesis 5

This passage in Genesis is the account of the generations from Adam to Noah. It's difficult to read because there's not a story tied with it. It's just names and numbers—big numbers. For example, can you believe Adam lived 930 years? The purpose of this chapter discussion is not the length of years lived by these people but to notice how important family is to God. Several times in the Bible, God has us stop and read genealogies. He lists the generations by name, giving them not only a place in history but the honor and dignity of their personhood—acknowledgment that they lived and had a place and purpose in this life. Somehow God exists in community with the Son and the Holy Spirit, and He quickly decided His first created man, Adam, should also live in community. Of course, we know the idea of family was planned from the beginning as Adam and Eve were obviously fashioned to procreate.

When the Bible talks about family, it is referring to at least three generations. Families at that time lived together throughout their lives, so a family may have included twenty to thirty people. Today we call that extended family, but then, a family consisted of the paternal grandparents, their sons (and their wives), and their sons' children. (If there were daughters, they would have gone to be part of their husbands' families.) There are many places in the world today where this is still the case, although the Western idea of the family of only mother, father, and children is becoming more common in those cultures (while the Western idea of family continues to change).

Prayer for Today

Thank God for the credible, historical account of His Word and for His design and intent of the family. Ask for His wisdom as we begin to look at our own families, that His Spirit will quicken your memory to things He wants to show you. Pray that your mind and heart will be ready and willing to receive these truths.

It's a Sin Issue

Most of us are protective of our family image, and we do not want to admit our families were dysfunctional. We can acknowledge our parents were not perfect (because no one is), and we may say they did the best they could, but it is difficult to wear the label "dysfunctional." Most of us try to honor our fathers and mothers, and we try to be good parents ourselves.

The truth is, however, there are no perfectly healthy families. As we read in our scripture discussion for today, from the first family created, there was dysfunction. There was murder between the first children ever born! Granted, there are different levels of dysfunction, but all of us come from families that practiced some unhealthy behavior somewhere.

There is a difference between families who have some traits or behaviors (discipline or communication practices, for example) that could be improved upon and families whose unhealthy traits and behaviors affect basic needs. The *McGraw-Hill Concise Dictionary of Modern Medicine* defines the term *dysfunctional family* as "a family with multiple internal conflicts" (relational issues, single parenthood, violence, or mental illness), or "external conflicts" (addictions, affairs, chronic unemployment, or any influences neglecting basic needs of the family).[1]

It is easy to see how a child's need for healthy love and belonging could go unmet in a home where domestic violence or alcoholism gets all the attention. It is also easy to see how these kinds of behaviors can affect generations. Not only are the behaviors often repeated, but so are the coping behaviors, communication patterns, priorities, and values.

There are many scriptures that talk about the sins of one generation being visited in the next. In Exodus 20:5–6, we see both a warning and a promise.

> You shall not bow down to them or worship them; for I, the Lord your God, am a jealous God, punishing the children for the sin of the parents to the third and fourth generation of those who hate me, but showing love to a thousand generations of those who love me and keep my commandments.

The Hebrew word for punishing is better translated "giving consequences," which also makes sense for what we see often happens in families throughout generations.

In his article "Can You Break the Cycle of Generational Dysfunction?"[2] Greg Thomas recounts the story of a family studied by the New York State Prison Board in 1874 when they noticed six family members were all incarcerated at the same time. They traced patterns of illegal behavior back to an ancestor in 1720. Among their 1200 descendants, they found several hundreds of them were homeless, alcoholics, prostitutes, or imprisoned criminals, including six murderers. The study further revealed the state of New York had spent over $1.5 million caring for this family—over $10,000 per year for 150 years—a considerable sum at the time! This family is surely an example of consequences to the third and fourth generation.

Thomas also tells of another family who lived in the same era. It is recorded the descendants of the famous preacher Jonathan Edwards (who also became the president of Princeton University) and his godly wife, Sarah, had eleven children. By 1874, their 1400 descendants included college and university professors and presidents, authors, doctors, attorneys, judges, and politicians, including senators, governors, and a vice president of the United States. That is quite a contrast of values passed down between these two families.

The good news is it only takes one person to break the cycle of dysfunction and unhealthy patterns in a family. You may not have prostitutes or murderers in your family of origin, but you may have abuse or addiction. Some of our backgrounds are dark and full of fear and sadness. I promise you are not alone. And shining the light of God's healing into your life will not change the past, but it can and will make a difference for generations to come.

This week, as we look deeper into our families of origin, I encourage you to be honest with yourself and your feelings. Some of this may feel as though you are betraying your family or dishonoring them in some way. Honoring yourself and God by speaking truth is what matters. And by honoring God, you bring great honor to your family.

What feelings come up for you when you think about the home you were raised in?

_____

_____

_____

_____

What are some positive memories you have of growing up in your family of origin?

_____

_____

_____

_____

As a child, how did you feel about your family? How did your family compare to other families you knew?

_____

_____

_____

_____

Were there unmet needs in your family or things you wish were different? Explain.

_____

_____

_____

_____

Day 2

Read: 1 Corinthians 13:11

Anyone who has a child or has been around a child for a while will relate to what today's scripture reading suggests—if you read between the lines of what the apostle Paul is saying. Paul is telling us there should be two processes going on simultaneously as we grow. "When I became a man" (or a woman) suggests the physical aging that takes place. A boy grows physically into a man. He gets tall and muscular, he grows facial hair, and his voice becomes deeper and more commanding. And he develops the ability to father children.

The rest of that sentence says, "I put the ways of childhood behind me." Another version says, "I put away childish things." This suggests the emotional process of aging. We no longer scream or cry for what we want. Instead, we learn to be patient and ask for what we want. And we understand we do not always get what we want. We learn responsibility by working instead of playing all day. We learn empathy and respect for others and how to handle conflict.

In this section of chapter 13, Paul is making a comparison for us. He is using our physical and emotional maturation as a metaphor for our understanding of what it will be like when we are made perfect in the afterlife. Just like it is impossible for a child to know and comprehend adult concepts and information, so are we unable, as imperfect beings, to fully know and comprehend eternal concepts and information. It is like looking through a darkened glass. How glorious it will be when the struggles and dysfunctions of this life are over, when we are made perfect in mind, body, and soul, and when we will fully know our Creator God.

Prayer for Today

Express gratitude to God for His amazing creative power that formed our bodies to mature in orderly ways, both physically and emotionally. Ask Him to show you places you may need to further mature emotionally, and praise Him for the coming day when we will be perfect like Him!

Healthy or Dysfunctional? That Is the Question

Our physical bodies require a healthy environment to grow properly. We need sunshine, air, food, and water. Our emotional side also requires a healthy environment to develop properly. According to American psychologist Abraham Maslow, to fully mature, there are five levels of needs. All humans need food, air, and water (physiological needs), safety and security needs, love and belonging, self-respect and self-worth needs, and appreciation and respect for the worth of others.

Each category of needs builds on the other, and when the needs of one level are not met, we cannot go into the next phase of growth. Such research suggests while a child continues to grow physically in an unhealthy environment, he or she may remain stuck emotionally at the age when a traumatic event occurred or when these important needs were neglected, barring a healing intervention of some kind.

It is generally agreed there are certain positive characteristics that healthy (or safe) families display. In these families, parents try to create an environment where every family member feels safe, heard, loved, and respected. These families clearly communicate with each other, are supportive of one another, and don't have a lot of conflict. [3] Families that are considered dysfunctional, unsafe, or codependent typically don't have these positive characteristics. They may also have additional issues like addictions or abuse of some kind that contribute to the dysfunction. You may have heard other terms to describe these families, but we will refer to them as dysfunctional versus healthy, and we will be looking at some characteristics of both types of families. As we discuss dysfunctional and healthy families, it may be helpful to think in terms of a continuum since there are no perfect families.

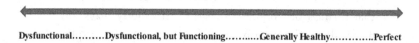

Dysfunctional..........Dysfunctional, but Functioning............Generally Healthy..............Perfect

What are the characteristics of families along this continuum? Although dysfunctional families are all different, they often share some principal characteristics.

Defining traits of a dysfunctional family include the following:

- **Lack of empathy** – No room for mistakes, lack of understanding of others' feelings, judgmentalism, every man for himself.
- **Poor communication** – Yelling, back talk, name-calling, criticizing, sarcasm, making fun of others, dismissing, individuals not feeling heard, no disagreeing allowed, triangling, alliances, not listening, lying, etc. Or complete lack of conflict, sweeping issues under the rug instead of discussion or pretending everything is always perfect, only certain emotions are allowed, and there are secrets and/or topics that are never talked about or mentioned.
- **Emotional, sexual, or physical abuse** – Hitting, pushing, shoving, throwing things, choking, frequent ridicule and criticism, threatening, bullying, controlling, shaming, jealousy, suspicion, withholding love or affection, rage, manipulation, guilt, or other mind games.
- **Addictions or coping abuse** – Hidden or overt abuses of drugs, alcohol, food, etc.
- **Perfectionism** – Extremely high expectations, never accepting failure, always pointing out the negative, failing to acknowledge any positive, can't show weaknesses, achievements are valued over people, adherence to rigid religious rules.
- **Fear and unpredictability** – Constant threats without follow-through, "Come here; go away" relationships, inconsistent discipline and affection.
- **Denial** – Failure to acknowledge the truth about issues, whitewashing or making excuses, constant blaming.

- **Enmeshment, disrespect of boundaries** – Everyone must feel/think/believe the same way, no privacy, differences are not tolerated or are made fun of.

Healthy families have also been found to share similar characteristics.

Defining traits of a healthy family include the following:

- **Clearly defined roles and boundaries** – Parents are united and in charge of training, discipline, and decision-making, appropriate sense of personal space is encouraged and practiced, parents are model for trust to develop between all members.
- **Effective communication** – Conflicts resolved quickly and productively, each member free to speak their mind and feel listened to, forgiveness is practiced, all emotions permitted and expressed appropriately, humor is plentiful and appropriate, big decisions are discussed and successfully negotiated.
- **Mutual respect and accountability** – Between all family members in words and actions, with responsibility toward each other for whereabouts, actions, and decisions.
- **Family resilience** – Promotes general healthy standards of diet, sleep, and physical activity, enjoys being together and plans family times, recovers from stress or trauma by leaning on each other for support and encouragement.
- **Promotes healthy growth** – Individuals are encouraged to dream, try new things, grow, and change, differences are acknowledged and/or celebrated, mistakes are allowed, return to family safety and nurture is welcomed.

Which of the two general *categories* most resembles the family you grew up in: dysfunctional or healthy?

_____

_____

As you read through the traits of the dysfunctional family, which specific *trait* or traits resemble your family most? Give an example of each.

_____

_____

_____

_____

Do you recall how experiencing those occurrences made you feel as a child? Can you describe your feelings?

_____

_____

_____

_____

Day 3

Read: Exodus 20:12, 1 Corinthians 13:4–7, and 1 John 4:7–12

Perhaps these scripture passages are quite familiar. The first one is part of the Ten Commandments God gave to Moses for the Israelites. The commandments were given to establish order to life and society. The first four commandments taught the Israelites how to relate to God. The last six taught them how to relate to their fellow man, beginning with father and mother.

The second scripture comes from the well-known "love chapter" where the apostle Paul details for us what love is and how important it ranks in life and society. Some of us will read these words with a resonating familiarity because this kind of love was not only taught to us as children but was modeled to us by our parents. Having parents who were patient, kind, protective, and not easily angered would make it simple to honor or respect them. That is how God intended it. Parents are supposed to model this kind of love and teach and train their children to love this way.

Why? Because of our third scripture. Because God is love. Because each of those descriptions of love Paul gives is an attribute of our Heavenly Father. His love is unfailing because He is love! Of course, no parent loves perfectly like God. But some of us cannot relate to the kind of love Paul describes because we didn't see it growing up, or if we did, it was very inconsistent and mixed up with harsh, demeaning words, a slap across the face, or worse. Some of us may have been told we were loved (and any thought to the contrary would provoke anger!), but actions and our feelings caused questions. Not only is it difficult to believe God is as loving as Paul describes love, but the whole honoring your parents thing can be confusing if our homes didn't make it easy to do. What do we do with all of that?

Prayer for Today

Ask God to be present with you as you begin to look honestly at your family of origin. Ask Him to safely guide your thoughts toward the truth without judgment and for the courage to do so. Thank Him for the healing He is preparing you for. Thank Him for being trustworthy.

What about My Family?

All cultures are built on the family unit, and each begins with parental authority. Children are taught early to obey their parents and show some level of respect or honor. Most young children consider whatever environment they are in to be normal; it's all they know. Some children are later exposed to other families through friends, relatives, or stories and can begin to see differences in how families function and relate to each other.

You may have learned your family did punishment and discipline differently from other families. You may have noticed they communicated differently. Maybe there was a lot of cursing or shouting in your family. Maybe things got violent and there was a lot of fear growing up. Or maybe shouting or anger was never allowed. Maybe disagreements were never addressed and you just got over it. Maybe one parent was always the one who got angry and the other did everything possible to prevent it. Maybe your parents got their parenting manual from a set of "church rules" and that became the standard by which everything was done in your family. Maybe your parents were proud of the way your family functioned and everything was always done "right," and anyone who did it differently was wrong.

Families all look differently and behave differently. It can be uncomfortable to talk about your family of origin, especially if things were mostly OK. After all, you may be thinking, *We turned out to be respectable adults with our own families, and besides, our parents just did the best they could.* All of that can be true and can also make us think finding any dysfunction means betrayal, which means disrespect or dishonor. That is not true. It is *not* either my family was perfect or it was a total disaster and the authorities should have been called. It is not an either/or situation. It can be a both/and situation.

You may have grown into a respectable adult and your parents may have done the best they could, and things could have been mostly OK and there may have *still* been dysfunctional patterns of communication, discipline, finances, or spirituality *and* you can still respect and honor your parents. Being honest with your feelings and honest about your past is honoring to yourself and honoring to God. Being healed from the past and breaking the cycles of dysfunction and sin is the best way to honor your parents.

In the weeks ahead, we will be examining specific patterns of relating and healing from those that are causing problems in our current ways of relating. But the prerequisite for healing is honesty. Honesty with yourself, with God, and ultimately with others.

As an adult, how do you feel about the family you grew up in?

_____

_____

_____

_____

Do you recall how you felt as a child about your family? Explain.

_____

_____

_____

_____

How does it feel to talk about your family of origin? Is there any resistance inside you? What is that resistance about?

_____

_____

_____

_____

Day 4

Read: James 1:20, Proverbs 14:12–13, and Philippians 4:4–7

It is no secret we are emotional beings who have the ability to express many different feelings. It takes less than a year of an infant's life to see we were created with a range of feelings and emotions, such as joy, sorrow, anger, fear, or jealousy. We also know from the story of creation that we were created in God's image. Therefore, we must conclude God also possesses feelings and emotions. However, our feelings as humans have been tainted by sin. Left uncontrolled, our feelings will bring about results that are neither pleasing to God nor beneficial to us. We are not to deny our feelings but to allow the Spirit to take control of our whole person, which includes our feelings. This is not simply a one-time decision and—poof!—like magic we are under a spell and will never wrestle with improper feelings again. Rather, it is an ongoing submission to God, bringing every situation, every part of ourselves, and every feeling to God in prayer and the reading of His Word.

Romans 12:1–2 tells us we are transformed by the renewing of our minds. In these times of meditating on the Word and praying to God, His Spirit consoles us, teaches us, and brings about a new perspective—His perspective—on the situation. The Spirit enables us to have a change of heart toward others or ourselves, and over time, we are transformed. Often, this transformation surprises even us. One day we feel joy or peace in circumstances we would never have before, or we respond with gentleness where once was anger. This is the transformation of Romans 12. This is the guarding of our hearts of Philippians 4. This transcends our understanding.

Prayer for Today

Praise God for our miraculous emotional makeup, that we can experience exuberant joy and the gift of sorrow that allows us to process grief. Ask Him to continue to transform you into His image for His purposes as you submit daily to His leading.

Feelings Come and Feelings Go

What are feelings anyway? Some people say not to trust feelings because they come and go. Other say always pay attention to your feelings and they will direct you. Some people seem to always display their emotions in a huge dramatic way, while others rarely show any emotion at all. Some children are told, "Go ahead and cry! It won't change anything." Others are told, "Stop that crying right now, or I'll give you something to cry about!"

Anger, joy, sadness, fear, hate, love, surprise, content, confused, hopeless, refreshed, offended, and happy—the list of feelings could go on and on. We are often held hostage by our feelings instead of being in control of them. Dysfunctional families either allow their feelings to rule them or they ban them altogether. To be in control of our feelings and move into heathier emotional patterns, we first need to understand the difference between feelings and emotions.

Feelings and emotions are different. Emotions are involuntary bodily responses to something that happens. For example, the teacher announces speeches will begin today and calls on you to go first. Your heart rate goes up, your hands might get clammy, and you may even get a little queasy in your stomach. The basic emotion here would be fear—fear of being unprepared, of failing, of not remembering the facts, etc. Feelings are our mental associations and reactions to an emotion. Later, when you describe the speech incident (how your brain recalled it), you became aware of how the announcement of speeches made you *feel*. You associated a *feeling* with the emotions you experienced. Our feelings are individual and are shaped by our environment, personal experiences, and beliefs. That's why some people describe speaking in public as terrifying while others see it as their time to shine!

Let's take it one step further. Let's suppose Amy and Emily are in the same third grade class and one day during school a tornado is spotted heading right for their school. The children are all whisked away to the lower level while the wind howls and they hear all the windows explode above them. No doubt all of the children and teachers are experiencing the raw emotion of fear. Their hearts are racing, their eyes may be watering with tears, they may be short of breath, or they be frozen and unable to move or open their eyes.

Later in the day when the storm had passed, the children were reunited with their parents. Amy's mother held her and kissed her and listened to Amy breathlessly explain everything that happened. Afterward, her mother told her while she was worried about Amy, she knew Amy's teacher would know exactly what to do. She was grateful Amy and her friends were not hurt and that, although an infrequent occurrence, now Amy would know better what to do if she was ever in a storm like that in the future. Amy was comforted and able to tell the story to friends and family in a more matter-of-fact manner.

Emily's mother also held her and kissed her but was crying hysterically. Every time Emily tried to tell her mother what happened, her mother burst into tears and wailed about not being able to get to her. As a result, Emily seemed upset for days and rarely left her mother's side.

Both girls experienced the same initial emotion of fear, but Amy later displayed feelings of concern and calm whenever there was a bad storm while Emily became agitated and at times hysterical. Their emotion was the same; their feelings were different based on their environment and personal experiences.

Feelings are important. They help us understand our bodily sensations and alert us to what we should do about them if anything. They also allow us to care for other people, to be concerned for them and create ways of solving problems about things that bother us, frustrate us, anger us, make us sad, or seem unjust. They also can be learned responses within families and passed from one generation to the next, as in our previous example. Amy's mother handled the fearful and serious situation in a healthy way. She helped Amy make sense of her fear emotion and validated it but also reduced it and used it as a learning experience for both caution and rationale. Emily's mother also validated her fear emotion but gave it more power than it deserved, especially since everything turned out all right. Perhaps her response was due to her own uncontrolled feelings of fear, but her reactions shaped Emily's feelings perhaps forever.

All feelings begin with a thought. Something happens and our bodies react involuntarily the same way they did at the initial occurrence. Later, when we *think* about what just happened (or what happened years ago that we stuffed or ignored), we assign a meaning to it. It was a good thing, a bad thing, a scary thing, a mean thing, an unfair thing, or another type of thing. As soon as we label what kind of thing it was, the appropriate feeling jumps right in! We are immediately happy, sad, afraid, hurt, incensed, or something else. Then we act or behave accordingly. If we decide later the good thing was really a bad thing or the unfair thing was really a good thing, then our feelings will change accordingly, and we can change our behavior as well.

So can we trust our feelings or not? The answer is both yes and no. We pay attention to our feelings. We examine them and hold them up against our beliefs, values, and logic. If we have been hurt and are feeling angry, we pay attention to that feeling. We ask ourselves if carrying that feeling of anger into a behavior we would later be sorry for, or that goes against what we believe or doesn't align with the person we want to be, then we reevaluate the situation. Logic may remind us perhaps the person who hurt us was having a bad day, or perhaps we misunderstood or took something too personally. Perhaps everything we felt *was* justified but acting on the anger would only fuel the situation. A few days later, after examining our anger, we don't feel quite so angry. We're annoyed and decide to set a boundary or have a conversation. The anger subsides and we learn from it. Or maybe we decide we overreacted and now we are feeling foolish. We paid attention to the feeling but in the end could not entirely trust it. Feelings do come. And some feelings go.

What is your understanding now about the difference between emotions and feelings?

_____

_____

_____

_____

How might this difference affect your understanding of how your family handled feelings?

_____

_____

_____

_____

As you think back to your own family or where you were raised, what feelings were OK to express? Were there any that were not OK to express or were "corrected"? What were they?

OK _____ Not OK _____

_____   _____

_____   _____

_____   _____

_____   _____

After writing these down, what feelings might you need to reexamine in your own life and why?

_____

_____

_____

_____

Day 5

Read: Deuteronomy 6:5–9

While the charge in our scripture today is specific to teaching our children about loving God first and foremost in our lives and with all that we are, from it we can get a clue into how children learn. If God intended His most important commandment taught in this manner, it is safe to assume it is a reliable method for children to learn other things as well. Children are so impressionable that some researchers believe by the age of ten children already know what their parents' opinions and decisions will be about most choices and issues they face. We also know from an early age children imitate their parents. They boss younger siblings in tones and with exact words a parent has used. They pretend to drive, cook, smoke, shave, apply lipstick, and do many other behaviors they observe.

When my oldest daughter was a toddler, I watched soap operas while I folded laundry. One day, my daughter ran across the room pretending to cry with her hand over her forehead and threw herself across the couch just like the actress on the show had just done. I turned off the television and never watched another soap opera.

Children learn by repetition, observation, and consequences. It makes sense then that we would learn what feelings were not acceptable, which were most often practiced, and which brought consequences we either desired or wished to avoid. God's ways are always wise, and we can be grateful if we had parents who continuously taught us kindness, gentleness, and assertiveness without aggression. For those of us who constantly observed anger, control, or manipulation (or who avoided feelings altogether), it is never too late for God's transforming power to do its work.

Prayer for Today

As we look at our feelings, ask God to keep your heart and mind open to memories of how we were shaped. Ask Him to help you accept His grace when you see patterns of behavior and handling feelings in unhealthy ways. Thank Him for His ongoing healing.

Focus on the Family Feelings

We could spend an entire week delving into the world of feelings. We all have them, whether we have tried to shut them off or they shoot out of us like water out of a fire hydrant. Some of us grew up in families where anger quickly turned into abuse. As a result, we came to fear the feeling of anger in ourselves, while others of us followed the pattern of letting our anger fly uncontrolled. Others of us were raised to believe anger was bad or wrong. This left us either to live as doormats for anyone to use or abuse, or we feel guilty for "sinning" every day because we cannot live up to such impossible standards.

Feelings are what make us distinctively human. Animals also have involuntary responses (emotions), to sudden danger, favorite snacks, and loud noises, for example, but these responses are only repeated by association to the stimulus—the coming car, the meaty bone, or the crack of thunder. They do not have the ability to translate their emotions into the feelings of "I was terrified, ecstatic, or startled!" We have the ability to think, reason, and make sense of the past and plan for the future by using our feelings to guide us into action. We can think back on words spoken to us and recall the emotion we had at the time, then reason how those words made us feel and vow to make changes to avoid it in the future or change the situation or never speak that way to someone else.

Some of us learned to stuff our feelings down, to ignore or dismiss them because tears were not tolerated or being scared was a sign of weakness, or anger was either squashed with even bigger anger or was sinful and not allowed. We quickly learned to ignore or mask or hide our feelings to avoid the pain of being hurt emotionally or physically.

The problem is stuffing, ignoring, masking, or hiding our feelings does not make them go away for good. They will quickly resurface any time we face similar circumstances or triggers. Evaluating how our experience with emotions was formed is key to understanding our own emotional makeup and is the beginning of changing what needs changing. In this section, we will begin looking at not only some key feelings in our families of origin but also some situations where we might reflect on how those feelings were used. Spend some time thinking about the questions below before answering.

How did your parents (or the person who raised you) handle conflict?

_____

_____

_____

_____

How did your parents (or the person who raised you) handle sadness or loss?

_____

_____

_____

_____

How did your parents (or the person who raised you) handle anger?

_____

_____

_____

_____

How did your parents (or the person who raised you) handle failure?

_____

_____

_____

_____

How did your parents (or the person who raised you) handle fear?

_____

_____

_____

_____

How did your parents (or the person who raised you) handle success or achievements?

_____

_____

_____

_____

How did your parents (or the person who raised you) handle secrets? What was not talked about?

_____

_____

_____

In the remaining space, examine how you handle each of these circumstances.

Conflict

_____

_____

Sadness or loss

_____

_____

Anger

_____

_____

Failure

_____

_____

Fear

_____

_____

Success or achievement

_____

_____

Secrets (or uncomfortable topics)

_____

What similarities or differences did you notice between how you and your family handle these circumstances? How do you feel about those?

_____

_____

_____

_____

Chapter 3

Instructions for Proper Attachment

Day 1

Read: Psalm 139:13–18

No scripture better prepares us for our discussion on attachment than this psalm. David so beautifully reminds us of God's most intimate and most loving attachment to us—the day He decided that for this exact time and place, the world would be lacking if you or I were not a part of it. Think of it! We were precisely what God planned the world would need, and the Almighty Creator set out to fashion us as a tiny, helpless, innocent baby deep within the body of our mother, hidden away from everything. And there, just as He designed it, He made sure all our needs were met—for nourishment, for safety, and for comfort until the day came when the exact days of our journey here on earth would begin.

Toward the end of our reading for today, David is expressing his numerous thoughts about such a loving and caring God. When we take the time to meditate on the many, *many* ways God provides for us, we cannot possibly name them all. Every second of every day we have air to breathe into lungs that continue to fill up and a heart that continues to beat. The countless beauties our eyes and ears constantly take in: the sky, the clouds, the birds, butterflies, flowers, music, and laughter, and "were [we] to count them, they would outnumber the grains of sand" (v. 18). Every single day of His creation holds more for us to be reverently thankful for than we can know or think of. Yet when all our world shuts down for us to stop, sleep, recover, and recharge, He is there watching over us, making sure it all keeps going.

Prayer for Today

Take a few minutes to picture in your mind God planning to put you in the world. Picture Him lovingly forming you—what the colors your eyes and hair would be, what your voice would sound like, and how tall you would be. Think about how beautiful you must have been to Him, and whether you believe that or not, thank Him for wanting you in the world and for putting all His heart into creating you. Thank Him for loving you and for considering you one of His beautiful creations.

Attach Yourself

We all know what it means to be attached to something. If you have children, no doubt you went through that stage of diligent parenting when it seemed the most important task was not to lose the blanket, the bunny, or—heaven forbid—the pacifier! Perhaps you can remember being attached to a stuffed animal or a doll yourself. Children can become attached to the most unusual things. It makes sense, developmentally, when all the child has known before is a deep and constant connection to their mother.

As the child begins to crawl and walk, they obviously cannot explore the world around them while always tethered to their mother. They are innately seeking independence, but the fear of being apart from all they have ever known is unthinkable. Often the child will accept, and soon latch onto, a suitable substitute for mom for short periods of time.

This temporary substitute most often will be soft like mom and able to be cuddled or stroked. Before long, the child is attached to this bunny, bear, blanket, or floppy dog and will cling to it for security in times of exploration, fear, stress, or hurt. Mom will always be first and best choice, but in her absence, the softy is the next best thing.

Besides being attached to blankets and bunnies, perhaps you have also heard the word *attachment* used in reference to the child/parent relationship or the marriage relationship. This type of attachment is what we will be discussing in this chapter. It also has its roots in the early developmental years, but instead of referring to being attached to a soft, cuddly substitute, this attachment refers to the bond between the child and his or her mother or earliest primary caregiver.

It is naturally by design we need to feel connected to someone. God's choice for procreation was that a child would begin nestled snugly inside his or her mother, completely dependent for survival, until birth. Even after birth, for the first years, the child depends on others for every need. Too often, in our society, we are eager to train for total independence, making any dependence frowned upon. Research has shown over and over that we need to be connected to others. In fact, loneliness and isolation are known contributors to stress, insecurity, anxiety, and depression and can even lead to physical ailments.

In the past, human behavior was seen on a continuum between complete independence at one end and overdependence on the other end. Researchers now believe we are all interdependent. They see our interdependence as either effective or ineffective according to how it plays out in our relationships. As it turns out, being both securely dependent and independent are two sides of the same coin, according to Susan Johnson, a well-known theorist and marriage and family therapist. The more secure our attachments in our formative years, the more self-confidence we have and the more effective our interdependence on others as we mature.[1]

As we discussed earlier, most young children go through some form of attaching to a blanket, bunny, or something else. Sometimes these connections are healthy, developmentally appropriate ties. Other times they can be beyond the scope of what is considered normal by age, circumstance, or insecure attachments. Perhaps the child is clinging to it well past young years. Or maybe the child shows an abnormal reaction to losing or misplacing it or shows great fear or anxiety to situations without its security. These responses may depend on how securely the child is attached to the primary caregiver. These are not the *only* signs of insecure attachments, nor are they always present as a sign at all. Also, a child who is securely attached may also display similar behaviors for a time. Obviously, we cannot assume meaning by a single action. However, this is the example we are using as our introduction to attachment. There will be other examples along the way, and you may have an example from your own childhood.

Knowing our own attachment style helps explain how we approach intimacy, closeness, and connectedness with other people. It helps us identify patterns in how we repair arguments and issues of security. This week, as we explore our own early attachments, it will give us a new understanding of our adult attachments to our spouses or intimate relationships in our past, and perhaps we can identify attachment patterns in our children. We will learn what attachment is, how it is developed, and what the different styles of attachment are.

God created us to be relational beings. He intended for us to have healthy, loving, effective relationships with people, some more closely than others. And He intended for us to have a vibrant relationship with Him. If you are feeling anxious or hesitant about digging into your early attachments, remember God desires to heal and redeem every part of our story. He has promised to work in all things to bring good (Romans 8:28) and to bestow beauty for ashes (Isaiah 61:3). Surely, He is at work and is trustworthy.

Write down any thoughts or questions you had while reading the introduction to the attachment theory.

_____

_____

_____

_____

Describe a time in your childhood when a special toy, stuffed animal, pet, or other object was a comfort or brought joy to you.

_____

_____

_____

_____

Sometimes it is easier for us to express our love for others than to accept or receive their love for us. Often, this is the case in God's love for us. How did you feel when reading today's verses in Psalm 139? Could you envision God loving you as He "knit you in your mother's womb"? Why or why not?

_____

_____

_____

_____

Day 2

Read: Philippians 4:19

Throughout the fourth chapter of Philippians, Paul reminds his readers of the secure relationship between himself and Jesus Christ. We assume that Paul practiced what he preached when he told his dear friends not to be anxious or not to worry about anything but to give those worries to God. He also mentions times he had been in worrisome situations and in great need. But he ends this chapter with the confidence that God will meet all our needs. And not merely meet our needs in a basic, paltry manner but according to the riches of His glory in Christ Jesus! That is having at His disposal more than we could ever imagine, to meet whatever needs we might have.

However endless God's reserves are, the focus of Paul's words here zeroes in on his assurance, his confidence, and his certainty that the God he knew and served would meet his every need. He would never go lacking, never be in want of anything he truly needed. That is evidence of the securest of attachments. Wherever Paul went on this earth, His Heavenly Father was always available and willing to meet any need he had. Paul knew it, he counted on it, and he lived by it.

Prayer for Today

As you pray today, ask God to open your eyes to His faithfulness to you. Be reminded in prayer of times past when you have needed a bill paid, a favorable outcome, or help finding a new church or home. We forget every breath is a miracle, but He gives us so much more. Ask Him to help you to rest in Him as your Heavenly Father who sees you, cares about you, and meets your needs according to His infinite riches. Then begin to thank Him for that.

Birth of a Fundamental Question

Theorists and researchers in the field of psychology tell us every human being comes into this world with unmet needs. Obvious, right? To survive physically, we need air, food, water, clothing, and shelter. How is a helpless newborn baby going to get these things by herself? Miraculously, the birthing process provides the means to get air. The food, water, shelter, clothing, and other needs are not automatically provided at birth, nor can the newborn do anything to get them. This helpless little person needs someone to provide these things to survive. Along with the birth of the newborn is the birth of a fundamental question. "Who is going to meet my needs?"

Babies cry when they're hungry, cold, tired, or hurting. The cry is an innate, natural response when baby senses something is not quite right. There is discomfort of some kind, and by God's design, the baby will try to get someone's attention to take care of the problem. Also by God's design, a crying baby is hard to ignore! However, for some generations, it was customary to allow a baby to cry for a bit to see if she would comfort or soothe herself. The thinking was the baby would be "spoiled" if her cries always brought immediate attention and relief.

That thinking was proven untrue in the 1970s when researchers Sylvia Bell and Mary Ainsworth studied two groups of thirty-two mother/infant pairs over a period of months. The first group gave an immediate, caring response to their crying infant. The second group practiced a more restrained response. The researchers found the infants in the first group, whose mothers had given the immediate, nurturing response, cried less by one year of age. These babies were more securely attached to their mothers and were less whiny than the second group of babies who did not receive an immediate response. The study further showed the bond these same mothers developed with their babies correlated with their early response. Mothers who did not respond immediately to their infants' cries found it harder to bond with their babies later, and those who responded immediately early on felt a strong bond and attachment to their babies.[2]

Why are we discussing infant and mother bonding? We are discussing it because there seems to be a correlation between our early maternal attachments and how we do relationships as adults. It would seem natural to repeat how we attach to our children when we become parents, but that same "attachment style" may also be repeated in all our intimate relationships.

Before we begin to think about that, let's stay with our maternal attachments for a bit. There are many reasons a mother may not be able to immediately bond with a newborn baby. Some children are adopted and this mother/infant bond never develops or is interrupted or cut off. There are other times mother and baby must be separated because of emergency situations that develop before, during, or after birth. There may be other underlying illnesses or issues that require one or both to remain hospitalized for days, weeks, or even months. Perhaps there are emotional or mental issues with the mother that prevent her from caring for her newborn. Even in cases where things seem to be developing normally, there may be other crises or stressors within the family that cause the mother to withdraw emotionally from her baby and become emotionally absent or unavailable.

All these legitimate and often unavoidable scenarios can set the stage for insecure attachment and result in unmet needs of the infant. The silent newborn question "Who will meet my needs?" may remain unanswered, even if the baby's physical needs are being met. Feedings can be done by nurses or family members, and diapers can still be changed, but the emotional bond between the mother and her baby may still be underdeveloped or missing. This may result in an insecure attachment and the baby's very early perception of uncertainty in whether they can count on their needs being met.

Some new mothers do care for their infants but do so inconsistently. Their own needs take priority for various reasons and sometimes the baby's cries are met with immediate care and lots of attention and other times no one is there. The baby can never trust his or her needs will be met.

Other new mothers may dismiss the emotional (and even physical) needs of their babies. The baby may be neglected altogether, or the mother may have a cold, businesslike manner of merely getting the job done. The mother may change the baby's diaper but never interact or even look at her baby. She may feed hurriedly or prop the bottle for feedings. Later needs for nurture or attention are also dismissed.

Still, there are some mothers, caregivers, or other parents who destroy the emotional bond by abuse or consistent neglect. These children learn to fear the very person who is supposed to care for them and keep them safe. They still crave an emotional connection but quickly learn it will be painful.

Fortunately, many mothers love and care for their babies well. They recognize this is a selfless period of time where another human requires their time and attention, and they genuinely love giving it. They delight in their connection with their baby, and despite exhaustion and occasional fail as a parent, they form a strong bond with their baby that continues throughout childhood and beyond.

This early bonding, or lack of, can serve as a model for future relationships. It begins the process of perceiving how the world works and how others respond to our needs. It makes sense that an insecure infant may become an insecure child who may become an insecure adult, and without realizing it, we are recreating these patterns from the past in our current closest relationships, romantic partners, spouses, or with our own children.[3] Like our fundamental question stated, the insecure infant or child will continue searching to get their needs met. Left unhealed, these insecure attachment patterns can cause strained, hurtful, or painful experiences in later relationships as the grown adult may seek to meet their needs in unhealthy ways. We may not choose the healthiest of partners, or we may choose someone with whom we can reenact relationship dynamics from our past (subconsciously hoping for a different outcome). Or we may unintentionally change or even destroy a decent relationship because of our insecurities or the unhealthy ways we learned to get our needs met.

The good news is early attachment wounds can be healed as we learn new ways of getting needs met and new ways of interacting with people, especially those we are closest to.

As you reflect over your childhood, how would you describe your relationship as a child with your mother or earliest caregiver?

_____

_____

_____

_____

How has this relationship changed as you grew to adulthood?

_____

_____

_____

_____

What feelings come up for you when you think about your relationship?

_____

_____

_____

_____

Describe any times you can remember (or were told about) when you experienced a separation from your mother or earliest caregiver. If it was an exciting time (like spending the night somewhere fun), describe that too.

_____

_____

_____

_____

Do you feel you were blessed with a secure attachment early in life? Why, or why not?

_____

_____

_____

_____

What did you miss as a child, and how did you get it? What are some healthy ways you do or could get it now?

_____

_____

_____

_____

Day 3

Read: Romans 8:1, 31–39

These verses written by the apostle Paul show us just how certain he was of Christ's love. His question in verse 31 is asked in such a way that any answer other than the expected one would be incredulous. It's as if Paul is waiting for us to answer, "Why, no one! There can be no one against us!" I have thought about that verse a lot because clearly it feels like there are many people who are often against us. I am sure the other apostles who were martyred because they believed in Jesus as the Son of God felt as though people were against them. What then can this mean?

As Paul states later in this same chapter, it means that we are God's children. If we have accepted His Son as our Savior, God has adopted us as His own with all the rights and privileges of His own Son, including the glorious inheritance of eternal life with Him in heaven. And if we are a child of God, He has at His disposal resources and abilities beyond our comprehension to help us in times of trouble. This same God, who tells the stars where to perch in the heavens and the oceans where to stop on the shore, and this God who spared not His own Son to bring us back to Him, will stop at nothing to help us and see us safely home. Nothing is too difficult for Him. Nothing.

So what of the dangers and disappointments, accidents, and tragedies of this life? What of illness and death? Paul's words at the beginning of this chapter and verse 39 at the very end tell us all we need to know. God knows our time on this earth is but a moment in time. He is working a greater plan that spans from the day He set Adam and Eve in the garden till now, and on to the end of life as we know it. And whatever we do not understand in this life, we will understand in the life to come. What happens to us in this life will be of little consequence compared to the eternity ahead of us. All that matters is that He made a way for us to enjoy that eternity with Him, and though we may die from this earth, we will live forever because Jesus was victorious at the cross in the awful battle with sin and darkness. We are no longer condemned to death (Romans 8:1).

And while we remain on this earth, no matter what else may happen to us, nothing in all creation, above or below, can separate us from God's love (verses 38–39). And that is a secure attachment!

Prayer for Today

If you have never trusted Christ as your Savior or aren't sure you would be with Him in eternity, now would be a good time to know you are included in God's promises of no condemnation and to always keep you in His loving care. If you know you have believed Jesus to be your Savior and have asked Him for forgiveness, thank Him for your salvation and for eternal life. If you would like to accept the amazing free gift of eternal life, tell God you realize you are a sinner in need of a Savior and ask Him to come into your heart. Then thank Him for saving you and giving you eternal life.

Four Attachments and Your Personal Attachments

Sadly, not everyone can say they started out with secure attachments and all their relationships have been without insecurities. The truth is probably no one's relationships have been completely without insecurities, even if they were blessed with secure attachments early in life. Most of us experience insecurities in relationships from time to time depending on how others treat us, our own self-image, which can wax and wane throughout our life span, and as we go through many other experiences in life. That is different, however, from identifying patterns we may begin to observe in ourselves when we stop long enough to reflect on failed or strained relationships.

To understand our patterns, it's helpful to explore the four main categories of attachment.[4] These four categories of attachment are

- anxious attachment
- avoidant attachment
- disorganized (or fearful) attachment
- secure attachment

Recall our examples yesterday of four mothers who each cared for their babies in different ways. Each of these examples entailed different attachment styles. Let's look ahead from these examples and see how each child may behave in relationships as adults. Of course, these are not foolproof predictions, only behaviors researchers found tended to develop from the type of attachment seen early in life.

Our first example was the mother who displayed inconsistent caregiving. Perhaps this mother was focused on herself or something else that required her attention. Maybe there was an illness, another issue, or other children who needed her. Maybe she was not ready to be a mother or simply cared for herself more than her baby. For whatever reason, sometimes the baby received immediate care and lots of attention and other times was ignored. This is known as an *anxious attachment style.* How do you think a child who can never trust his or her needs will be met will be in relationships as an adult?

It would not be hard to envision a child who experienced such confusion may have felt frustrated and angry at times while still craving the attention they did receive sporadically. This child develops fears of losing the connection and begins to feel they must not be deserving of love. Consequently, you can see how these thoughts and feelings could develop into patterns of underlying anxiety in important relationships as they grow into adulthood. These adults now are still uncertain they are loveable and often have a negative view of themselves. When they find someone to be in a relationship with, they can be clingy or needy. They may tend toward jealousy and can be aggressive or easily angered out of fear they will lose the relationship. If their personality is not prone to anger, anxiety may overtake them in stressful times. They find it difficult to trust and may not ever fully trust, because remember they believe they will eventually be left and disappointed yet again. They have *anxious attachments.*

Another one of our examples discussed the mother who avoided developing an emotional bond with her baby. The baby was neglected or dismissed or needs were met in a cold, businesslike fashion. This is known as an *avoidant attachment style.* Perhaps the mother was not ready to be a mother or didn't want a baby at that time, or not at all. Babies who grew up displaced into foster homes or orphanages where there may have been a lack of love and nurturing learned early to shut off their emotions because no one cared. (Thankfully, not all orphanages or foster homes are like this.) As all these children grow up and begin to do things for themselves, they learn to become self-reliant and independent. They may grow to have a positive view of themselves but a negative view of others. "I can take care of myself, thank you. No one else is going to anyway!"

This child may also become an adult who does not trust others but for different reasons. They are not simply unsure whether anyone will be there for them, but they also are convinced no one will be. Of course, they still desire to be in relationship. That's how we were created! But adults with an *avoidant attachment style* find it difficult to be vulnerable or get close to anyone. They put up walls and avoid true intimacy. They are actually detached from their own needs and fail to meet the needs of others. They are often quick to leave during conflict because, after all, "I don't need this!"

The third example was the parent who harmed the baby's emotional growth in some way, abusing him or her physically, emotionally, sexually, or verbally. These children learn they are not worthy of being protected and grow up with a negative view of themselves and a negative, distrustful view of others. They develop the thinking *There must be something wrong with me* and may become a self-loathing adult characterized by addiction, self-harm, or repeating their abuser's actions. But because they too were created for relationship, they still desire closeness, but their messages are conflicting. "Come here; go away" messages are hallmarks of their relationships. These adults may often be depressed or angry. They may seem unresponsive in relationships because they are so disconnected with their own emotions. Every important relationship they have had results in pain of some kind, and if it doesn't, they will create pain because it's all they know and feels familiar. They have a *disorganized or fearful attachment style.*

Finally, we came to a *secure attachment style* in our examples. There are many mothers who feel the responsibility to intentionally pour into their children so they will develop into healthy, loving, empathic adults someday. They are not perfect, but they teach their children their needs will be met until they are old enough to meet them for themselves. The child who develops a secure attachment learns her needs are important and trusts her needs will be met. Further, the secure child learns to meet her own needs in healthy ways without manipulation, control, anger, whining, or demanding. These children also learn the needs of others are equally important. They are attached to what theorists refer to as a "secure base" that allows them to feel free to explore the world around them, knowing they are protected and can return when necessary. They have a positive view of themselves and a positive view of others. They are interdependent and comfortable with intimacy, asking for what they need and happy to meet the needs of the special people in their lives.

It is important to note that researchers are now seeing these different attachment styles as more on continuums of avoidance and anxiety. You also may lean toward one style with a spouse with whom you have worked through some of these issues, while still feel stuck in a different style with your family of origin or one parent. The diagrams below will help you visualize these continuums and characteristics of each attachment style and may help you better recognize where you are as an adult.

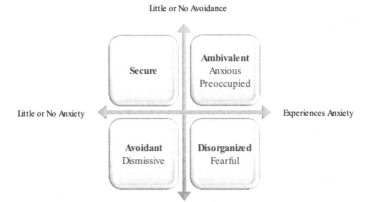

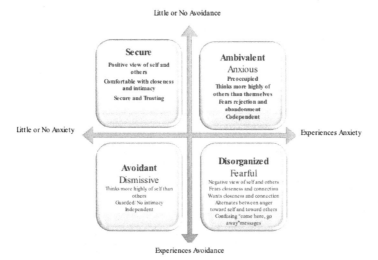

From the discussions on the four different attachment styles, which style do you feel fits you best during infancy and childhood?

_____

_____

_____

_____

What factors may have affected the type of attachment style you developed as a child?

_____

_____

_____

_____

As an adult, what are some difficulties you have experienced because of this attachment style?

_____

_____

_____

_____

Do you believe you are still operating under this attachment style? Why or why not?

_____

_____

_____

_____

List any concerns you may have concerning your attachment style.

_____

_____

_____

_____

Who do you want to move toward a more secure attachment with, and what kinds of changes could you make that might help you become more securely attached?

_____

_____

_____

_____

Day 4

Read: Psalm 23 and Matthew 18:12–13

In this most beloved chapter of the psalms, David introduces us to the kind shepherd. The sheep attach themselves to their shepherd because they learn he is the one who will take care of them. They can roam and graze freely because the shepherd is keeping watch. He is a good shepherd, and they are totally dependent on him unaware.

Sensing their needs before they do, He leads them to places of rest and refreshment. He keeps them on the right path, using his staff as necessary to ward off any predators or clear a thorny way. The sheep come to rely on their shepherd in treacherous conditions or when danger comes near.

We know from the first words of this psalm David is comparing God to everything he knows about shepherding, having been one. He speaks of the abundant, overflowing mercies and provisions God blesses us with. He compares the giving of these mercies and provisions to the lavish practice of David's day of graciously and generously pouring oil over guests' heads and allowing it to run down recklessly.

David further expresses his assurance in God's loving faithfulness for however long his life may be. He is confident of God's continuing love and mercy, but I love how David says God's goodness and mercy will follow him. He is not saying that everything we face in life will appear or seem good. Often, it is much later we can look at past circumstances and see God's goodness in those experiences. We may see how he prepared us or took care of us or how he used it for our (or others') growth or benefit.

Then there are the messes our choices often make. That's where, as in David's case, God's mercy following us is indeed a good thing! Mercy can be thought of as withholding whatever consequences our poor choices or actions deserve. Thank God His mercy follows us.

Our second reading takes mercy a step farther. We know sheep are prone to wander, and the shepherd allows them. But a good shepherd will make every effort to rescue and bring back the wandering one, rejoicing as he does so.

In His great mercy and goodness to us, God, our good shepherd, is searching for us when we have gone astray and our choices have made a mess of our lives. He is searching for us when we are off the beaten path, bleeding and wounded from others' choices. He is longing to bind up our wounds, offering healing to our broken places. He wants to take us in His arms and bring us safely home. What a kind and gentle shepherd!

Prayer for Today

Close your eyes and sit in His presence. Imagine you are lost and alone on a dusty, dirty path. Imagine the kind shepherd comes along beside you. What do you want to say to Him? What do you need to ask for? He wants to bring healing from all that is broken in your life. Tell Him what is holding you captive and what you are angry or bitter about. Tell Him the losses you have suffered. And thank Him for His ability to lovingly rescue, heal, and bring restoration and joy to your life.

Fixing What's Broken

We have been talking about attachments this week and perhaps you have recognized places in your early life that have formed insecure attachments. For some, those early experiences may be difficult to recall. Maybe you have heard stories or pieced together bits of information here or there or have had to come up with your own reasons for the some of the patterns and insecurities in your life. Sometimes it is easier to work from the present. Sometimes it is more beneficial to explore current struggles, regardless of how they started or where they came from.

Let's look at some possible symptoms that could have an insecure attachment as the root cause. These are possible symptoms because there are other events in life that may also contribute to these behaviors. Generally, you can look back over your own life and note impactful events that changed you or you can look to your own family of origin and get a sense of where behaviors began. These are also only possible symptoms because this list is not exhaustive.

Examine your thinking, feelings, and behaviors in your important relationships and check any of the symptoms below that resonate with you. You might also try rating yourself on each one from 1 to 5, with 1 meaning you rarely or never relate to that symptom and 5 meaning it describes you very well.

_____ I have little or no self-worth or esteem, no matter how many compliments I receive.

_____ I am self-reliant to the point that I won't ask for or accept help.

_____ I can't stand being alone but can't stand being with people.

_____ I will do anything to keep from being alone.

_____ I like friends until they get too close.

_____ Fear of abandonment.

_____ I fly off the handle, sometimes over silly things.

_____ Will go to great lengths to keep the relationship. Just don't leave me!

_____ Jealous and threatened when my partner moves away emotionally.

_____ Something in me resists intimacy with my partner.

_____ My relationships build the physical attraction first.

_____ People would say I have an addiction to alcohol, drugs, food, spending, or working.

_____ I find myself constantly seeking reassurance in a relationship.

_____ I'm generally untrusting or extremely slow to trust.

_____ I cannot bear it when my partner needs more from me.

_____ When conflict arises, I can't find the door fast enough.

_____ I am a hopeless caretaker.

_____ I'm often depressed, sad, or feel empty inside despite having a good life.

_____ I cycle between "I want to be near you" and "I don't want to be near you."

_____ I have no idea what I'm feeling!

It can be challenging to admit even to ourselves we have some dysfunctional traits in relationships. All of us share some of these feelings from time to time, depending on circumstances, life stressors, current mood, and many other factors. Relationships that are always difficult to maintain, however, may be due to a failure to bond with each other in a healthy way.

Being aware of the difficulty and being able to pinpoint the struggle is the first step to healing the relationship. Once we are aware we behave in some of these ways, we can look back over past hurts and discover any correlation between the message we received from the event and the behavior we adopted as a result. For example, the child who was abandoned and perceived the message she was not worth staying for may adopt the behaviors in adult relationships of constantly seeking assurance and doing anything to keep a relationship, even if it is a bad one. Or the child who has been abused may have perceived the message they were despised or unlovable and may have adopted the behavior or feeling in adulthood of having no self-worth, despite constant compliments, or may not trust even the best partner.

Beside past hurts being a roadblock to bonding in a relationship, we also may have picked up negative messages from parents, family members, teachers, coaches, or other authority figures. One comment by a trusted adult to a vulnerable child can embed itself in that child's mind and serve to inspire or brand her for life. Perhaps you are thinking of a comment right now that changed the way you saw yourself and made you believe something about yourself to this day.

Other negative messages may have been adopted simply because they were constantly modeled before us. Parents who constantly make their financial, relational, or medical worries known to their children often cultivate fears in them of scarcity, abandonment, or death. Taking time to uncover some of our negative messages can lead to freedom from untruths we have been living with for a long time.

What can be done to stop relying on these destructive behaviors and repair our insecure bonds to begin to build stronger, healthier relationships? There are many ways we can begin to heal our relationships. You have already taken the first step of acknowledging the need. Further journaling as you ask God to help and heal you can be an effective start to the process. Perhaps you may find it helpful to seek counseling to discuss what you are discovering. This group study has proven helpful to many others.

No matter which insecure style you identify with, everyone can gain healing from going to God and asking Him to reveal ways you can change. The following exercises and future chapters will be helpful in finding new ways to think, feel, and act. With God's help, you *can* create healthier, secure attachments with those you love.

Were you able to be completely honest with yourself in looking at the symptoms list? Why or why not?

_____

_____

_____

_____

What did you learn about yourself in the symptoms list? How do you feel about what you learned?

_____

_____

_____

_____

How have these behaviors or symptoms affected your adult relationships? Be specific.

_____

_____

_____

_____

What were some of the messages you received from past hurts, experiences, or environments that impact you as an adult?

_____

_____

_____

In what ways did they impact you? Be specific.

_____

_____

_____

If you could say something as an adult to someone from your past whose words or actions impacted your life in a negative way, who would that be and what would you say?

_____

_____

_____

_____

If you could say something as an adult to someone from your past whose words or actions impacted your life in a *positive* way, who would that be and what would you say?

_____

_____

_____

_____

Day 5

Read: 1 John 4:18

This beautiful verse reminds us of two amazing facts. One, that unlike us, our God loves us with a love that is perfect. And two, when we are loved with a love that is perfect, there can be no fear present. That is really thought-provoking. Obviously, there is a relationship inherent in this verse and the ones preceding. This relationship between God, who loves perfectly, without error or misunderstanding every single second of every single day, and us who cannot go one day without error or misunderstanding in our relationships, requires a giving of love and a receiving of love. The giving part, the part God does, He does so freely and without any guarantee of getting anything in return. The receiving part, the part we do, is a choice we make. And we're always hoping to get something in return, even in our receiving.

The next thought presented in this verse brings in even more head-scratching. Perfect love casts out fear, or fear cannot be present in perfect love, because fear has to do with punishment. That takes us right back to our attachment discussions! It makes sense that if we, as children, were fearful of being punished, harmed, dismissed, or ignored in some way, it would definitely affect how we related to our caregivers, right? And children are not fearful for no reason, right? If fear were present, does that mean we concluded we were loved and adored perfectly? Of course not! We would have concluded the opposite; either love was messed up or there was no love at all.

What element would have to be present in this relationship for us to not be afraid and to conclude we were loved and adored? Trust! We would have had to trust our parents or caregivers were loving and caring toward us and that any punishment rendered was done so deservedly, fairly, and in love.

Since God loves us perfectly all the time, if there is any fear on our part, it is because there is a lack of trust on our part. It would also follow then there may be an attachment issue there.

Prayer for Today

Thank God today for His perfect love. Name all the ways He shows His love to you. Acknowledge to Him you cannot love perfectly and confess those times you could love better and don't. Ask Him to help you love Him and those around you better, and pray for help in trusting His perfect love.

Your God Attachment

If we understand anything about God, we know He wants to be in relationship with us. God didn't create humans because He was lonely or needed us to run this world He had just finished creating. He needs nothing. Acts 17:25 says, "And he (God), is not served by human hands, as if he needs anything. Rather, he himself gives everyone life and breath and everything else." He created us because He wants a relationship with us. He wants a relationship with all of us as a world of people, as well as you and me individually.

Your desire (or lack of desire) for a relationship with God, however, may be based on several things. For example, you may not believe in God or believe a relationship with someone you cannot see is even possible. You may be angry with God over losses or disappointments in your life and may not want a relationship with Him. Perhaps your earthly father didn't show you love or didn't protect you. Why would you want a relationship with a Heavenly Father, if that is the only idea of a father you have?[5]

The truth is God is unlike any earthly father we may have had, good or bad. Remember yesterday we discussed His ability to love with a love that is perfect, never misunderstanding us, and always giving us exactly what is best for us. Earthly fathers with the best intentions cannot do that. We must try really hard day after day to comprehend how deeply and perfectly God loves us. And even then, we won't fully understand it until we meet Him face-to-face. There are, however, some scriptures that can give us glimpses into how great God's love is for us.

Ephesians 3:17–19 says,

> And I pray that you, being rooted and established in love, may have power, together with all the Lord's holy people, to grasp how wide and long and high and deep is the love of Christ, and to know this love that surpasses knowledge—that you may be filled to the measure of all the fullness of God.

These verses tell us God's love is so huge for us that it goes beyond what our brains can understand or know and that it starts with being rooted and established in this love. It suggests God and His love for us as that secure base from which we grow and mature and explore and learn to love Him more and more until we are filled up with His love.

Isaiah 43:1–3 gives us these most beautiful words:

> But now, this is what the Lord says—he who created you … he who formed you … "Do not fear, for I have redeemed you; I have summoned you by name; you are mine. When you pass through the waters, I will be with you; and when you pass through the rivers, they will not sweep over you. When you walk through the fire, you will not be burned; the flames will not set you ablaze. For I am the Lord your God, the Holy One of Israel, your Savior … Since you are precious and honored in my sight, and because I love you."

These are some of the most comforting words in the Bible. For those who have insecure attachments, these words are healing. For those abandoned, abused, dismissed, or misunderstood, these words are what your hearts craved from infancy. For those blessed with secure attachments, these words show an even deeper, more perfect connection is possible. For those whose adult relationships lack intimacy and understanding, or are full of conflict and strife, these words promise hope that connecting and trusting in this secure base can bring positive changes.

The end of that same forty-third chapter of Isaiah promises God is at work in this relationship, and you are not alone. He is doing His part in the relationship, working to heal and change your insecurities and your life.

Isaiah 43:18–19 says, "Forget the former things; do not dwell on the past. See, I am doing a new thing! Now it springs up; do you not perceive it? I am making a way in the wilderness and streams in the wasteland." Even the best-intentioned earthly fathers can wound us and make mistakes. Regardless of the father you had, or didn't have, your Heavenly Father wants to do a new thing. He desires to lead you on your journey and refresh you when you're weary. What a promise!

Compare and contrast your earthly father (or father figure) with your Heavenly Father.

_____

_____

_____

_____

How would you describe your God attachment? Why?

_____

_____

_____

_____

Compare the attachment style in relationships you described yesterday to your God attachment style and give reasons why they are similar or different.

_____

_____

_____

_____

Do you feel you are included in God's perfect love for us? Why or why not?

_____

_____

_____

_____

Describe your feelings when you read the Isaiah 43 verses in today's lesson.

_____

_____

_____

Chapter 4

Ain't It a Shame!

Day 1

Read: Romans 8:1–4

The first verse of our reading for today is powerful beyond words. No matter what we may have done in this life or what may have been done to us, the sin of it is completely and utterly obliterated once we have been rescued from sin by accepting Christ's free but costly gift. The thought of that is amazing and the reality of it is unbelievable! But it's true! There may still be earthly consequences for these things, but our eternal consequences for sinning against a Holy God are wiped away.

Sometimes we are more preoccupied and fearful of our earthly consequences than we are about eternal ones. We are more upset about paying a traffic fine for speeding, being sentenced to prison for robbery, or getting pregnant too young than we are that we may have sinned against God. He doesn't promise to eliminate our earthly consequences, but He promises not to condemn us to hell if we trust in Him.

This passage talks a lot about the flesh—our human nature—and how weak it is. Never is that more obvious than when we have done something wrong or have suffered from someone else's sin. Sometimes we give into the flesh by committing the sin ourselves, and sometimes we give in to the flesh by allowing someone else's shame to cover us, if it were our own. Either way, Christ Jesus condemned sin in the flesh! The last part of verse 4 encourages us to live according to the Spirit and not the flesh. That goes for both sin *and* shame!

Prayer for Today

Begin your prayer today by thanking God for the incredible gift of salvation that keeps us from being condemned to eternal death. If there are sins you have not confessed, do that now. He has promised to forgive you and not hold those sins against you any longer. If there are times you have been a victim of someone else's sin and bear the shame of that, ask God to heal you of that shame and help you to live according to the Spirit when you are tempted to climb back under the shadow of shame.

Ain't It a Shame!

Shame is a powerful feeling. Left unrecognized, shame can distort our thinking, causing us to believe things about ourselves that are not true. Shame can alter our behavior and cause isolation and withdrawal. Shame can lead to emotional and psychological disorders and even affect us physically. Yes, shame is powerful, but it doesn't have to be all-consuming. Understanding what shame is, how it affects us, and where it comes from can help us grow through it and heal from its effects.

The feeling of shame is always a response. It is often a twofold response to something that was said or done to us, or something we did, that first caused an intense desire to hide (figuratively or literally) and second caused a feeling of being flawed, bad, or worthless.[1] Shame can be a momentary feeling of humiliation (the intense desire to hide), or it can be with us our whole life like a second skin.

Where does shame come from? What causes it? We have all seen or heard about someone who was made fun of on the playground at recess. Perhaps you experienced it. Children typically speak their minds and can say cruel things if they have not been taught empathy. Children who are the recipient of such name-calling, or bullying, can bear lasting scars in the form of shame for years to come. The bully's message of dummy, ugly, fat, or not good enough sticks like glue and you can recall the incident forty years later like it happened yesterday. That's shame. Bullying can cause shame.

Other potential causes of shame are childhood traumatic events or long-term neglect, abuse, poverty, or other conditions that could cause embarrassment. Sometimes failure or public disgrace can be a cause of shame. Physical challenges or mental health disorders that elicit (real or perceived) judgment from others or self can cause shame, as can rejection, betrayal, divorce, job loss, and other events where people feel exposed, judged, and vulnerable.

These are all potential causes of shame because for shame to become more than a temporary feeling of humiliation, it must be internalized, resulting in a devaluing of self. Any one of the above potential causes can be overcome when we realize these feelings do not have to overcome *us*. We can realize these feelings are often not ours to bear but should be borne by those inflicting the humiliation. Or we might realize everyone fails sometimes and it's nothing to be ashamed of; we will just learn from it! Perhaps with some good counsel we can realize our physical or mental health disorders may indeed be judged by others, but that is only because they have no idea what it's like to be in our place. If they were, they may not handle it as well as we are! Shame does not have to control us.

Shame is not, however, as easy to recognize or heal as it sounds. Often the messages we received or the events that brought shame happened when we were not mature or developed enough to recognize the lies. They became part of us, and we were defenseless. The feelings of being a bad person, or worthless, insignificant, ugly, or dumb, are strong and don't leave without a fight. They may be such a part of us we aren't even aware we carry shame.

If you wonder whether shame has taken up residence in you, here are some of the most common behaviors people with shame exhibit. All of us have these thoughts or feelings from time to time, but if any of these resonate deeply, as though they're part of your DNA, you may be carrying shame.

Common Shame Behaviors

- often find yourself being taken advantage of
- are extremely shy and feel awkward around people
- have been told you are overly sensitive
- feel like no one likes you
- find yourself always being the first to apologize
- feel more comfortable with hairstyles that partially cover your face or eyes
- have an acute sense other people are talking about you
- keep your thoughts mostly to yourself
- would rather die than be the center of attention
- have poor posture
- cry every time there's conflict
- feel like you don't belong anywhere
- wish you could let loose and have more fun
- feel invisible or constantly overlooked
- find it uncomfortable to look people in the eye
- freeze up when people talk to you
- lash out or become defensive when criticized
- always take the blame when being criticized

Without recognizing shame, and taking steps to heal it, the long-term effects can be devastating. It is possible to live an entire life missing God's best, engaging with people, contributing to family and community, and enjoying everything life has to offer. In addition to missing out, the physical effects shame can lead to could potentially cut life short. Much research has been done on mental stressors and their effect on our bodies.

Shame is a constant mental stressor and can lead to social withdrawal, addictions, depression, anxiety, and serious physical conditions.

Earlier we said the feeling of shame is a response to something said or done. One of the reasons shame is so powerful is because it most often associates itself with secrecy and silence. Shame counts on you to carry it around without exposing it. It counts on you to remain silent and never speak about why you are feeling shame. How often do you talk about the things that bring you shame?

Throughout the Bible, sin is equated with darkness. The idea that Satan desires to destroy us by luring us into sin is most often done silently. Most of us are not apt to run out and commit a crime in broad daylight or announce it ahead of time. Most of us are probably not likely to run out and commit a crime at all. But we might be tempted in our silent alone times to do something we would not do in broad daylight or in front of our family or friends. That's how sin works. In the dark, where no one knows. And that's how shame operates. It grows and feeds on itself (and silently destroys), as long as you keep it in the dark and tell no one.

Unlike plants that represent life, whatever sin and shame you keep in the dark grows. Sin loves the dark, the secrecy, and the silence. But it dies a little each time you bring it into the light. Do you want to know how to rid yourself of shame's hold on your life and begin the healing journey from shame to life and grace? Bring it into the light. Tell someone your story. Confess your sin or shame to someone you trust. Dare to be vulnerable with another human being and let God's grace flow through them. Keep bringing it into the light, refusing to keep silent, and shame will die.

Did you relate to any of the shame behaviors? Which ones?

_____

_____

_____

_____

In what ways have these shame behaviors affected your life?

_____

_____

_____

_____

What shame messages have you believed about yourself that are lies?

_____

_____

_____

_____

How has believing these messages affected your life? Your relationships? Be specific.

_____

_____

_____

_____

Where did these shame messages come from?

_____

_____

_____

Have you had any experience with the secrecy and silence part of shame in your life? Explain.

_____

_____

_____

_____

Sharing your story brings the shame into the light. What feelings come up for you when you read that? Why?

_____

_____

_____

_____

Day 2

Read: Isaiah 41:10

Can you imagine the God who created everything we see, and the eyes to see it all with, telling you not to worry because He is going to help you and hold you up? I don't know about you, but there have been times in my life where I needed someone to hold me up and tell me everything would be all right. What a great and loving God we have!

These words were written by the prophet Isaiah to God's chosen people in Israel. Isaiah prophesied for sixty years through four kings. He had witnessed the invasion of the northern kingdom of Judah by the Assyrians and watched the Israelites there be scattered and taken captive. Horrible! He was also watching as the people in the southern kingdom were following in the footsteps of their northern brothers and sisters who had turned away from God and followed after idols. Isaiah was warning them they too would see the same fate if they failed to heed the warnings against idolatry. He warned them the Babylonians were going to destroy their beloved land.

And amid the dire warnings, God, in His lovingkindness, speaks tenderly to His faithful children who are not among those going astray but who will also have to endure the pain of the coming doom. "Don't be afraid," He tells them. "Don't be discouraged. I am going to give you strength and help you. I will be here every step of the way, just like I have always been. I will hold you up, and you will be able to endure through it all."

We have many questions when it comes to suffering and God's children. He certainly is powerful enough to stop any and all suffering. He certainly loves you and me and declares us worthy of His love and care. So why is there still suffering? I never liked the answer that God hurts when we hurt. I'm sure there is truth in that, but it sounds like He is sitting up there unable to do anything about what we are going through except to cry with us. I much prefer this image in Isaiah of a strong God who says, "Yes, I know it is painful now, but it is only for a season. I am right here giving you the strength to get through this. You can do it! I will hold you up and help you and you *will* come through it! And what awaits you when you do is beyond amazing!" Fear not!

Prayer for Today

God is always available to hear your prayers. He cares. Tell Him how hard it is for you sometimes. Tell Him what you are struggling with and what you do not understand. Give Him your pain, and ask Him to help you through it. Tell Him you are counting on Him to give you strength and to hold you up. Then thank Him for His faithfulness. He will do it!

Trauma Drama

We started off this week talking about shame. We talked about how bringing your story into the light (or sharing your story) can take some of the power of it away. That can be scary, especially if you have never told anyone before. Typically, when someone is carrying or experiencing shame, the event that caused the shame was traumatic in some way. Shame is only one of the issues that may result from a traumatic event and dealing with the shame is only one of the steps you can take to heal. In other words, healing from shame is different from healing from trauma, even though recognizing and dealing with the shame component can only help. We are going to spend the rest of this week discussing trauma, understanding how it operates, and how it affects us.

Let's get very basic about trauma. When something happens in our lives that that is emotionally disturbing or life-threatening, we all know our bodies respond. Our heart rate increases, and it takes our minds a minute to get a grasp on exactly what is going on. For example, suppose you are driving along minding your own business and suddenly the car next to you swerves into your lane, causing you to instinctively swerve into the next lane and hit the car next to you. Brakes squeal, horns honk, and people scream. Then everything is quiet. Immediately you determine no one is seriously hurt, the police report is filed, and you are back home to deal with all the insurance claims and car repairs. It may take a day or two to come down emotionally, but eventually you do. Your brain understands what happened; it all makes sense to you because, no doubt, you have told the story multiple times. It may have felt traumatic in the moment, but there are no devastating long-term effects. Your body did what it was designed to do in a crisis or dangerous situation. After the initial shock of what was happening, the part of your brain that was overwhelmed by the shock and fear was soon calmed by the part of your brain that took in the facts and determined everything was OK. The *emotional* part of your brain can now return to normal functioning thanks to the *reasonable* part of your brain.

When something shocking or frightening happens, the "fight, flight, or freeze" hormones kick in, giving a temporary surge of strength, a heightened sense of awareness, or quicker than normal responses. The reasoning part of the brain works in tandem assessing the situation and sending messages of action or calm back to the nervous system.

When trauma happens, however, the emotional part of the brain becomes overwhelmed and remains in that "fight, flight, or freeze" state. You are unable to reset your mind, your emotions, and as time goes on, perhaps even your body. Instead of the reasoning part of your brain sending out messages of action or calm, your brain becomes disconnected or short-circuits. The two parts (emotional and reasoning) are no longer working in tandem sending messages back and forth. They function as if they are disconnected.[2]

Trauma creates a failure to return to normal functioning. Your ability to cope has been hijacked and has long-term effects on normal functioning and well-being. That is because trauma takes place in the emotional part of your brain *first*. The split second your body senses something bad, shocking, or frightening is happening and you are helpless to prevent it, the adrenalin and other neurochemicals that rush to the brain now record memories as intense and emotional fragments of what happened. Those fragmented and intense memories play on a continual loop, disconnecting the emotional part of your brain from the reasonable part. The reasonable part of the brain is unable to help the emotional part of the brain get away from the trauma. These memory fragments are stored as visual images, smells, sounds, tastes, or touch.[3]

After the traumatic event, parts of the brain remain disconnected or offline. There is no calm and there is no cohesive story to make sense of. There are only sensory fragments. Consequently, your brain can easily be triggered by sensory input, reading normal circumstances as dangerous. Things you see, smell, or hear or certain touches are misinterpreted, and the brain loses its ability to tell the difference between what is threatening and what is not.

Perhaps as you are reading this week about shame and trauma you have experienced some uneasiness or some resistance to the material. That's OK. Just acknowledge it is there and keep going. It may be your body and mind trying to protect you from something it fears may cause harm. Healing is often uncomfortable, but it never causes harm.

Were there traumatic events or periods of time in your life? Will you be courageous enough to write them here, knowing this is the first step toward healing?

_____

_____

_____

_____

Do you remember feeling a sense of shame about these events? Explain.

_____

_____

_____

_____

What message or messages did you begin to believe about yourself because
the shame?

_____

_____

_____

_____

How do you feel about shedding light on your shame by telling your story?

_____

_____

_____

Use the rest of this page and the back, if necessary, to write your story. This
is a confidential first step to sharing your story and may help you when
you are ready to share. _This portion will not be discussed in the group right now._

_____

_____

_____

_____

Day 3

Read: Jeremiah 23:23–24 and Isaiah 54:10

The first two verses for our scripture reading today were written by the prophet Jeremiah, whose only message for forty years was warning the people of Israel of God's coming judgment because of their sin. These verses are amid verses written specifically about other prophets and priests of the day who were glossing over the sin of the people, instead of holding them accountable. Right in the middle of Jeremiah's discourse, he gives us this stark reminder: God sees all. There was nothing the people could do that God didn't see. There was no turning a blind eye by the prophets or priests that slipped by God. There was no hiding.

That also goes for any denial we may be living under. It is possible to ignore or shove down something we don't want to acknowledge long enough that we begin to fool ourselves. The Bible says in several places we can deceive ourselves. First John 1:8, for example, tells us we are deceiving ourselves if we say we are without sin. We also deceive ourselves when we deny the truth about our past or any faults or failures our parents may have had. Aside from God, there is no such thing as a perfect parent (and thus, a perfect childhood), yet many of us like to believe ours was (or everyone but ours was!), and we live in denial hiding the truth even to ourselves.

It might feel scary or uncomfortable to think about God seeing and knowing everything. It can also be quite comforting, however, because of His mercy and compassion. The beautiful words of Isaiah 54:10 show us how committed God is in His love and care for us. You see, whatever you have been through in your life, God was there. He heard every hurtful word. He saw every rejection and mistreatment. He knows what you did to survive. He knows how hard you try to hide from the pain even today. But He also wants to set you free from it. He wants you to come out of hiding and let Him heal your pain. He will never expose us or embarrass us. How freeing!

The irony of it is, once we decide to step into the light and decide to stop hiding, He covers the vulnerable places for us. He becomes our hiding place, our shelter, our safe haven. We no longer need the hiding places that did nothing but bring us more shame. He removes that shame and lovingly brings us into the shadow of the Almighty, where no evil or darkness can come near us.

Prayer for Today

Today is a good day to sit quietly before God and just tell Him you want to stop hiding. That's all. Just tell Him and sit quietly and let His spirit wash over you with tenderness and compassion. It is the deepest intimacy to be fully known and fully loved, and that is His desire for you.

Take Off Your Mask

On day 1 this week, we talked about how shame can be caused by words, events, or periods of time when we experienced dysfunction. Often, when something in our lives cause us to feel shame, we may begin to see ourselves as different from others. We may come to believe we are not as good as others or are unlovable or damaged. However, to function and participate in life, we must hide the shame we feel from others. We often do this by wearing an invisible mask, hoping no one will find out what we believe to be true about ourselves—that we are unlovable, damaged, or not as good.

Sometimes we may feel the need to overcompensate for this flawed person we feel we now are. We may strive to prove we *are* as good by achievements in academics, sports, or music. We may become the perfect daughter or bend over backward for a boyfriend or husband to prove we *are* loveable. To prove we are not damaged, we might avoid dating or embrace the single life, or we might choose a career or life that aligns easily with remaining single, such as the military or a missionary life. We might also move somewhere far away from family and friends. These are all ways we might mask our shame.

There are other masks as well, and shame can affect people differently. For example, not everyone feels the need to prove they are not what they fear is obvious to others. We might not have the "I'll show you" personality, so masks will look different. Perhaps it is easy for us to accept or believe we are not as good as others, so we settle. We never try. We don't live up to our potential. We settle for average or lesser grades, jobs, or dating partners, and we for sure never put ourselves out there for fun activities where we might look foolish.

If we accept the label "unlovable," it might show in our careless appearance, or it could play out in rude, disrespectful, or self-sabotaging behavior. We might *prove* we are unlovable by making sure no teacher, coworker, or boss has anything good to say about us or by running off every potential suitor or important relationship. And if our personality leads us to fully believe we are damaged, we might become wild or promiscuous in our dress or behavior. After all, we feel we're already ruined!

You might have your own name for the mask you wear to hide shame and protect yourself from being hurt like that again. We have talked about what we might call an overachiever, an invisible person, and a troublemaker. Perhaps you tried on a clown mask long ago, always making jokes to hide the pain, or maybe you became controlling, trying to make up for a situation where you had no control. You may have found a victim mask fit you well or a frozen mask where you never showed emotions.

Whatever mask you chose, you did it to survive. You did it to protect the child that you were the only way you knew how. Just as we said shining a light dispels the darkness, so does recognizing our masks and the shame they hide. When we recognize the mask we wore to cover our shame all began with something said or done to us, or an event or period of time we experienced, a little light is shed, the darkness diminishes, and healing begins. As we go through the rest of this week, begin to link in your mind the events of the past that caused you shame and the mask you wore or wear to hide it.

What events in your past have caused you to feel shame?

_____

_____

_____

_____

Do you recall feeling different from other people because of the shame? Explain.

_____

_____

_____

_____

Did you try to hide or mask your shame? How? From whom?

_____

_____

_____

_____

How do you think hiding behind a mask helped you cope with life?

_____

_____

_____

_____

What might you have missed out on in your life because of hiding behind the mask(s)?

_____

_____

_____

_____

What would it take to remove your mask(s) and begin living without it? How might your life be different?

_____

_____

_____

_____

Day 4

Read: 1 Peter 5:8–10 and Galatians 5:1

Our readings for today remind us of the familiar question "Which do you want first: the good news or the bad news?" Since the past couple days may have been rather heavy for some, it would seem best to start with the good news. Unfortunately, we're not going to do that. But fortunately, there is good news to follow.

It is important for us to remember that all suffering, all evil, all abuse, all dysfunction, and all trauma in the world are a result of sin entering God's perfect creation when Satan first tempted Eve. Everything bad that has ever happened to you in your life we could say was Satan's fault, and we could blame him all day long, and we would be justified. However, we are still accountable for our own choices because of the sin nature passed down to us from Adam and Eve's first sin. That's the bad news.

Of course, knowing how sin entered the world is just part of the story. We also need to remember the devil still continually works to destroy the good in the world. The first scripture urges us to be as alert as if we were alone at night on the savanna hearing a deep, menacing roar of a hungry lion. Peter likens the devil to a lion on the prowl looking for his next meal. The hunt. Choosing the prey. The setup. The pounce. The devour. The carnage left behind. And he always has a next meal coming as long as he roams this earth.

Tucked into this same verse, however, is the good news! There is hope in the instruction to resist the devil. Because we are instructed to resist him, we know it is possible. We can remain firm in our faith, and we don't have to give in to his ways. We don't have to listen to him when he brings up our past and tells us we are no good, worthless, or not enough. We do not have to be a slave to him and his lies.

And this brings us to even more good news! Paul tells us in Galatians we have been set free! No longer are we victim to the lion's snare or his evil tricks or lies. We can choose Christ every time and refuse to submit to the yoke of slavery we have been bound by our whole lives. We can claim our freedom in Christ, throw off the shame and the masks we have worn to hide our shame, and take on our new identity in Christ. His beloved child, His heir, His treasure!

Prayer for Today

Thank God today for His authority over sin and the devil's snares. Thank Him we do not have to be a victim of his lies. Tell Him you want to live a life set free from sin and shame!

Author of Trauma, Father of Lies

It is true Satan wants us to stay stuck in the sin and dysfunction of the past. He is the reason for the sin, dysfunction, and trauma of our past and is responsible for the lies we believe about ourselves because of it. From the beginning, he has been the author of trauma and the father of lies. He has perfected his craft and used it on every generation since the beginning of time.

The Bible has much to say about the generations and the sins of the fathers. It's easy to see how generational sin passes from one to the next. Habits, attitudes, beliefs, and behaviors are learned from a young age just by observing. They also pick up bad language or coping habits and behaviors like yelling, hitting, drinking, and others. Often children grow up thinking everything that happened in the family was normal, only to learn later it was not. The enemy cleverly confuses what is truth and what is a lie.

Recognizing and acknowledging the truth of our past is an important first step toward healing. No wound can be healed if it is not recognized and addressed. Trying to cover it up and forgetting about it only causes more problems later. But neither is acknowledging it enough. We can say we will never repeat the sins or dysfunctions of our parents, but rarely is that possible, and it often brings guilt and more shame when we fail. Simply acknowledging our past and the truth of what it looked like will not heal the wound. We must look at the truth of the past, allow Christ to set us free from the bondage of it, remain vigilant against the enemy of our soul, and claim our true identity in light of what God's Word says about us. John 8:36 says, "So if the Son sets you free, you will be free indeed." Sadly, setting us free does not mean we are magically rid of the scars we carry or the masks we have worn our whole lives. That's where staying vigilant against Satan's constant efforts to hold us under water is vital. No longer are we bound by the labels we wore as a child. We are free. No longer are we cursed by the shame of an event. We are free. No longer are we condemned by our own sinful mistakes. We are free. No longer are we alone, abandoned, or abused. We are free! But that doesn't mean Satan will leave us alone. He won't. We will constantly face situations, conversations, or memories that will tempt us to go back to those feelings and beliefs about ourselves. And every time we refuse to go back, every time we remind the tempter (and ourselves!), we are no longer bound to those feelings and beliefs about ourselves. Every time we practice saying no, we grow stronger and the old fades away as the new takes hold.

Getting healthy and healing from the past takes work and isn't for weaklings. But for some reason, Jesus has brought you to this place at this time, and He will be with you every step of the way. Having a supportive group of people who are also on a healing journey is a gift from God. When you are tempted to give up, they will spur you on. When you are afraid to look at something or take the next step, there will be those who have already taken that step and will be there to encourage you.

There is healing in Jesus and often there is a part for us to play in our healing. Jesus almost always gave a command as part of His healing. "Get up." "Take up your bed." "Come forth." "Go wash." It's not that we wouldn't be healed without doing those things. Those commands were not given so Jesus could heal. They're not for Him; they're for us! They're part of His authority, for us to listen to His words and to obey what He tells us. It's also wise on Jesus's part, because He knows healing brings changes—changes we may or may not be ready for.

Some of us have lived as victims of our past. Changing that identity is hard. Being a victim requires no accountability. We can simply go through our lives claiming we are how we are because of what happened to us and there's nothing we can do about that. It's why Jesus asked the man at the pool of Bethesda if he wanted to get well. Are you kidding? Who wouldn't want to be healed and be free from spending your whole life lying helplessly with a bunch of other invalids? But it's all he knew. It was his life. His normal. No doubt these were his friends. They commiserated together and supported each other's invalidness. If Jesus were to heal him, he would have to give up the familiar life he knew. There would be a new normal. He would need new friends. He would have to find somewhere else to live. He might have to get a job. He might start thinking it was all too hard, and he would just stay where he was, thank you very much. And Jesus knew that.

When God heals, He can use any means at His command. He can heal immediately, and He can use doctors and modern-day medicine. His healing may require time, patience, and setbacks. But He will guide you to deal with every last dysfunctional piece as He feels you are ready. In the days ahead, ask God to bring to your mind anything and everything He wants to heal you from. There may be areas you are completely oblivious to that need His healing touch. Stay open and follow the Spirit's leading.

Some of you may not completely relate to having great trauma in the past that needs healing or didn't experience damaging dysfunction in your families growing up. Use these sessions to ask God how He wants to use this material in your life. Maybe your trauma happened later in life. Perhaps He has brought or will bring someone into your life who has experienced past wounds that need healing. Or maybe you will become a more compassionate person as you recognize the woundedness in others. Wherever we find ourselves in life's journey, we have all experienced or will experience some measure of trauma or suffering and God wants us to know it is not His intention for us to stay stuck in the effects it can have on us or the lies we have believed about ourselves or Him, because of the trauma or suffering.

In what ways have you recognized Satan's part in your trauma or in helping you stay stuck in the results it created? Explain.

_____

_____

_____

_____

When was the last time you were triggered by an experience, place, conversation, or comment that caused you to believe the lies about yourself created by shame?

_____

_____

_____

_____

What is it you want healing from?

_____

_____

_____

_____

Are you prepared to walk away from the shroud of shame, the masks, and other systems that have kept you in the place of being a victim (or from the guilt of your own bad choices)? Why or why not?

_____

_____

_____

_____

Day 5

Read: Romans 12:2–3

These words of the apostle Paul are helpful for us in so many ways and at so many times in our lives. As we discuss shame, trauma, and hidden things from the past, the principle of renewing our minds may be a familiar concept to you. You may have already learned the importance of renewing your mind with the truth of what God say's about you rather than the lies the enemy tried to sow in your heart and mind years ago.

But did you ever consider that hiding our shame by masking it with a belief or behavior could be a way of conforming to this world? Initially, of course, we did it to protect ourselves or to survive, and we probably weren't aware we were doing it at the time. As God sheds light on our thoughts, beliefs, and behaviors, He is inviting us to accept the truth of our past and allow Him to cover it with His grace instead of hiding it.

Often when we look at the dysfunction of our families or the indignities of our past, it seems easier to deny than to face the reality and embarrassment if someone found out. That's the way the world deals with disgrace and humiliation too. It's hidden, masked, and denied it ever happened. It is the pattern of the world. We never want others to know we were poor, abused, failed in school, or that our parents were alcoholics. We want to hide all the dysfunction and appear normal.

These verses encourage us not to think more highly of ourselves than we ought. Nor do we want to believe we are less than, because Christ has adopted us as His children and we are His heirs. But we are to think of ourselves with sober judgment. Acknowledge the truth. Accept the denial. No more humiliation. No more shame.

Prayer for Today

Today as you come before Him, who overcame rejection, humiliation, and shame, pour your heart out to Him about the painful parts of your past you have tried so hard to hide. Ask Him to help you bring them out of hiding and to cover them with His grace so there is no more denial. Ask Him to make you an overcomer who can humbly and truthfully tell your story because it is a testimony to His amazing ability to bring beauty from ashes.

Whose Shame Is It Anyway?

Shame is powerful. Shame can cover us, control us, consume us, and change us. That shouldn't surprise us, since we have already acknowledged who is behind our shame. The Bible tells us Satan is a deceiver, and that is exactly how he does business. He takes whatever trauma we have been through and embeds it deeply within us where the seeds of shame begin to grow. He waters the seeds with thoughts of not being good enough or being damaged—somehow different and not as good as those around us. He uses other events, people, discussions, or comments throughout our lives to nourish these thoughts, confirming over and over to us that we are indeed damaged and not as good as those around us. And soon, as the shame grows, it becomes a truth we own—a truth we live by.

Here is where Satan's deceit works its magic, layering shame upon shame. Not only are we now living and believing the shame, but we are also most likely acting as if we have no shame! And we think no one else does either! We become so committed to keeping our own shame camouflaged we may even forget it does not belong to us in the first place.

We accepted this tremendous burden of shame like an undercover setup. Then we carried it for so long we forgot it wasn't ours. We made room for it in every situation. We covered it and molded it to fit us, and it has become so much a part of us we can't go anywhere without it. We have become a master of our own disguise as we blend in and pretend everything is all right when deep down, we know it is not. This works fine until we are triggered by a conversation, a comment, or a circumstance that feels a little too uncomfortable, a little too exposing. And it all comes flooding back.

The most deceitful part of this cheap trick of shame is that when we are triggered by an uncomfortable conversation or a comment or a circumstance, what comes flooding back is often *not* the distinct memory of the original trauma. What floods us are the feelings of shame *about* the trauma! All of the lies we have believed about ourselves, because of the shame, scream in our ears for one reason and one reason only: so that we will forget who the shame really belongs to.

No doubt you have seen it all too often. Someone does something wrong then turns around and blames the fallout on someone else. It's the pattern of the world. A mom loses her temper with her little children after a bad day at work and blames them for not being good. A guy rapes a young girl, and she gets blamed for walking down the street alone. A husband cheats on his wife, then blames her for not meeting his needs. Do you think the battered children come to believe they deserved the beating? Do you think the girl comes to believe she somehow contributed to being raped? Do you think the betrayed wife comes to believe she caused her husband to cheat? If Satan gets his way, that's exactly what happens. When the little children and the young girl and the betrayed wife forget who the shame really belongs to, it's a double win for evil. First, the one who is guilty gets away with their sin and can be manipulated to sin again. Second, the victim begins to live a life contrary to who God made them to be, which can hinder their usefulness in the kingdom of God.

It may sound counterintuitive to say that living in shame is conforming to the pattern of this world. After all, we are to have compassion for those touched by trauma and living in shame as a result. And indeed, we are. When we find ourselves in that situation, and we are one of God's children, there is no longer any condemnation. We indeed show compassion. But that does not mean we are to *remain* living in shame. Once we know there is healing for the shame we carry, once we recognize the shame is not ours to bear, we can be cleansed of the shame and go on to live unaffected by someone else's shame. Not only do we look on others with no condemnation, but we also look on ourselves with no condemnation. To remain living in shame is to choose the pattern of this world.

We will learn in the weeks ahead more about this healing from shame and how to live a shame-free life. For now, it is enough to recognize the shame you carry does not belong to you. If the source of your shame is a failing, a neglect, or a willful sin by someone else, the shame belongs to them. Refuse to carry their shame. If the source of your shame is a failing, a neglect, or a willful sin of your own doing, confess that failing, neglect, or sin and know you are no longer condemned. The shame of it belongs to the deceiver. Refuse to carry his shame.

How do you feel about carrying shame that belongs to someone else?

_____

_____

_____

_____

Has the shame you've carried been the result of someone else's failing, neglect, or willful sin? Explain.

_____

_____

_____

_____

Has there been any shame of your own failing, neglect, or sin? Have you experienced forgiveness? Explain.

_____

_____

_____

_____

How do you feel about the idea that continuing to carry shame is a way of conforming to the patterns of this world?

_____

_____

_____

_____

What would change in your life if you refused to continue to carry the shame you've been carrying?

_____

_____

_____

_____

How might your life be affected if you continue to carry the shame? How about your spiritual life?

_____

_____

_____

_____

What needs to change for you to refuse to carry the shame any longer?

_____

_____

_____

_____

Chapter 5

No Suffering for Me, Please

Day 1

Read: 2 Samuel 6:12–23 and 1 Chronicles 15:29

Our reading today is about a woman named Michal, who was one of King's Saul's five children and his youngest daughter (1 Samuel 14:49). Our story focuses on what we would all probably read as a jealous outburst by Michal toward David, who had recently been made king (replacing her father) and was now her husband. That's right! Michal went from being Princess Michal, daughter of the king of all the tribes of Israel, to Queen Michal, wife of the new king of Israel, one of several wives of the king.

The Bible gives us an interesting peek inside the marriage of these two. David is ecstatic and is rejoicing over bringing the Ark of the Covenant back to its rightful place in Jerusalem after years of being taken. The scriptures tell us Michal watches from an upper window as her husband, the king, dances in worship before the Lord. She is not pleased, to say the least. In fact, she accuses him of intentionally showing off his physique to all the young maidens.

Whatever provoked such a jealous reaction from Michal, we can infer it may have been due to a lack of trust on her part. She was watching from an upper window, not walking by catching a glimpse. She was watching. Perhaps she was watching for his arrival into the city after having been gone a few days because she missed him and was excited to have him home. But then why wasn't she down worshiping with him? And why when she saw him entering the city all happy and jumping and dancing around did she "despise him in her heart" (verse 16?) Sounds like there was trouble in paradise. What could be the reason for Michal's attitude and lack of trust?

Michal is caught in the middle of some interesting relationships. First, Princess Michal is head over heels in love with her big brother's best friend (1 Samuel 18:20). Her brother Jonathan (listed as first of King Saul's children in 1 Samuel 14:49) is David's best friend, and her father eventually gives her in marriage to David, but purely for political reasons. Thanks, Dad. Then there are years when her father spends every waking moment trying to kill her husband! Let's say that again. Her father was trying to kill her husband! She even lied to her father to save David. That's a lot of family dysfunction right there.

Meanwhile, her husband also has other wives. Michal wasn't his one and only, despite him being hers. He was also married to Ahinoam, Abigail, Bathsheba, and several more, according to genealogical records found in 1 Chronicles 3. As if that isn't bad enough (even if it is your culture), her father decides to rip her away from her husband and her royal digs and forces her to marry someone else while David is running for his life (1 Samuel 25:44). Michal is used as a political pawn once again. Her husband, the king, doesn't try to get her back until years later when, you guessed it, it makes sense for him politically (2 Samuel 3:12–16). Notice David doesn't refer to Michal as his wife here but as the king's daughter.

Notice also whether David the king actually loves her or not, her current husband surely did. After these things, we see Michal's father, the previous great King Saul, die by intentionally falling on his sword and her three brothers die in the same battle (1 Samuel 31:8). As if these losses weren't enough, Michal dies never having children (2 Samuel 6:23).

Michal was a manipulated princess, a political trophy wife, a barren rose in a thorny harem, and a pawn in a tug-o-war. Perhaps we can relate to the trust issues she may have had, even if we faced different circumstances.

Prayer for Today

Sometimes the accounts of people in the Bible have pieces of our own lives in them. We may not be married to a king, but we can relate to some of the broken dreams, betrayal, or feeling used. Ask God to show you how pieces of your story have caused you to have trust issues, especially with Him.

The Whole Trust Thing

Trust means placing confidence in someone or something. As humans, we all experience trust. We must trust to live. Without *some* measure of trust, we would fail to breathe or move and would eventually die. Without trust, fear rules. We learn to trust as newborn infants when we take our first breath. Without knowing it, we trust the air we inhale and the lungs that take it in will continue to work on their own with no effort on our part. We learn to trust someone will feed us when we cry. Later we learn to trust our legs and muscles will hold us up and allow us to walk. Trust builds in every little thing we do every single day of our new lives.

Eventually, our trust becomes something we choose. Perhaps unknowingly, at first, but as we experience interactions with people and things around us, we get an inner sense of who and what we can trust. We learn if we continue to climb on a broken chair, we will also continue to fall and hurt ourselves. That chair is not trustworthy. We learn if someone continually promises to give us a cookie or take us to the store but never comes through with the cookie or always leaves us behind, that person may not be trustworthy.

Our early experiences shape our sense of trust. If we have been hurt, shamed, or abused, we will naturally develop walls of mistrust to prevent further pain. Likewise, if our parents, caretakers, or authority figures were consistently unreliable, we learned not to depend on anyone else but ourselves, setting us up for mistrust of others. On the other hand, children who grow up neglected may be so hungry for love and attention they become too trusting, at the hands of people and situations that are not good for them. This can lead to living in denial about poor choices and outcomes rather than risk losing perceived love and attention.

It is no stretch to see how these attitudes of trust can be projected onto our Heavenly Father. If there have been instances when someone we esteemed or respected and whom we should have been able to trust abused that trust, perhaps we equate those behaviors with God, whom we are also asked to esteem, respect, and trust. At the very least, we might be skeptical and keep our distance.

A similar result can come from someone who is hungry for love and overly trusting. Just as in earthly relationships, we might live in spiritual denial, pretending everything is great, but secretly we keep our distance behind spiritual walls that surround our hearts.

The antidote for trust issues is both truth and grace. We must begin to tell ourselves the truth. The truth about our past, about our relationships, and the about how we are protecting our hearts with walls of mistrust. And we then begin to trust ourselves. We begin to trust we have the wisdom and discernment to know who we can trust and who we cannot. We get to choose! We give ourselves grace for times past of not trusting those we could have and for trusting those we should not have.

We begin to trust God as we look back over our lives and see how He has been faithful, no matter what we have gone through. We begin to go to Him giving Him a little more, and a little more, of ourselves as He proves He is trustworthy. We can trust Him to be with us, to never leave us, to guide us, and to direct our thoughts as we seek Him.

We may always feel vulnerable in the trust department. After all, most all of us can relate to disappointments or wounds where our trust in how things are supposed to be was shaken or destroyed. Rebuilding that trust is not easy, and we won't do it perfectly. But as we grow in our trust, we will realize we each have a responsibility to be trustworthy and someone else's lack of trustworthiness is not about us. There is only One we can totally and completely trust, and He is the foundation on which to build our trust.

Have there been people or situations in your life that have shaken or destroyed your trust? Explain.

_____

_____

_____

_____

How have those experiences affected your relationships today?

_____

_____

_____

_____

How have those experiences affected your relationship with God?

_____

_____

_____

_____

How might your life be different if your trust issues were healed?

_____

_____

_____

_____

Day 2

Read: Psalm 91

"He that dwells in the secret place of the Most High shall abide in the shadow of the Almighty. I will say of the Lord, 'He is my shelter and my fortress. My God, in whom I trust.'" What comforting verses! I remember the helpless panic I felt when my world fell apart. When the final divorce papers were signed, I could hardly breathe. I plopped in my red chair sobbing, and I cried out to God, "If this were physical, I would be calling 911. I need an ambulance or something! I'm dying here, and there is no one to call and nowhere to go. There is no 911 for this!"

As soon as those words left my lips, I felt an instant assurance in my heart. "Oh yes, there is!" The voice was not audible, but it was definitely spoken. "Dial 91:1" It was like someone put an oxygen mask on me. I could breathe! I ran over to my desk and flipped through my Bible to the book of Psalms. In that moment, I wasn't sure if any other book had ninety-one chapters, but I knew Psalms did! When I read the words of Psalm 91:1, I wept for days. I said them over and over and over. I read them, I memorized them, and I wrote them. They became my theme. "I need your secret place. I want to hide out in your great and mighty shadow safely sheltered behind you as my fortress. I am trusting you. I am trusting you!"

God's Word for us in times of suffering can be a healing balm—even if we can't focus completely, even if we only remember part of a verse, even if we don't understand the whole passage. Do you know why? Because these are God's words to us. He speaks them directly to us just when we need to hear them. They are words of peace and comfort or instruction and conviction. They are praise and adoration. His words tell us who He is and what He wants for us. When all around us are chaos, pain, and confusion, His words are a shelter and a fortress. Dwell in His secret place and abide in His Almighty shadow.

Prayer for Today

Today thank God that He knows everything about your life. He knows the pain, suffering, fear, and confusion. Praise Him for being a kind and compassionate God who is never too busy to listen to your heart's cry. Thank Him for His Holy Spirit who interprets your groanings even when your heart is so burdened you can't pull together a sentence or don't even know what or how to pray. Thank Him for being all wise and all understanding. Ask Him to give you what you need today in this very moment.

The Truth about Suffering

Some people have the idea that receiving Christ into our lives means all our troubles and trials will go away. He will heal all our diseases, perform miracles in our finances, bring our wayward children home, and restore all our relationships. Certainly, Christ is able to do any and all of those things, and He often does. Those of us who have followed Christ for a while, however, know suffering and trials are a part of this life whether we follow Christ or not. But we also know when we give our hearts and lives to Jesus, we are acknowledging He knows things we do not know, and we trust Him to work on our behalf for His good purposes.

We may also be familiar with John 16:33, where Christ Himself assures us. "In this world you will have trouble. But take heart! I have overcome the world." We can be sure God cares about our troubles, trials, and sufferings that are certain while "in this world." Sometimes, because of sin, things happen that cause us to suffer, so sometimes suffering may be at the hand of Satan. In that same scripture, Jesus tells us to "take heart." This is meant to be an encouragement or a comfort. We don't lose hope or become discouraged; rather, we can have confidence in Him for our future because He has overcome everything this world and Satan could possibly throw at us, including death!

I like what Carolyn Custis James says about suffering. While God may permit suffering in this life, He "harnesses the sufferings of his children and compels the bad things that happen to us to serve His good purposes for us and for our mission in this world."[1] God not only uses suffering during and after the fact, but He also has a planned purpose for our suffering—even though He may not let us know why He is allowing our suffering or what His purposes are.

In his 1996 book *The Fire of Delayed Answers*, Bob Sorge [2] suggests many purposes God has for the suffering and waiting periods of our lives, including these:

1. For obedience. Think of a child who is disciplined, not punished for bad behavior but disciplined, as training to teach right behavior and sometimes to teach consequences. Psalm 119:67 says, "Before I was afflicted, I went astray, but now I keep your word."

2. To deepen our knowledge of Christ. The more Christ suffered, the more He pressed in and sought His Heavenly Father, even to the point of sweating drops of blood. It is always through pain that we grow closer to God. When things are good, we tend to go on autopilot. God can use suffering to draw us closer.

3. To awaken us to the spiritual. Sometimes we need a wakeup call to begin to see where we have been failing. For example, recall the suffering of Samson after the Philistines gouged out his eyes! Samson was raised by godly parents, and he had a divine anointing in the power of the Spirit that flowed through him. Yet he continually refused to follow God's laws for his calling. Only after losing his eyesight did he really begin to see! He was awakened to the spiritual in prison where he was humbled and returned to God. Samson did more to save the Israelites in his few remaining years of blindness than in his entire life. God can use our suffering to align our priorities.

4. To strengthen our faith or refine us. We realize how much stronger our faith becomes during trials as reliance on God is all we can do. First Peter 1:6–7 says,

> In all this you greatly rejoice, though now for a little while you may have had to suffer grief in all kinds of trials. These (trials) have come so that the proven genuineness of your faith—of greater worth than gold (which perishes even though refined by fire), may result in praise, glory and honor when Jesus Christ is revealed.

5. For greater compassion for others. We become more sensitive to the suffering of others and can relate to their plight once we have experienced similar circumstances. Second Corinthians 1:3–4 says,

> Praise be to the God and father of our Lord Jesus Christ, the father of compassion and the God of all comfort, who comforts us in all our troubles, so that we can comfort those in any trouble with the comfort we ourselves receive from God. We know this to be true that often after we go through a period of suffering God puts someone in our path going through a similar experience, and we are better able to comfort and encourage them because of what we have endured.

6. To reveal God's glory. Bob Sorge reminds us, "When God does move or rescue or heal, He always gets the glory. Every time he healed in the NT, His glory was revealed. But first, there was suffering or pain or waiting."
7. For greater spiritual maturity. Most of us would prefer less character to more suffering, but we are no longer our own; we were bought with a price (1 Corinthians 6:19–20). We are urged to grow up in our faith and pursue Christlikeness as the Holy Spirit does His work in us. Romans 5:3–4 states, "We know that suffering produces perseverance; perseverance, character; and character, hope." As one builds on the other, we are maturing spiritually.

Likewise, James tells us,

> Consider it pure joy, my brothers and sisters, whenever you face trials of many kinds, because you know that the testing of your faith produces perseverance. Let perseverance finish its work so that you may be mature and complete, not lacking anything. (James 1:2–4)

Not many of us can say we consider trying times pure joy. But persevering through trials we may better relate to. Perhaps we can take comfort in knowing our perseverance is maturing us and making us whole.

None of us have a dream in life to suffer. Yet all of us will suffer at some point in our lives. Like birth and death, it is the one thing in life we all have in common, even though our sufferings look different and seem to come in varying intensities. One person may be devastated by something for which another person would gladly trade. Different parts of the world seem to experience different sufferings, as do different socioeconomic levels. Yet there is so much suffering in the those who appear to have it the easiest, and so much joy in those who appear to have it the hardest, it all remains a mystery only God can understand. We must not compare our sufferings, only endure those that befall us.

And as part of that enduring, we must ask ourselves these two questions:

- What kind of person does God want me to be in this suffering?
- What am I supposed to learn from it?

Are there any trials or sufferings in your life for which you believe you know the purpose? Explain.

_____

_____

_____

_____

Are there trials or sufferings you have experienced for which you saw no purpose? Do any of God's purposes discussed in today's reading seem to be possibilities for those sufferings? Explain.

_____

_____

_____

_____

What would you like to tell God about the current struggle you are facing?

_____

_____

_____

_____

Day 3

Read: 2 Corinthians 11:23–33 and 12:7–10

When we think of the apostle Paul, we think of a spiritual giant who was sent to straighten out the early church and prevent them from moving away from the true gospel of Christ. And that he was for sure! We know about his beatings and imprisonments, but I think sometimes we gloss over them, as if the reason Paul was able to make it through such suffering was because he was made of such strong stuff. After all, he was quite the heavy persecutor before he became a believer, right? But what if it was the other way around? What if Paul was made of such strong stuff because he went through such suffering?

We see in our readings for today that Paul did much self-examination about his former life as a persecutor, his sufferings, and his relationship with God. He stays true to what God has called him to do, despite the hardships. We might argue if we were walking along and a bright light blinded us and a voice told us to change our ways, we would stay true to that as well. No doubt, however, many of us have had undeniable and powerful encounters with God in our lives that have faded to the background when trouble comes knocking. Paul had one trouble after another, yet he never wavered. He continued to do what God wanted him to do and to be the man God wanted him to be.

Not only did Paul not waver in the face of trouble and suffering, but he also used those circumstances to learn from God. He learned more about his own calling and task and more about God and his relationship with Him. The hardest part of this to understand is how God taught him these lessons. Here was Paul, a man God obviously handpicked to carry His message, to build His church, and to leave behind for us his legacy of lessons. We would think Paul had God's ear on every prayer he prayed! And he did. We would think Paul would be a teacher's pet or God's favored child! And he was (as we all are). We would think whatever Paul asked of God, He would do! But He didn't.

That's the interesting thing about suffering and God. Sometimes He heals and changes our circumstances and sometimes He doesn't. But He *always* listens and sees us, and He always walks with us and teaches us about Him, about ourselves, and about our relationship with Him.

Prayer for Today

Today as you pray, take time to tell God how you feel about your suffering. Confess the helplessness and hopelessness you feel. Ask for His peace and comfort. Then sit quietly and wait for Him. Finally, ask Him to help you stay true to the person He wants you to be and the things He wants you to do and to teach you what He wants you to know.

Two Practical Questions

Suffering comes in all shapes and sizes and looks different to different people. Some people in the Western world think they are suffering when they have to cancel a vacation, while elsewhere in the world walking two miles for water is part of daily life and not considered suffering at all. In this regard, we could say suffering is relative as it exists only in relation to the perceptions and circumstances of those involved. That's why it can be at once challenging to share our sufferings and to listen to others' sufferings.

To be sure we often need the support, and sometimes the help, of other people when we are going through some sort of suffering. The truth is, however, there are some sufferings we must go through by ourselves. As close as we are to our family, friends, or even our spouse, no one else truly knows what we are thinking or feeling when we get a cancer diagnosis or receive our first chemotherapy treatment. No one can feel our pain after surgery or know the anguish in our heart from a shattered relationship. No one else knows the searing loss from the death of a child or the fear and concern from losing a job or a home. No one else can feel the anger of things not turning out liked we hoped or planned.

Of course, we know we are never alone. We know God is there with us and fully understands our sufferings. But these are the times when it doesn't *feel* like He's there. These are the times when we feel abandoned and left to deal with all the fear and pain alone. So what do we do? How do we deal with these feelings and walk through these circumstances that may or may not have an end to them?

There are two practical questions we can ask ourselves during these times to help us stay true to who God called us to be. The first question is this: "What kind of person do I want to be?" We already know the kind of person God wants us to be, and frankly, sometimes in times of suffering and hardships, it feels impossible to measure up to that. (Thank God for His patience and compassion.) Asking ourselves, "What kind of person do *I* want to be?" puts the decision and the choice back on me. It reminds me I have chosen to follow Christ and I want to live up to values and standards I can be proud of.

Having lived a memorable portion of my life in Nashville, Tennessee, I came to appreciate the candor of country music. Many of the lyrics offer us a plethora of options on how to deal with sufferings and tough times. One catchy tune and perfect rhyme advises the betrayed lass to bash in the headlights of his prized sportscar and take a knife to his leather seats. Another equally creative song reminds girls their mamas expect them to dry up their tears, put on their lipstick, swallow down their hurt, and act like life is perfect. Others suggest everything from crying in beer to making lemonade to simply getting a new attitude. Most of these are not my glass of sweet tea, but I do believe the Lord might get a kick out of some of the revenge tactics humans think about—as long as we don't go through with them. However, it likely also pains Him greatly to see the many ways humans try to deal with trials instead of coming to Him and practicing the ways He has taught us.

"What kind of person do I want to be?" is not a question that reminds me others may be watching, asks what kind of witness I am being, or asks all the other self-focused questions we have been taught to ask ourselves. Those questions can lead to vanity and pride. This question is different. It is introspective and leads to humility and growth. It's the kind of question that says I can lay my head down at night and know I have carried myself to the best of my ability as the child of God I want to be. I have held my tongue and resisted complaining or lashing out. I have examined my motives and stopped myself from doing things out of bitterness, revenge, anger, fear, or even pain. This question is an arrow on the compass of my life that points to true north and guides my every word, action, and response. It is the answer to who I want to be in the face of suffering. What kind of person do I want to be?

The second question that helps us walk through these trials and sufferings is "What am I supposed to learn from this?" The answer to this question may not be immediately known. In fact, we may not know the answer in this life. But wrestling with this question and keeping a journal or taking note of what we are learning from our suffering is vital to not being sucked into the suffering itself. This question can have spiritual implications, relational implications, and physical, financial, emotional, and mental implications. The very exercise of asking ourselves (and asking God), "What is my lesson in this?" creates room for us to evaluate where we have been in this journey and what we have learned along the way. It can bring hope and surprise at how much we have changed and grown, and it can lead to setting goals of going even farther and living for the day when things might be different or better.

You may have heard people say trials are here in this life to teach us lessons and we will continue to face the same trials over and over until and unless we learn whatever lesson we're supposed to learn. I don't recall that being anywhere in scripture, but I do know people who still suffer trials who have learned how to walk through them with a grace and dignity that is beyond humanly possible. Jesus is our perfect example of suffering with grace and dignity. Being mocked and ridiculed, beaten and hung on a cross, He was not angry, offered no resistance, and asked for forgiveness for His persecutors. For us, He is present and faithful in our suffering, and His grace is sufficient. His power is made perfect in the very times we are weak. And that is how we walk through suffering with a grace and dignity that is beyond humanly possible.

What kind of person do you want to be in the struggle you are facing?

_____

_____

_____

_____

What would you have to change or do to be that person in this struggle?

_____

_____

_____

_____

What are some lessons you have learned or are learning from your current suffering or trial?

_____

_____

_____

_____

How will learning those lessons be helpful to you or others in the future?

_____

_____

_____

_____

Do you feel God's grace is sufficient for you in your time of weakness? Why or why not?

_____

_____

_____

_____

Day 4

Read: Isaiah 40:25–31

In Isaiah 40, we get the rare opportunity to actually see a portrait of God! A self-portrait! God Himself speaks through the prophet Isaiah and lovingly describes Himself to us. We know this is all done in a loving way because God is using the prophet Isaiah to speak to a people who were about to suffer greatly. God wanted them to trust in Him and turn to Him in their suffering. These words are spoken much like a mother or father would assure a child who was afraid for their very life. This is the same compassion God is using in these verses. God tells Isaiah He is aware of the suffering of the Israelites and how long they have waited for the Messiah, waited for a Savior, waited to be saved and rescued from their pain and wandering. God tells Isaiah to comfort His children with these words. As you read the words of this chapter, picture Him talking right to you, comforting you in your waiting, in your suffering, as He asks, "Who can you even compare Me to?" Then rest as He takes your chin and gently lifts it to look at the starry night sky and begins to give this self-portrait of who He is.

First, He tells us He is Creator. He is a loving Creator who has taken the time to give a name even to every star. Somehow, He keeps track of everyone, and science tells us there are billions. He is also present and attentive, despite our ability to feel Him or see Him. He is the eternal Creator from before time. He is the rightful owner and ruler of it all. He never needs rest, sleep, recharging, or rejuvenation. Who He is, what He knows, and how He works—no one can begin to comprehend. He will fully never make sense to us in this life.

When we feel like we cannot take one more day of our circumstances—when we are that weary—He is the reason we can make it through the day, and He is the reason we wake up the next morning. He is sustainer; He allows us to bear it, to withstand it, and to endure it.

He explains to us that even the strong, energetic teenagers around us who seem to have boundless energy eventually get tired and have to sleep. And although they seem so sure-footed, nimble, and athletic, even they occasionally stumble and fall, so of course we will get tired and weak— and occasionally we will stumble and even fall. There is none among us who can bear up perfectly under the strain of life all the time without periods of complaint, unhealthy coping, becoming depressed, or failing in some way.

However, here comes the secret to the whole thing: Those who hope in the Lord (or wait on the Lord!), those who by faith rely on Him and count on all these reliable characteristics He has just revealed about Himself, will have divine resources to draw from during trials. If we commit to His ability to sustain and renew and provide and protect—that's hoping in the Lord—He will not fail us! He will give us the strength to endure, the strength to bear, the strength to suffer, the strength to wait, and the strength to come through to the end of the trial. And as we do that, we are taken into a place with Him where our souls soar into His presence, entering into the holiest, most indescribable place that makes us know Him and know we can make it through.

Prayer for Today

Take time to read the entire fortieth chapter of Isaiah, and then just sit in God's presence—the presence of the Almighty. Bask in the reality that this God who is so amazing and so holy sees you, knows all about your struggles, and is at work on your behalf. Ask Him to help you know Him more and trust Him more during your most difficult times.

The Truth about God's Answers

There are many scriptures in the Bible we go to and hold onto when we are faced with some type of difficulty or suffering. As you read the following scriptures, pay attention to how you are feeling inside. Is there a jubilation or a contentment at what you read? Or do you sense a resistance or perhaps a private shame because you can't quite believe them?

- James 5:13–18 (ESV): Is anyone among you suffering? Let him pray. Is anyone cheerful? Let him sing praise. Is anyone among you sick? Let him call for the elders of the church, and let them pray over him, anointing him with oil in the name of the Lord. And the prayer of faith will save the one who is sick, and the Lord will raise him up.
- Psalm 37:4–5 (ESV): Delight yourself in the Lord, and he will give you the desires of your heart.
- Matthew 21:21 (ESV): And Jesus answered them, "Truly, I say to you, if you have faith and do not doubt, you will not only do what has been done to the fig tree, but even if you say to this mountain, 'Be taken up and thrown into the sea,' it will happen."
- 1 John 5:14–15 (ESV): And this is the confidence that we have toward him, that if we ask anything according to his will, he hears us. And if we know that he hears us in *whatever we ask*, we know that we have the requests that we have asked of him.
- John 15:7 (ESV): If you abide in me, and my words abide in you, ask *whatever* you wish, and it will be done for you.

Look at the power and the certainty of the words here! These scriptures can be quite confusing. Based on what we read in scripture, and what we are taught about God, we believe God will be true to His word, don't we? And sometimes, He is true to His word, and He answers yes, giving us what we pray for: the healing, the finances, or the good outcome. At other times, He seems not true to His word, and He answers no and doesn't give us what we pray for—no healing (or even death), loss of job or home, or an outcome we would not call good at all. And still other times, we don't know whether He will say yes or no, and we are in a waiting period.

We know what to do with the yes answers, don't we? We praise, worship, offer gratitude, maybe tell others, and then go on with our lives! Most of us eventually deal with the no answers too. We grieve, cope, grieve some more, maybe use or abuse, and finally spiral downward, deal with it and accept it, or make something good out of it (ministry, help others in some way, learn from it and make changes). As they say, such times can make us better or bitter.

But typically, we are not good with the wait. And often the no.

We know what to do with the yes answers, but it's the wait and the no we have trouble with. Perhaps there are two things that may be happening when we are in these spaces of no and wait. When the answer is not what we want or need, or isn't what we were hoping for, it instinctively raises two questions.

The first main question is "What does this say about God?" We then begin to question to God's character and possibly His existence. Other questions follow. Is He good? Does He love me? Is He even *there*? Does He care? Is He too busy? What about His promises? Sadly, we begin to assume God is not what we have been taught He is, or who He claims to be, rather than first assuming God is not who we *thought* He was. If we ask ourselves what kind of God we had conjured up in our minds and compare that to who God says He is in His Word, we will soon discover it is our image of God that has misled us, not God Himself.

Still, we are left with this huge no or wait answer that we simply cannot resolve. If God is indeed a good and powerful God and has answered many other prayers throughout history, then that instinctively raises our second question.

The second main question is "What does this say about *me?* If God isn't the problem, then it must be me. Again, more questions follow. Does God love me? Is there still a purpose for me? Can I make it through this? Does God care about me? Does *anyone* care about me? If we again take the answers we are feeling and compare those to what God's Word tells us about whether He loves and cares for us (see Matthew 6:25–34), whether we have a purpose (see Jeremiah 29:11), or whether we can make it through whatever we are facing (see our scripture for today), we will again discover it is our human frailties that cause us to believe such distortions.

When we pray and trust God to answer our prayers, our trust is often based on conditions created by our own understanding. We assign God motives and traits like ours, *our* understanding of compassion, *our* understanding of need, *our* understanding of a desperate situation. Our prayers, our trust, and our God cannot be based on *our* understanding. It all must be based on the *person* of the Triune God who operates not on conditions but on His supremacy, His sovereignty, His goodness, and His justice, all attributes we cannot possibly fully understand.

We must base our prayers and our trust on *Him*, not what we think should happen or what we think would be best. Will we be disappointed? Yes. Will our hearts be broken? Yes. Will things always work out how we think is best? No. But when we pray in His will, we remain confident He is able, and we rest in the confidence that He is indeed willing, *when He thinks it's best.*

As Timothy Keller, the *New York Times* best-selling author and successful Christian evangelist, tweeted in 2014, "God will either give us what we ask for in prayer or give us what we would have asked for if we knew everything He knows."[3] Trusting God when He doesn't do things the way we think He should is not easy to do. When we remind ourselves He is a loving Father and His plans for us are perfect, we can live with not understanding. We will not always understand. We cannot know what He knows. But we can know He is trustworthy.

Describe a time when you received a *no* or a *wait* answer from God for a prayer you desperately wanted a different answer for.

_____

_____

_____

_____

What questions or uncertainties did you have about God during that time?

_____

_____

_____

_____

What questions or uncertainties did you have about yourself at that time?

_____

_____

_____

_____

How has that experience affected your relationship with God?

_____

_____

_____

What would you like to say to God about that experience?

_____

_____

_____

_____

What do you imagine God would say to you about that experience?

_____

_____

_____

_____

Day 5

Read: Psalm 34:18 and 2 Corinthians 4:16–18

We have two readings for today, because both ideas are necessary for healthy grieving. The first idea we read in Psalm 34 is that God grieves with us. His heart breaks when we suffer loss at the hand of death or because of sinful choices (ours or someone else's). Healthy grieving requires a time for sadness, for tears and for evaluating the weight of the loss and what could have or would have been.

But staying in the season of sadness is not meant to be forever. There is no timetable for grief, and depending on the loss, sorrow can be months or years. Still, a complete trust in God as the One who knows our situation, fully understands the loss we have suffered, and whose purpose for us has not changed moves us from this heavy burden of sadness to a more hopeful, accepting place.

Whatever losses we have suffered, there is reason to hope. Losses from suffering may include loss of dreams. Whether the suffering is physical, financial, emotional, or relational, there may be some common losses. We may not be able to function like we once did, or like others do. We may not have the career, the home, or the family we wanted or had. We may need to adjust expectations and learn humility. Things in our life have changed because of the suffering in ways we never wanted or planned for. Nothing about our life may be what we want or planned for. And if suffering is the result of the death of a loved one, there is a finality there where suffering only begins.

Whatever your circumstances of suffering, the promise found in our reading in 2 Corinthians today can bring hope when nothing else will. When all other hope is lost, thank God we can know that the promises of eternity are real. Whatever we have lost in this life will be regained, restored, or reunited in eternity. And however huge our losses here, they will seem insignificant compared to the glory we will experience in eternity. Hard to fathom, but that's a promise!

Prayer for Today

Thank God for being our comfort in times of suffering and loss. Thank Him for being near to the brokenhearted. Ask for His help, strength, and encouragement in grieving. Ask Him to help you remember that all your long, hard sufferings here will seem momentary and insignificant compared to what He has planned for us in eternity. Thank Him for this incredible promise and this great hope.

Grieving the Losses

Experts tell us there are many different events in our lives that create feelings of loss. Most losses have an element of suffering with them, even if it is minor or temporary. For example, getting married is typically an exciting time for the couple. Happy and anticipated as it may be, there may also be feelings of loss—loss of the freedom of being single, loss of living in the only home you've known or with the only people you've ever lived with. Dealing with these losses may only require a fleeting private acknowledgment or a nostalgic conversation with someone close.

Other losses, however, are not so minor and bring with them greater suffering with no happily ever after. They may also have built-in trickle-down losses, known as secondary losses. For example, a divorce brings with it the obvious loss of a marriage and the dreams of the life planned at the altar. But it also may bring secondary losses of home and possessions, friends, income or lifestyle, identity, time with children, etc. These secondary losses may not be realized initially but may unfold or pile on as things change down the road.

The list of losses that bring suffering and the suffering that brings losses is at once personal and universal. We may experience suffering that brings loss from a personal injury or illness, loss of a job or a career, legal issues or imprisonment, or past unresolved issues of abuse, addiction, abandonment, etc. We may also experience loss that results in suffering such as marital separation or divorce; death of a child, spouse, close friend, or family member; sudden accident; injury; natural disaster, financial fallout; etc. We may have prayed earnestly for something or someone only to have received a no or a wait answer, resulting in loss.

Any loss—tangible, physical, relational, financial, or having to do with plans, dreams, or lifestyle—is significant if our healthy coping skills cannot process the loss or if the loss affects our normal functioning (eating, sleeping, thinking, working, or interpersonal activities). When our healthy coping skills of crying, conversation, reminiscing, mental processing, prayer, journaling, or other healthy activity are enough to heal the loss in time, we are said to be grieving well. When our healthy coping skills are not enough and lead to unhealthy behavior, such as compulsions, addictions, lingering out-of-control emotions, extreme isolation, or depression, then we are not grieving well and may need some professional help in the process.

According to Elisabeth Kübler-Ross, the Swiss American psychiatrist, there are five stages of grief that are necessary for grieving a loss such as death.[4] Depending on the scope of the losses in your life, you may have skipped or glided through some of these stages with little concern, or you may find yourself stuck in one or more stages for a prolonged grieving experience. As said earlier, there is no timetable for grief, and the process is different for every person and every loss.

The five stages of grief as described by Kübler-Ross are:

LOSS	DENIAL Disbelief, Confusion, Shock	ANGER Frustration, Irritability, Outbursts
BARGAINING Search to Understand, "What-ifs"	DEPRESSION Emptiness, Isolation, Loss of Purpose	ACCEPTANCE "I'll be OK", More Good Days than Bad

While these five stages are often followed in order, it is equally common to cycle back through stages, skip stages, repeat stages, and linger in a particular stage. Often when a loss occurs, there is a period of shock or disbelief whereby the brain tries to comprehend what has happened. This is the *denial stage*. It is going from "What is happening?" to "This is really happening!" Depending on the severity and whether it was at all expected, this stage may last a short time or several days or weeks. Even when other stages are at play, there can still be sudden periods of feeling "This just can't be true!"

Once reality sets in, most people experience some sense of anger over what has happened, entering the *anger stage*. Depending on the circumstances and personality, the degree, duration, and expressions of anger will look different. The anger resulting from the senseless death of a loved one caused by a drunk driver may be very different from any anger that may result from the slow death of a ninety-six-year-old grandmother, though both are losses. Passing through the anger stage may take years or be short-lived. It may look like a tearful rage, or it may be angry thoughts that pass to the pages of a journal. This stage may also look like numbness or avoiding the anger or the pain. Anger may happen only once, or it may rise up again long after it was in the past.

Sometimes happening simultaneously, or even before the anger stage, is the *bargaining stage*. This is the stage where we would do anything to undo what's been done and our minds desperately search for a way to make that happen, even though it makes no sense. "What if I had left earlier?" "What if I hadn't allowed her to go?" "Maybe if we would have tried a different treatment or medication." These scenarios are subconscious attempts to postpone the sadness or prevent further pain. They may either alleviate or take on guilt or feelings of responsibility, but all unwittingly and desperately search for hope in alternate scenarios, albeit false hope.

At some point in suffering and losses, there is a *depression stage,* which like the anger stage looks different and has different durations for each person and each situation. Missing a loved one, adapting to a reduced lifestyle physically or financially, and realizing this is the new normal and life will never go back to the way it was can result in profound sadness. Life can feel empty and without purpose, and motivation to do the most mundane and routine tasks can completely disappear. Like the anger stage, the depression stage may also turn into feeling numb and avoiding feeling anything at all. Depending on the amount of outside support and inner strength, this stage can be dealt with effectively or can lead to complex grief that requires professional help.

The final stage of grieving a loss is the *acceptance stage*. This does not mean we are no longer sad over the loss or OK that it happened. Rather, it means we have come to accept that it *did* happen and we know we will be OK. We have decided (with the help of our friends, family, faith, professional help, etc.) there is still purpose in life, and we have motivation to keep going despite the loss. We know our life will go on, even though we may not know exactly what that will look like. We may still grieve from time to time, we may still be sad, we may still wish for the way things used to be, and we may still experience feelings of anger as we are reminded of certain memories, but somehow our life is going on, one step at a time.

The interesting thing about grief is there is no statute of limitations or an expiration date on losses we need to grieve. If we have experienced a loss at any time in our lives and have not properly grieved that loss, we can still heal by grieving it. How do we know we have not properly grieved a loss of the past? If it still interferes with our thoughts, our peace, our behavior, or our relationships, we may need to do some grief work. And we can deceive ourselves on whether a loss in the past is interfering. So ask someone who knows you well and whom you trust. Then listen to them! Pray about it, and ask God to show you and to give you the courage to grieve this loss.

How do we properly grieve losses? Again, some of it is a natural process and no doubt you have experienced some of the above stages. Perhaps you have cried (a lot!) and felt like you were done grieving. And maybe you were. Only your most honest heart knows if you are truly at peace with whatever losses you have experienced. If not, here are some helpful ways to process grief:

- Determine what stage of grief you may be stuck in.
- Begin to talk about the loss in a journal or with God, friends, family, or a clergy member.

- Allow yourself to feel the feelings associated with your words when you begin to talk about it.
- If you feel overwhelmed by the feelings or the fear of them, consider talking to a counselor or doctor.
- Be gentle with yourself during the process. Accept whatever feelings come up as part of healing.
- Consider joining a support group. Hearing others' experiences and perspectives brings insight to our own.
- Do something for someone else in need. Getting outside our own problems is healing.
- Dabble in your old hobbies or activities. If it is not enjoyable at first, accept that and try again later.
- Create some sort of memory marker for yourself or for your loved one. "This is the day I decided to live again."

What losses (or suffering that resulted in loss) have you experienced in your life? List them here.

_____

_____

_____

_____

In what ways has your life been affected by these losses?

_____

_____

_____

_____

Do you feel you have grieved the losses in your life well? Why or why not?

_____

_____

_____

_____

For any losses you have not fully grieved, what steps could you take to further the grieving process?

_____

_____

_____

_____

Chapter 6

Let the Healing Flow!

Day 1

Read: Genesis 16

Today we read the story of a woman who went through what I believe was a traumatic experience. The Old Testament story of Hagar is helpful for us because what happened in Hagar's life was both done to her but also something she had a part in. Her story is one we can all relate to. Those of us who bear shame from the actions of others committed against us will relate to Hagar being used by both her mistress, Sarai (Sarah), and Sarai's husband, Abram (Abraham). Their actions seemingly disregarded Hagar's personhood and dignity. They counted her as a servant to do with as they pleased.

The other piece to Hagar's story is the part she played. This part may resonate with those of us who carry shame not for things done to us but for things we may have done in our past. The Bible says when Hagar found out she was pregnant, she despised Sarai, her mistress. Her hatred of Sarai, and whatever behavior that may have involved, led to Sarai mistreating her so badly she had to flee. Of course, this story has enough blame to go around on everyone's part, and overall Hagar was clearly the victim. But we cannot overlook the breakdown of how our thoughts and attitudes or actions belong to us, how they affect our circumstances, and how we are accountable for them.

It is easy to understand how Hagar may have felt when she found out she was pregnant. Some of us may know exactly how she may have felt. But why would that make her despise Sarai and not Abram? Perhaps she knew the plot was Sarai's idea all along; we don't know. Perhaps she was angry and fearful that her child might be raised by another woman and she would have to watch that. Perhaps she was oblivious to their scheme and became fearful of being a single mother and fearful of her uncertain future and that fear simply turned to anger and hatred of someone who had it so good in life. We can only surmise.

Whatever Hagar's reasons for turning on Sarai, we now see her alone and scared sitting by a stream in the desert. (Thank God for the stream!) Again, we can only guess what is going through her mind. She is so kindly, and so providentially, visited by an angel of the Lord, and she confesses, "I am running away from my mistress." Full disclosure and full accountability. She doesn't lead with how she was used or mistreated or how it was anyone else's fault that she is dangerously alone in the desert with no provisions and nowhere to go. This tells us she has been doing a lot of honest reflecting. "I am in this situation because I ran away." Period. She doesn't go into "What choice did I have?" or "Anyone would do the same thing!" None of that. "I am here because I ran away."

It also tells us she is desperate and ready to accept any help this person may possibly offer her. It may have been bad at home, but it's really bad now! And two things happen at this point. One, she pays consequences for her attitude that played a part in her current situation. She is told, "Go back to your mistress and submit to her." Not easy! And two, somehow in that exchange, her shame is taken away, and in its place, she finds grace, forgiveness, and healing. She gives God (the angel of the Lord, perhaps Jesus, or His representative), the name El Roi, "the God who sees me." She no longer felt abandoned, scared, shameful, or angry. She felt known and taken care of and loved. The exchange was so real she was indeed able to go back and submit, knowing that even if Sarai never accepted her again, she was accepted by God, Most High, and she and her son would be cared for, provided for, and blessed beyond any human deserving.

Prayer for Today

Lord, it can be so painful to look back at our past. To look at things we have done and things that were done to us. We don't always think or act in ways that are pleasing to You when shame overwhelms us. Thank You for being El Roi, the God who sees us. Thank You for looking on us with compassion and healing. Help us to have the courage to do what it takes to accept Your healing for our shame. Guide us through Your healing so we can live freely and fully. Amen.

A Deeper Look at Your Story

In day 2 of chapter 4, you wrote down your story. For some of you, this was the first time you did that. For others, it may have been the first time in a long time you thought about your story. Others of you may have told your story to someone already, maybe many times. Each time we revisit our story, we see new things we hadn't seen or thought of before. A new memory may rise to the surface. We may connect the dots to parts of our lives, decisions, or circumstances we hadn't connected before. But almost always our story becomes more a part of us. The truth of it sinks down into us like water being poured into a bucket of sand. We become more familiar with ourselves, hopefully humbly pleased, and grateful for what we have overcome. That is part of the healing process.

Another important part of healing is sharing our story out loud with someone. This can feel terrifying, but it doesn't have to be. Satan would like you to think your story is so shameful and worse than anyone else's. Or he may suggest your story is nothing compared to others and you have no business feeling any shame at all. These are both lies from the deceiver, and you mustn't listen for even one second. I assure you your group will listen with compassion and El Roi will be among you. It takes courage to be honest with ourselves about our story, courage to accept it as part of our journey, and courage to share it with others. God has brought you to this place for healing. He will be with you, and He will help you.

Sharing your story will be easier and more beneficial if you are prepared to share. That is what we are going to do today. Follow this checklist to prepare your story for sharing:

1. Go back to chapter 4 and read over your story. See if there are any pieces you left out that you would like to add. Note those additions in the margin. At this point, don't delete anything. You will have a chance to do that later. This will be your first draft.

Typically, when a group shares stories, each person has a certain amount of time, depending on the size of the group. Your group may choose to stay on this chapter for several meetings until everyone has shared, or you can do abbreviated versions in less time. This means you may not be able to share every little detail. And often the details are more interesting to us than they are to other people.

2. Using your first draft as a guide, you will rewrite your story. Begin by grounding your story for the listener. Open your story with time and place. How old were you, and where does the story take place? Briefly tell any other *important* background information. If you were ten years old and your story takes place in Antarctica, the listeners might want to know how and why a ten-year-old is in Antarctica. But everyone can probably relate to being at Grandma's

house or living on a farm without many details, even if they've never been there.

3. From here, simply write your story. Tell the facts.

- Who was involved?
- What was the length of time involved?
- What happened?
- How did it affect you?
- Do you recall how you felt at the time?
- Did you feel different later? How so or why?
- Who else knew about what was going on or what happened?
- Were there any consequences involved?
- How has your life been affected since then?

4. Next, include any shame messages you have carried because of your story and how your life will be different without the shame.

5. Now pray over your story. Ask God to reveal anything you should add. Ask for courage to leave in things you are tempted to take out but that are important for you to share. Be sure that the things you share about other people are accurate and truthful. There is no need to use names if you don't want to. Also, you can refer to "a close family member" instead of saying "my uncle" or "my grandmother." You can say "one of my parents" instead of telling which parent. The idea is not to smear your family or others, nor is it to cover up for them. It is simply to tell *your* story as *you* lived it. Ask God to guard your heart and help you share humbly but truthfully.

6. Finally, practice sharing your story out loud. Set a timer to see how long it takes you. Try to keep it between five and ten minutes as people tire quickly, even though it may be interesting. If your story is considerably over ten minutes, edit out the parts that are not critical. If it is considerably less than five minutes, perhaps there are pieces you are leaving out on purpose. Consider asking the group if they have any questions about your story. If there is a question you don't feel comfortable answering, just say so.

Some of you may prefer to read your story. That is fine. Others of you may wish to use the "Talking Points Story Card" printed at the end of this session and just talk to your group. However you choose to do it, after you have shared your story, you will no doubt feel relief, but you may also feel happy and free as though a weight has been lifted.

Later, the enemy may try to steal your freedom and this part of your healing by telling you that you shouldn't have shared, that you have dishonored your family or friends, or some other lie to try to bring you back into the shame you have been freed from. Do not listen to him. If you have been honest with yourself in writing your story, it is your story to tell. Any guilt, shame, or embarrassment belongs to those who were in the wrong. When you are tempted to feel any of these things, remember Romans 12:1–2. "Therefore, there is now no condemnation for those who are in Christ Jesus, because through Christ Jesus the law of the Spirit who gives life has set you free from the law of sin and death." Then call someone from your group and share with them what you are going through. You probably won't be the only one.

Talking Points Story Card

1. STORY GROUNDING- (*important* background information)
   "The story I want to share with you today begins in ____, when I was ____."
   Time
   Place
   Age

2. STORY FACTS – (important details of your story)
   Who was involved?
   What was the length of time involved?
   What happened?
   How did it affect you?
   Do you recall how you felt at the time?
   Did you feel differently later? How so or why?
   Who else knew about what was going on or what happened?
   Were there any consequences involved?
   How has your life been affected since then?

3. SHAME MESSAGES –
   "The messages I began to believe about myself were_____."

4. SHAME-FREE CHANGES –
   "The things that will be different for me without the shame are _____."

Day 2

Read: John 5:1–8

This is a favorite story of Jesus healing the invalid at the pool of Bethesda. First, let's look at the word *invalid*. It simply means someone who is not able to care for themselves because of an illness or injury or old age. But look at the word again. *In-valid*. It reeks of shame. It declares an unworthiness. The dictionary would also say the word refers to something that is no longer current or useful, something that is expired, like a license or certification. It needs to be renewed.

Surely the man at the pool of Bethesda was not able to care for himself as he had been there for thirty-eight years hoping to be healed. That makes us think he was desperate for healing. Thirty-eight years is a long time. Was he the poster child for positive thinking? Or had he given up hope and his life at the pool had become a way of life? Surely none of us would blame him if the latter was the case. Perhaps we would have given up after a year or two!

Jesus thought the man had given up too. He knew this man's story. He knew the exact moment he had given up hope. But he didn't heal him out of pity. Compassion, yes. Pity, no. Jesus knew this man had allowed himself to become a victim of his circumstances. He knew the man had perhaps become bitter. But Jesus wanted more for this man. And He asks a most unusual question. "Do you want to be healed?"

We would think this man would cry out, "Are you kidding? Of course, I want to be healed! Why else would I be lying here day after day for thirty-eight years hoping for a chance to get in the water first!" Instead, he doesn't answer Jesus's question. He unknowingly reveals his bitterness and complacency as a victim. "There's not anyone to help me get into the pool. Someone always gets in before me." What he has revealed is not that he is a blamer or a quitter. He has revealed that his condition had become his security.

It had been so long since he had walked (if he ever had), the joy of freedom and the satisfaction of taking care of himself had long passed. He had become quite OK hanging with his friends and allowing whoever brought him food and took care of him to do so. This was who he was now. The thought of anything else would bring too many changes, require too much work, and be too hard and too scary. This was his identity. *In-valid.* No longer current or useful. Expired and unworthy of anything else.

Jesus knew all of this, yet Jesus wanted more for him. No judgment, no pity, no criticism. Only *renewal.*

Prayer for Today

Today in your prayer time, tell God your fears about laying down your masks and your shame and how it might feel to live without them. Don't be afraid to be honest and vulnerable. Tell Him if you are afraid to feel courageous, competent, and confident. Tell Him if you are afraid it will be hard or that you're afraid you won't be able to give up your coping mechanisms. Ask Him to help you through this. But express to God your desire to be healed.

Do You Want to Be Healed?

It is easy to see how our dysfunctional ways have not worked for us. Thinking back to the early days of these sessions, we were quick to share what wasn't working. It was easy to scratch out what was wrong in our relationships, our finances, our social groups, or our private lives. It was easy until we began to connect the dots from how we were raised to how we handled emotions or how we did relationships. Then we could see our part.

It is not so easy, however, to see how our dysfunctional ways *have* worked for us. It's not easy to admit we have not always been honest with ourselves and therefore not honest with others. But this has gotten us through an argument or avoided an argument. Perhaps we have pretended to be something we weren't around certain people, which helped us feel accepted or even be accepted. Many of us have manipulated circumstances or people to get what we wanted or what was best for us. There may be substances or other habits we have used that no one knows about that helped us make it through a tough time or even a normal day.

All of these examples, and more, are common behaviors we discussed in chapter 2 regarding traits of dysfunctional families. They become a part of who we are, and we can live a long time, even trying to be a good person, while still unconsciously practicing these behaviors. Like the man at the pool of Bethesda, we learn how to make our shame-based dysfunction work for us, we become its victim, and it becomes our security. Honestly, thinking about doing things differently is scary. There may be repercussions in our families if we try to change. We may feel like we're losing our identity.

All these feelings are normal and legitimate. We wouldn't be human if we didn't feel apprehensive about such changes. Just like the man at the pool, God knows this about us too. He doesn't judge us. He wants to heal us. He wants us to be free of the bondage of shame and dysfunction and to know the joy of what that freedom feels like. Can you imagine the joy the man at the pool felt? I'm sure once he was healed, he didn't care about how he would handle any of the things he was fearful of. God is trustworthy. We can trust Him with our healing for things done to us, for things we have done, and for whatever we had to do to survive or cope.

How do you feel about knowing complete healing may include changes in the ways you cope or the patterns of behavior you may have used to survive?

_____

_____

_____

_____

What are some of the behaviors or coping mechanisms that come to mind when you read this session?

_____

_____

_____

_____

Do you have any apprehensions about being healed in this way?

_____

_____

_____

_____

Do you want to be healed? Explain.

_____

_____

_____

_____

If your answer was no, what is holding you back from wanting healing?
Be honest.

_____

_____

_____

_____

Would you be willing to talk to your group about this? Why or why not?

_____

_____

_____

_____

Day 3

Read: 2 Samuel 12:1–19

Our scripture reading for today is about an honest but clever confrontation by a prophet of God who also happened to be a faithful and trusted adviser to King David. We know from reading about the prophets that these were men who devoted their entire lives to doing and saying whatever it was the Lord told them to do or say, often at great personal cost. Despite their devotion, we know they were normal humans who often wrestled with their difficult assignments.

But here we have Nathan who must have wrestled with his assignment. Can you imagine going straight to your boss, the king, and saying, "After everything God has given you, why did you show hatred toward Him by acting so evil?" Which would no doubt be quickly followed by "Uh, my lord, my liege, sire!" Nathan was no dummy. He knew he would lose his head had he approached the king that way. Eventually he was able to say almost those exact words, and more, which was his assignment all along. But he was clever enough to confront the king's actions by using a made-up scenario to get the king's attention. It certainly couldn't have been easy. In Nathan's case, he went through with it because God Almighty told him to! That's a high purpose. He had no other motive.

In the end, King David confessed and was forgiven. But he still suffered a terrible consequence for his sin. Sometimes it happens like that. We often find it unfair or harsh when consequences are served after a true confession is made. We forget that when we sin, or when we break the law, those actions may demand a consequence. Confessing does not erase the action. The act was deliberately done and deserves punishment. If mercy is shown, it is just that—mercy!

The beautiful thing about David's shameful story with Bathsheba was that he was truly broken because he sinned against God. Despite the severe consequence of losing his son, he was not bitter toward God (or Nathan!). We read his words in Psalm 51, David's prayer of repentance. "My sacrifice, O God, is a broken spirit; a broken and contrite heart you, God, will not despise." May we all be as courageous and honest as Nathan and as humble and contrite as David.

Prayer for Today

As you pray today, thank God for His forgiveness and His mercy. Thank Him that He does not always give us the punishment we deserve. Instead, He lavishes grace upon grace with every sunrise and every breath. Ask for humility and a teachable spirit when we do face consequences because of our sin. And ask Him for the courage to speak truth in the face of confronting those who have wronged us.

Speaking Truth

There is nothing easy about confronting someone about a wrong they have done to us, especially if we are or were in close relation with them. It is much easier to call out a stranger who stole something than someone we know well or trusted. By now you may have guessed that today's session is going to involve facing the people who either wronged us or played a part in our shame. But don't worry; it won't be as scary as it seems. This is an important part of our healing journey.

Imagine that a student brought dollar bills to school every day for a bus ride home and kept them in her desk. After the first few weeks of school, she noticed a couple of dollars missing every now and then. On days she didn't have enough for bus fare, she felt humiliated and was often shamed when the other students saw her walking in the cold or the rain. After some time, she discovered it was her teacher who brazenly took a couple of dollars for the vending machines every few days.

The girl was too afraid to confront the teacher. Who would believe such a story? She would be even more of a laughingstock with the students. How could she be sure the teacher wouldn't fail her if she told? Although this continued to happen the entire school year, the girl said nothing.

This is a far-fetched story, but the intent is to discuss her choice in confronting the teacher. She could say nothing, leaving the teacher to think he got away with it and triggering her every time she saw a schoolgirl walking down the street. And who knows? She may not have been the only student he stole from. She could say nothing, holding her head high, knowing she had overcome all the ridicule he caused her. She could alert the school office and share her story, which would inevitably be her word against his. Or she could walk into his room one day after school and tell him she knew all along that he was taking money out of her desk and it was wrong for him, an adult with authority, to take advantage of an innocent child. She could tell him how not having bus money caused her to feel ridicule and shame from the other students and could have cost her life because she had to walk so far home alone. She could leave by saying all the shame and humiliation was no longer hers because she now knew it belonged to him and that's where she was leaving it.

It would be up to her whether she took it further to the administration or perhaps even to the school board. But whether she did or not, do you see how differently she would have felt going off to college having spoken her truth versus going off to college without confronting him?

When there are people in our past who have wronged us in some way and have changed our life stories by the shame they caused us, speaking up helps us to, in a sense, reclaim what was taken from us. It may be our innocence, our independence, or our ability to feel safe. It may be opportunity, power, or our right to say no. It could be making our own choice about something, a chance at a better life, or our need to feel loved and cared for. We may not be able to get back whatever was taken, nor can we undo what was done. But we can stand up for ourselves in a way we were not able to at that time. We reclaim ourselves.

It all comes down to the motive and purpose for confronting. For some, there is a hope something will change—that the person will see the error of their ways and apologize or ask forgiveness. For others, the outcome isn't as important as doing the right thing, standing up for yourself, speaking your truth, or taking back the control you were unable to have at the time. It's not about vengeance or revenge or necessarily about consequences. Although in some cases there may be consequences, like there was for King David, seen later in the chapter of today's scripture reading. But we can leave the consequences to God, or the law, and simply do what we feel is right for us. This step of the healing process is for *us*, not for them.

Some of you may be terrified at the suggestion of confronting the person or people in your past. You may be thinking this is not possible because the person is no longer alive or you'd rather forget the whole thing. Maybe they can't be found, or maybe it is a close relative and confronting would start a family feud. Before you close the book and give up on your healing journey, remember we said this step is *for you,* not them. It isn't always necessary to confront the person face-to-face. It can be done in a letter. And it may not even be necessary to ever mail or give the letter. What matters is that you speak truthfully to whomever in whatever manner helps you heal.

Speaking your truth promotes your own healing. It removes whatever invisible gag was placed on you years ago or whatever verbal or physical assault you silently endured. In the next section, you will be given an opportunity to speak your truth. Before you begin this section, pray and ask God to show you who you may need to speak to and to give you the courage to say what needs said honestly and humbly but confidently.

When you think about your story, who is the person or persons responsible for the shame you have carried?

_____

_____

_____

_____

Choose one of the people you just listed. What would you say to that person if you were to confront them? What exactly did they do that you now are speaking up about? Try not to censor your words.

_____

_____

_____

_____

How did you feel at the time? Again, don't censor.

_____

_____

_____

_____

How was your life different because of their actions? What shame did you begin to take on? How long?

_____

_____

_____

_____

The previous questions are a good format for confronting the person or people who wronged you. Use this blank page to write a letter to each person or to those you need to speak your truth to. Follow the format above for the letter or letters. End the letter by giving them back their shame you have been carrying. Use a separate sheet of paper if needed.

Dear _____,

Day 4

Read: Isaiah 53:3–5 and Hebrews 4:15

Both of these scripture readings are perfect foundations for our next two sessions. Isaiah 53 is one of the Old Testament prophecies of the Messiah that paints a picture for us of He who is to come. And we know that He did come and that He did suffer all of the pain and humiliation that Isaiah prophesied. The suffering that Christ endured not only paid the price for our salvation, but it did so much more. It gave us this all powerful, Almighty God in a human form that we could relate to when we must endure trials. For more than two thousand years since His brutal death on the cross (and victorious resurrection!), people of all walks of life have been consoled by the fact that Jesus Christ also relates to us. He knows what it's like to suffer physical pain unto death. He knows what it's like to suffer shame, ridicule, criticism, and humiliation.

Hebrews 4:15 reminds us we indeed have a High Priest who empathizes with our infirmities and weaknesses because He also experienced the same. Whatever physical or emotional pain you suffered, whatever dread or fear you endured, and whatever shame you bore as a result, Jesus understands. He was mocked and beaten. He was led through the streets barely able to walk, for people to jeer, ridicule, and spit on. His hands and feet had spikes driven through them to hold Him to a wooden cross. Then He was lifted up to hang there until He died. Jesus gets it. And He too was innocent and deserved none of it. He understands. And because of that, He has great compassion and sorrow for what you went through.

This is a good time to pause and check in with ourselves and where we stand personally with Jesus. Have you received the gift Christ provided by His death on the cross? His willingness to die for the sins of the world satisfied Almighty God's just requirement for the penalty of all our sins. This is something we could never do on our own. None of us are without sin. All of us have at least been dishonest in thought or deed, and many of us have done worse. No matter how good you are, you can never measure up to perfection. And no matter how bad you have been, you are included in the everyone that Christ died for. Accept His gift now, and you will immediately become His child with the promise of eternal life with Him when your life here is over. His spirit will guide you through all your days. The benefits are immeasurable.

Prayer for Today

Today when you pray, ask the Holy Spirit to show you afresh the sufferings that Jesus endured for you. Ask Him to help you imagine the pain He suffered. Ask Him to help you feel the mockery and humiliation. If you haven't already, tell Him you confess your need for Him in your life, and accept His gift of salvation. Then thank Jesus for willingly going through all of that to save you from every sin you ever committed so you might have eternal life in heaven when your life here is over. Ask Him to give you the courage to bring your sufferings before Him in these next sessions, knowing that He understands and has compassion for you.

Inner Healing: Part 1

Today and tomorrow, we will end this week inviting God into our stories and our wounded places. It is critical to our healing to take today and tomorrow seriously and to vow to spend some extra time on these sessions. Don't rush through them to get your work done. These two sessions will be structured a little differently from the others, and you are encouraged to take your time working through them. You may also choose to do these two sessions as a group or with someone in your group whom you trust.

✣ Paula French ✣

Your group may choose to spend an extra week or more going through these sessions.

All the work you have done up this point is important. All the therapy or counseling you may have done throughout your life is important. But they all led up to these two sessions. No healing is complete without God's healing playing a significant role. In fact, there *is* no healing without God's touch.

We see Jesus being revealed in the New Testament as the Healer. We read the many accounts of Him healing all sorts of diseases and spiritual or emotional illnesses. He is known for being able to heal. Even before Jesus's time, in the Old Testament, God is referred to as Jehovah Rapha. In Hebrew, this means "the God who heals." Bible scholars tell us this healing is indeed physical, but it also refers to more than the physical healing of our bodies. Other times in the Old Testament, the name is used to mean "to restore." Jehovah Rapha is the God who heals and restores. Psalm 42:1–2 says, "The earth is the Lord's, and everything in it, the world, and all who live in it; for he founded it upon the seas and established it upon the waters." There is nothing that exists that God did not create and nothing He does not own. We have been given this life, this world, and everything in it as a gift from God, and we have sorely corrupted it. It is His intention and His work to restore and bring all things under heaven and earth back into God's original perfect state. And when He reveals the New Heaven and the New Earth in eternity, it will be perfect and without blemish—no more sickness, pain, tears, decay, sin, or corruption (Revelation 21).

So if all things belong to God, then all healing belongs to God. Hebrews 2:4 reminds us He is the one who gives us the gifts or talents we have. He is the one who wove together all the intricacies of how our minds and bodies work. He has created the very possibility for therapeutics and medicines to even work! That means He directs the healing through all medicine, all doctors, and all therapies. All healing is God's healing.

Anytime Satan steals from one of God's children or distorts a truth God has pronounced over us, God longs for us to be healed from that. God loves when someone acknowledges the truth and denounces the lies of the enemy. He longs for us to see Him present in our circumstances and trust in His sovereign goodness. Often, we can only see that after the fact, sometimes only years later. Eventually, we come to be able to trust He is always with us, always looking out for us, and always working for our good and His glory.

Our human minds can't conceive how suffering here could in any way be good, but we cannot see the whole movie. We see only a few scenes or screenshots compared to what God sees and understands. Learning to trust that and trust Him takes away the anxiety and fear of having to control our lives. Knowing Satan is responsible for much of the pain, humiliation, and shame we have suffered, and knowing God is able to work these things for our good and His glory, is a step toward healing.

Today we are going to take another step toward healing. It is important to create a quiet space and an hour or two for the rest of this session. If you do not have that availability right now, set aside a time in the next day or so to do this. As you wait, pray continually for God to begin to prepare your heart and mind to meet with Him. If you have decided to do these sessions with another person or your group, make sure there will be no interruptions or distractions. It may be helpful to play some soft music quietly in the background.

Begin by spending some time in prayer. We are about to bring our past before the Lord in a different way from how we have done before. Instead of telling God about the things that happened to us that caused us hardship and shame, we are going to be asking *Him* about these events. This requires listening to His spirit and trusting ourselves and Him that He is present and wants to heal and restore.

Begin by prayerfully reading a favorite passage of scripture. If you have no favorite scripture, consider reading Psalm 103. Now ask the Lord to help you clear your mind so you can hear His voice. Thank Him for His presence and healing. Sit before the Lord quietly for a few moments as you acknowledge His presence. Space is provided below for you to write your prayers or record anything you feel the Lord may be saying to you. You may use it if it is helpful.

_____

_____

_____

_____

Ask the Lord to place His protection around this session—protection from distractions and interruptions and from Satan, who has no power over Jesus's presence or healing.

_____

_____

_____

_____

Tell God you are seeking healing from an emotion, a pattern of emotions, or some shame that has overshadowed your life. Ask Him to show you in your spirit exactly what that emotion or pattern or shame is. Sit quietly and wait before Him. Do not be afraid of what words come to your mind.

_____

_____

_____

_____

Tell God what you heard Him say in your spirit, and ask Him to give you some insight as to what that emotion or pattern or shame is about and when it first took place in your life. It may or may not be what you are expecting. It may be about the things in your past you have been dealing with in our previous sessions, or it may be something else entirely. It may be something or some event or period of time that seems insignificant. It's OK. Ask Him now to tell you what it is about and when it first took place in your life.

_____

_____

_____

_____

Spend the rest of this session journaling quietly about your experience. Record your feelings, such as your inhibitions, any uncomfortableness, any thoughts, or any feelings about the process itself. Then record anything you may have heard the Lord speak to your heart. If you were not able to hear anything, journal about that. Don't be discouraged. This is not easy work. You may find trying it again in a different location or a different time may help. If you were alone, consider asking someone you trust to be with you. If you were with people, consider doing it again by yourself. Use the back if necessary.

_____

_____

_____

_____

_____

_____

_____

_____

_____

Finally, finish your session thanking God for His healing presence, for His ability to relate to your suffering, and for His love and care for you. Then leave it all with Him.

_____

_____

_____

_____

_____

_____

_____

_____

_____

_____

_____

_____

_____

_____

_____

_____

_____

Day 5

Read: Isaiah 61:1–3 and Luke 4:16–21

Today we have another word from the prophet Isaiah that speaks to the coming Messiah and His purpose on earth for His people. We know this because Jesus Himself reads these verses in the synagogue in our second reading in Luke.

It is hard for us to imagine being a Jew two thousand years ago. For centuries before, their ancestors had prayed and awaited the Messiah. They held dear the stories of God's miracles and provision for His people, and they were now confident the Messiah would come rescue them from the stern and ruthless rule of the Romans. Yet here He is, their Messiah, the Son of God come down, and many don't recognize Him, while others consider Him a dangerous imposter and blasphemer. How would you have responded when Jesus admitted that this beloved passage of scripture was written about Him?

Perhaps we, like many of them, would be so caught up in the politics of it all that we failed to see what was really going on. He was bringing good news (salvation) to those who were poor in every way. He was freeing people from their prisons of sin, shame, habits, and addictions. He was opening the eyes of those who had been blinded, both literally and figuratively. He was breaking the chains of oppression and lavishing God's favor on those who were outcast and deemed unworthy. He was declaring and gifting joy, freedom, beauty, healing, and restoration!

The amazing thing is He is still doing that today! But many of us are also caught up in the politics of it all. (What will people think? It all feels too weird. I wasn't raised that way. I don't believe in all that stuff. It's just a crutch!) We can come up with a hundred reasons to resist him, instead of reaching out and taking hold of the healing Jesus is offering right in front of us.

This was His purpose. This was why He came: to restore all things back to a Holy God that was severed when sin entered the world. How loving! How caring! How patient and longsuffering to deal with us for millennia while extending His healing hand all along the way! Amazingly, His healing hand still extends today.

Prayer for Today

Today in your prayer time, thank God for His plan of salvation that included sending the Messiah to be our healer. Thank Him for seeing beyond our brokenness and beyond our shame and into our stories. Thank Him for what He did in the last session, and ask Him for courage to continue.

Inner Healing: Part 2

Again, today we will be inviting God into our stories and our wounded places. Plan once again to arrange extra time in your schedule, especially for today. If you do not have the time or the privacy today, plan a time when you do. If it worked for you to do the past session as a group or with someone in your group, please do that again.

Sometimes when things happen to us, especially when we are younger, we wonder where God was when we needed Him. We may feel He abandoned us or that He allowed what happened to punish us in some way. We may even blame God or become angry or bitter at Him for not intervening. Perhaps we have even lost faith because of what happened. After all, if He is so powerful and sees everything, why didn't He stop it? These are difficult questions to answer and are certainly understandable. The incredible thing about God is that He understands these questions. He does not judge us for thinking such thoughts or asking such questions. He remembers how we were formed. He remembers that we are dust (Psalm 103:14).

God hates the sin and all the wickedness in our world even more than we do. It pains Him to see His children mistreated, abused, neglected, or used. And that is why we are glad there will be a day of reckoning. Remember God is restoring all things. He is bringing all things back into their original state of perfection without sin or corruption. It may be difficult for us to reconcile a loving God with a God of wrath and judgment, but it is easier to understand when we ask ourselves if we would want a child abuser to go unpunished. Of course not! Someday we will *all* stand and give an account for our lives. Thankfully, God provided a way for guilty sin to be covered by the blood of Jesus Christ. And we are *all* guilty of sin, and we *all* deserve punishment! But those who acknowledge this and accept Christ's free gift of salvation by His death on the cross will not be punished. God lovingly provided a way out for anyone who will take it. He did this to demonstrate His justice (Romans 3:25). Anyone who does not take the way out will be justly punished for their sin.

Just because God is holding off that time of punishment for those who refuse the way out does not mean He does not see or care about the sinful actions of men now. He does see and He does care, and He weeps over it, but not in a helpless or powerless way. Far from it! In the same way a father may hold his little crying daughter when she is being pricked with a needle; he knows she will not understand it all until much later. Just like we could say the little girl's suffering is, in effect, a result of a disease in the world, so was our suffering a result of the disease of sin in the world. For now, God walks with us through those times of suffering, and one day He will rid the world of all sin and evil. God hates what happened in your life, and He longs for you to trust His sovereign goodness.

Look at the verbs in our readings for today from Isaiah—all the actions Jesus came to take on our behalf.

He was anointed *to proclaim* the good news of salvation, *to bind up* the brokenhearted, *to declare* there is freedom, and *to free* the blind from darkness. He was anointed *to announce* both favor and vengeance, *to comfort* the grieving and *to provide* for them, *to crown* them with beauty and *remove* the shame, *bringing joy*, *wrapping* them *in secure praise*, and *setting* them *apart* as strong and righteous just to display His splendor—the splendor of His complete and majestic restoration! He is the restorer of broken things, and His great joy is to make us beautifully free from the shame of the past.

Let's bring our broken places into His presence where He longs to speak to us about these particular places. Some of us may have more than one place where we were wounded, more than one memory that needs healing, or more than one event in our past that still grips us today with a coping habit or fear. Remember Jesus heals completely. You may find yourself needing to repeat this time of solitude with Jehovah Rapha, God the Healer, more than once. Or perhaps you have the time and can focus long enough in this sitting to hear Him speak to your heart about all of it. Whatever you and God find works the best is fine.

What exactly can you expect from this time with God? We will go through a series of suggestions for you to pray, and you are to simply sit before the Lord, listening humbly and with an open heart and mind. You can talk to Him about anything you are thinking or feeling and ask Him to make things clear to you. He may give you a word, a phrase, or a scripture that feels healing to you in a meaningful way. He may ask you a question or give you something to consider. His Holy Spirit may convict you of something you need to confess. He may bring another memory to your mind or ask you to relinquish or trust Him with something. His healing ways are as numerous as broken people, and He will deal with you personally and in ways that make sense to you. It Is important that you spend this time unrushed and that you lean into Him and trust Him completely.

I once worked with a blind man at the same time I had been praying about a nagging half memory in my own life that I desired healing from. In one of my prayer times, I heard God say gently to my heart, "Just as this man will not regain his sight, you will never fully regain this memory. It is not for you to know, but you can trust that I know it, and I'm protecting you." That was all the healing I needed. It never bothered me again, but He confirmed later that I wasn't making the memory up in my head by showing me evidence of what little I *did* remember. I believe He gifted me with that because I trusted His word to me. I felt so loved. He cares for us in the most personal and meaningful ways. Remain open to whatever

God has for you without any expectations. In this final session, space is once again provided for you to write your prayers or record anything you feel the Lord may be saying to you. Use it if it is helpful.

Begin again by prayerfully reading a passage of scripture. Consider asking God to guide you to what He wants you to read. These are His words. Again, ask the Lord to help you clear your mind so you can hear His voice. Ask Him to surround you with His presence. Sit quietly before the Lord as you feel His presence surrounding you. He has promised to be with us. Thank Him for His presence and offer your whole heart and mind to Him for this inner healing time. Ask Him to free you of distractions.

Allow your mind to go back into the past and into the painful memory, trauma, or experience. You can do this because Jesus is surrounding you in this moment. (You might be reminded of an experience or time that is different from what you thought. It's OK. Keep your heart open to whatever God wants to show you.) See yourself as the child or younger adult that you were at that time. What feelings or thoughts do you have about her as you see your younger self in this setting?

_____

_____

_____

_____

Notice the space where you were at that time. Notice if anyone else was there and who that was or might have been. What questions do you have now, looking back at this experience? Ask God these questions.

_____

_____

_____

If you do not sense Him there already, invite God into this memory, into the place in your heart where the wounding took place. Ask Him what He has to say to the wounded part of us. Ask Him for His healing word to your heart. Allow His spirit to draw the shame and woundedness out of the shadows and into the light of His compassion and healing. Be still before the Lord and let Him speak to you.

_____

_____

_____

_____

Finally, ask God to show you anything in your life you have used to cope, as a result of your woundedness. Ask His Holy Spirit to reveal any shame messages, habits, addictions, or anything or anyone you have turned to for comfort instead of Him. Confess these to Him and ask Him to break any strongholds Satan has tried to put on you. Relinquish these things before God and ask for His complete healing and forgiveness.

_____

_____

_____

_____

Take some time now to sit with God and thank Him for His healing. Ask Him for faith to hold onto the healing you have received. Ask Him to confirm in the days ahead what you have heard Him say to you. Use the rest of these pages to journal about your experience. It will be a helpful practice to occasionally come back to what you have documented when you are tempted to doubt His healing.

Chapter 7

Living in the Truth

Day 1

Read: Matthew 4:1–11 and Ephesians 6:10–17

By now you are keenly aware of the two worlds our lives are sandwiched between. The heavenly realms, owned and operated by the Almighty God, and the earthly realms, also owned and operated by God but temporarily influenced by the dark forces of Satan, the enemy of God and all things heavenly. In your life, you have experience with both worlds. Whatever dysfunction or trauma you endured in your past was brought to you by the creative, slimy genius of Satan himself. And like our first reading today, he will continue to influence your life with lies, just as he did Jesus in the wilderness. Just because you have experienced a healing in your emotional life doesn't keep him from trying to pull you back into the world of shame and deception. He is not satisfied with wounding you; he seeks to destroy you.

Thankfully, God does not leave us helpless in the earthly realm where evil tries to reign. God is always available and wants to pull us from the darkness into His light. But people are often lovers of darkness, preferring to remain in the dark, even when the Light is waiting to rescue (John 3:19); therefore, God will not force Himself on anyone. His Holy

Spirit will remind us, warn us, convict us, and stand ready to provide a way out, but ultimately the decision is ours. And that is where our second reading for today comes in.

Verse 10 says, "Be strong in the Lord and in His mighty power." We can be confident in His healing words to us and therefore strong in the Lord. His power is mighty, and He heals completely. We need not fear the attacks of the enemy when we keep ourselves ready with the impenetrable armor He provides for us. Stand firm in His truth, girded with Christ's righteousness. With ready feet planted in His peace, ward off evil arrows with a shield of faith, knowing you are covered by His salvation. And go confidently into battle using the Word of God.

Prayer for Today

Tell God how you feel about living in a war zone where the enemy may attack at any minute. Then ask Him to help you be confident knowing it is His strength you are leaning on. Thank Him for His mighty power and all the armor He provides for you to be victorious. Pledge to Him you will use the armor daily as He did and thank Him again for the healing you have received.

Goodbye Lies, Hello Truth

In case you hadn't noticed, we are turning a corner in our healing journey. We are leaving the pain of the past behind and moving into life in the truth of who we were meant to be, not in what the enemy or other people's shame or bad behavior tried to mold us into. We do that by "taking every thought captive to make it obedient to Christ" (2 Corinthians 10:5). This does not mean that we stop at every single thought we have like a robot or a computer. But it does mean every thought that is negative, critical, judgmental, lustful, proud, or rebellious needs to be examined before Christ.

Do you know why it is necessary to examine our thoughts? Because God, in His wisdom, knows that thoughts beget feelings and feelings beget behavior. In other words, when we begin to dwell on something in our minds, we develop feelings about it. We can become angry, jealous, vengeful, fearful or begin to think of ourselves as better than we are, worthless, or even undeserving of love or life. Once the feelings set in, we act on those feelings. We may lash out or get even, we may stop trying new things, we may treat others as less than, we may shrink back and demean ourselves, or we may even take our own lives. Taking every thought captive requires intentionality. It's about training yourself to examine, according to the Word of God, the thoughts, feelings, images, and beliefs that arise in your daily living.

Foundational to this process of taking every thought captive is your willingness to invest in an intimate relationship with Jesus through personal times of worship, reading God's Word, and being led by the Spirit. Intimacy with Jesus is the key. In His presence, you receive both revelation and grace to become intentionally aware of your thought life.

Practically, when you have a thought that comes into your mind, pause and examine it to see if it agrees with God's Word. Of course, many times our thoughts are from God and are good and encouraging. When they are, establish them in your heart, meditate on them, and ask God to transform your heart with them. If you realize, however, that the thought isn't from God, then reject the thought and replace it with the truth of God's Word. If the thought happens to be one that you have bought into for a long time, confess this to God. Tell Him you will no longer agree with the lies of the enemy and ask the Holy Spirit to show you His truth. Find a scripture that reflects the truth He is showing you and make it your own. Write it down, memorize it, and practice saying it over and over to yourself. Write it as God speaking directly to you about your situation and use it to combat the lies of the enemy when they come back.

For example, you are feeling left out and rejected because of something someone did. The familiar message begins to swirl in your mind that you are not loveable and will never be accepted because you are simply not enough. Instead of spiraling down, with God's help you become aware you are thinking that about yourself. You pray, "God, I know these thoughts are not from You. I recognize the enemy has wracked me with these messages for years, and I confess that I have bought into the lie that I am worthless. My desire is to see myself as You see me. Will You show me in the days and weeks to come Your thoughts toward me? Help me refuse any thought that is not from You as You transform my heart and life. Amen."

In searching for scriptures that affirm your value to God, you come across Isaiah 43:1–4. You especially feel comforted and connected to the end of verse 1 and the beginning of verse 4, so you write them down. "Do not fear, for I have redeemed you; I have summoned you by name; you are mine … Since you are precious and honored in my sight, and because I love you …" You keep a three-by-five card on your bathroom mirror with these words written on them so you read it when you first get up in the morning and when you go to bed at night. You keep one taped on the dash of your car and carry one in your purse for a quick reassurance while you're out. Soon you become comfortable with the fact that you are precious to God and He really loves you!

This may sound like a lot of work. It might be. Anything in life worth achieving requires effort. This is the process of renewing your mind as we are encouraged to do in Romans 12:2. If you have been plagued all your life with messages of worthlessness and defeat, taking time to change those thoughts will soon prove worth it. As you practice taking every thought captive, you will begin to more quickly recognize the lies of the enemy and replace them with the truth of God's Word. You will become accustomed to turning your thoughts toward God and enjoy the intimacy of His care over you as He assures you of His constant love and acceptance.

Did you feel any resistance to today's discussion? Why or why not?

_____

_____

_____

_____

Do you remember the last time you gave in to your old shame messages? What was that like for you?

_____

_____

_____

_____

Do you think this process of taking every thought captive and renewing your mind will be difficult? Why or why not?

_____

_____

_____

_____

What do you hope to gain by taking every thought captive and renewing your mind?

_____

_____

_____

_____

Day 2

Read: Isaiah 30:20–21

Our scripture reading for today is part of a longer prophecy the Lord spoke to His people through the prophet Isaiah. He was warning them of a coming destruction to Jerusalem and Judah. In this chapter, He was chiding them for not heeding the warning. Some went to the Egyptians for help, while others simply ignored the warning. Some, however, listened and turned their hearts toward God. To the ones who did this, God was being gracious to them telling them He would be with them every step of the way and would see them through the trouble and bring them out on the other side.

This is exactly where you have been. You can count on God to walk with you throughout your healing journey guiding you each step of the way. At times it seems we are not making progress at all in our healing. It may even seem like we have regressed or relapsed into our old ways of coping or behaving. In these times, we can be certain God is waiting for us to turn to Him for help. When we do this, our ears will hear behind us, "This is the way. Walk in it."

Prayer for Today

Today when you pray, ask God to help you learn to hear His voice. Thank Him for His willingness to see you through your healing journey and His patience when you fall a step behind.

Listen Up!

How are you doing in your healing journey? Are you feeling lighter and happier? Are you nervous or fearful it won't last? Have you already slipped back into old coping patterns and feel defeated? All of these responses are normal and are no cause for worry. If you think everything is going great and you are one of the "lighter, happier" ones, there is a good chance you will eventually have a down day or two. If you have already experienced a down day or two (or more), fear not. Brighter days are ahead.

Learning to live in the new world of a healthier relationship with yourself and others is like learning to ride a bike. You have no clue how to do it at first. It feels strange and requires a desire to learn and a lot of patience. Oh, and you'll likely fall off a time or two. Surrounding yourself with a good support system of people who can encourage you and understand what you're going through is certainly important and helpful. Sooner or later, however, you will need to take off the training wheels and learn to ride on your own.

Thankfully, we have something better than training wheels, and we are never truly doing life on our own. The Holy Spirit is available to help every time we face something that triggers us and tempts us to return to old ways of thinking and coping.

Think for a moment about Jesus and His life here on earth. In the human sense, He grew up learning about His environment just like every other baby. Crawling, walking, learning right from wrong and who to trust and who not to was also natural for Him. But we forget He had an existence before His life here. He was used to glory, peace, and all heavenly beings happily doing the will of the Father every moment of every day, year, decade, century, or however they mark time up there. The point is I wonder if it was at all strange for Him to be on earth where He was now met with sin, temptation, sorrow, and pain. He had a mission to accomplish and a father He wanted to please and obey but had to do so in the confines of a decaying human body, imperfect and dysfunctional relationships, and generations of people who couldn't possibly understand Him.

For Jesus to live through each day of His ministry with no job or wages, no wife as a helper, and no home for comfort and support, He had to *completely* depend on His Father. He had to wholly trust Him when He spoke words of healing to the paralytic or touched the blind man's eyes. He had to know for certain the fish were going to be there when He told Peter to let his net down on the other side of the boat. He had to know His Father would provide His next meal and see Him all the way through to the other side of the crucifixion. Only one time do we see Him question His Father's presence and help, and that was at the end of His life as He completed His final task here on earth.

As we walk through the next days and weeks of what may feel like a strange new existence in the land of healthy living, we can be as certain of Jesus's presence and help as He was of His Father's. How can we know that level of certainty? The same way Jesus did. He was always slipping away to talk to His Father, always making time to pray. He *knew* His Father's voice and could sense His Father's direction at every turn.

God wants to do the same for us as we navigate family gatherings possibly with people who will not understand new perspectives or even believe in the experience of healing. We can call on Him to help in these and other circumstances. There will be times we will want to go back to old coping ways. We will also need to hear His direction or His ideas for how to respond to people or how to approach certain situations, and to do that, we need to know His voice.

Learning to hear God's voice requires practice and can be different for every person. God can and does speak through His Word, the Bible. The Bible is living and often surprises at how the same passage can be read many times but will speak in a special way one day. Asking the Holy Spirit to direct our reading and speak to our heart is the first, best way to learn God's voice.

Taking certain passages of scripture and reading the words to God as a prayer can also help form an intimate relationship with God. Asking Him to teach us to hear His voice in the days ahead, and then paying attention to times there is a pause in our heart or thinking, will also help us learn His voice. Perhaps a new thought or question will pop into our mind, or we'll hear a comment that makes us stop and think. Those are the times to ask God to confirm that it was His voice speaking through what was said or heard.

We are spending this day on learning to listen because it is so critical to healing. God is the ultimate healer, and no healing is complete without Him since He alone knows the smallest detail of our past and the biggest obstacle of our future. He has a good plan for our life and wants to give us everything we need to succeed in that plan. As we spend more time with God in prayer and Bible reading, we are practicing being in His presence. The more we practice being in His presence, the more we learn to hear His voice.

Although there has hopefully been a significant healing in the past days, the process of healing is not an overnight thing. There are always broken places God wants to heal and new places we will need His help. Regularly connecting with the divine avails us to further healing and awakens us to His constant presence. Taking the healing journey with God as our healer will prove rich and rewarding.

How adept are you at hearing God's voice in your life? Explain and give an example, if possible.

_____

_____

_____

_____

What is most challenging for you in hearing God's voice?

_____

_____

_____

_____

What obstacles or situations do you foresee where you will need God's help navigating?

_____

_____

_____

_____

What do you most need God to do for you as you walk through your healing journey?

_____

_____

_____

_____

Day 3

Read: Ezra 7:6–10, 9:1–5, and 10:1–12

These verses in the book of Ezra give us a brief summary of what Ezra, the holy prophet of God, faced as he returned to Jerusalem with the now second group of Israelites who had been exiled into Babylon for more than seventy years, away from their homeland, their temple (where God resided at that time), and their holy practices. Being placed in a pagan land with pagan gods and practices had left some of them vulnerable to falling into pagan lifestyles. And they did.

They knew who they were—God's chosen people. And they knew what was expected of them. But they fell into doing what they thought was necessary (or convenient) to survive their existence in a foreign, pagan land. But now here they are back in their homeland, a place many of them had never known, and the expectations were for their lifestyles and spiritual practices to match up with their new lives. This new life, which was supposed to be an occasion to celebrate, was at first challenging as Ezra called them to put away their old pagan practices and live in the new life God had provided for them. With Ezra's prayer and petitions for God's forgiveness and help, the people learned to walk in obedience and enjoyed God's blessing as a result.

Prayer for Today

Today sit in silence as you ask the Holy Spirit to show you where in your life you may still be thinking or acting as a victim of your past. As instances are brought to your mind, confess the old ways and ask Him to give you examples of how you could respond, think, or act. Then determine that with God's help you will walk in the newness of God's healing.

No Victims in My Safe Harbor!

If you've ever been out on the open sea during a storm, or even on a boat on a lake, it can feel anywhere from unnerving to downright terrifying—depending on who's at the helm! I have been at sea on a cruise ship in a storm and on the ocean in a boat in a storm. One was a little unnerving and the other downright terrifying. I'll let you guess which was which. In both cases, there was such great relief, such a release from anxiety, when we finally pulled into the harbor to dock. Just knowing we were safe and had made it back to shore and all things secure was as memorable a feeling as the fear I left behind.

For many of us, living in the turmoil of dysfunction for so long can feel like being in a storm at sea. And being healed from the past and its shame can feel like coming into the safe harbor. Leaving the chaos of the past behind is a relief and a memorable feeling. Equally memorable, however, are the old habits, roles, and behaviors we adapted to deal with the chaos of the past.

Putting away old habits is never an easy thing. Ways in which we have functioned for years and roles we have played have created patterns of thought and behavior that are difficult to change and can be difficult for those around us to accept. We may have become a pleaser as a way to fit in or find self or others' acceptance. Those around us have come to rely on us to be the one to volunteer even when it is most inconvenient for us. Along with that, we don't like conflict, so standing up for ourselves would never happen.

But here we are now, having realized why we became a pleaser and healed from shame we took on that was never ours. We are grateful for the realizations and the healing we have received, and we are looking to God for help and continued healing. And while it may be easy to picture and live out our new lives when we are by ourselves, when thrown into situations with people who know us as a pleaser, it's easier to be who we've always been. The problem is that now it no longer gives us the same feelings of being needed and accepted. We may feel resentful now, or we may see how we have allowed people to take advantage of us. We feel uncomfortable now because we no longer *need* their approval or acceptance. We have discovered our own worth and we see that our time is just as valuable as theirs.

Or perhaps you grew up in a family that uses sarcasm for humor as a way of always needing to be smart or right to gain acceptance. Questions asked are met with answers, such as "Now where do you *think* it would be?" or "Seriously? Everybody knows *that!*" It's a way of making one person superior and the other person inferior. You might as well attach the word "dummy" to the end of those remarks because that is exactly what is being conveyed. Whether you were the one doling out such remarks or were often the recipient, both are equally challenging to change.

If you are the one who uses sarcasm (calling it "joking"), when you begin to simply answer a question without sarcasm giving dignity to the one asking, they may be taken aback at first. People expect us to be who we've always been. And to be fair, sometimes people can ask dumb questions that have seemingly obvious answers. Changing the way we respond to people, giving them the respect and permission to ask "dumb" questions isn't only about suddenly seeing *them* differently. It is more about being the kind of person *you* want to be. It's about no longer needing to feel superior at the expense of someone else. Your worth is no longer attached to having to be smarter or righter than anyone in the family or in the room. You are valuable no matter how much you know or don't know and so are they.

Likewise, if you were always the recipient of the sarcasm, you may have shut down or simply walked away. Because of their sarcasm, you may have actually believed you *were* everything they said you were. Standing up for yourself now may be scary or may stir up conflict.

On top of that, we may now become frustrated or disappointed in ourselves when we fall back into our old patterns. Don't lose heart! Remember this is a process, and we won't do it perfectly. You are no longer a victim of your past and you will learn new ways of thinking and being. This can be difficult work. Most of us have been acting in these roles and using these coping behaviors for many years. In fact, it can be comfortable to continue that way and uncomfortable to change. Deciding that being a victim is no longer an option is a decision that may have to be made more than once along the way. It requires determination and grit that will eventually grow into confidence and self-respect.

In couples counseling, there is a measure of time counselors often ask about that can tell a lot about a couple's relationship. When a couple has a disagreement or argument, it is interesting to know how long it takes them to return to a good place together. After mutual forgiveness, there is a feeling of extreme comfort, like coming home where all is well. It is like finally returning to a safe harbor after a storm. The sooner you can return to that feeling of safety, the better the relationship.

We can use that same analogy in our healing journey with God. When we return to our old victim ways of thinking and behaving, leaning on God for help returns us to that feeling of coming home. Each time we catch ourselves or allow the Holy Spirit to check our thoughts or behavior, and once again determine not to be a victim lessens the occurrences. Before long we will prefer the safety of the harbor and feel less comfortable living like a victim. We will even risk conflict and begin standing up for ourselves by learning to say no when it's best for us. We may stop allowing or using sarcasm or other coping behaviors and begin to treat others and ourselves with the dignity and respect we all deserve.

All these changes will be made because there is no longer a need for unhealthy ways of getting approval or feeling included, important, or enough. Slowly the victim life will be more and more uncomfortable and less and less like our true selves, at home, in the safety of the harbor.

In what ways were you living like a victim of your past before you received healing?

_____

_____

_____

How difficult has it been for you to step out of the victim role since you began this healing journey? Explain.

_____

_____

_____

_____

How did you feel about the analogy of the safety of the harbor? Explain.

_____

_____

_____

_____

What has helped you the most so far in making changes from being a victim of your past?

_____

_____

_____

_____

Day 4

Read: 1 Timothy 6:11–20 and Colossians 3:2–10

Because the enemy of your soul has free reign while here on this earth, he will use every opportunity possible to pull you back into your old ways. Staying true to the real you requires vigilance and a commitment to renew your mind daily as you turn to God for help. Thankfully, God has given us in His Word several instructions on how to win out over the enemy, and two of those are our readings for today.

The types of things Paul encouraged Timothy to work on leave little room for thoughts of shame, self-degradation, or vengeance toward others. Thoughts that deal with pride, worthlessness, slander, self-loathing, and whether we're too much or not enough all have no space when we are diligently pursuing the righteous life. This is not to say we are earning our righteousness; it is a gift. Because Satan is hard at work, however, we must do everything we can to turn from evil, commit to the faith, put our hope and trust in God, and imitate Christ in our good works and attitudes.

That is exactly how we accomplish what Paul also encourages the Colossians to do. We are to set our minds on things above, run from evil and the lies Satan would have us believe about ourselves because of sin and a dysfunctional past. And we are to practice believing the truth about ourselves, about God, and about others. These are not always typically the first things that enter our minds, especially during failure, conflict, or trials. We train our minds to think differently and ask God to help us and slowly we are transformed according to the truth of His Word.

Prayer for Today

As you pray today, ask God to seal in your heart the truth of His Word. Ask Him to be present when you read it and search scriptures that show you His heart. Tell Him you desire a vibrant relationship with Him in the reading of His words to you. He will be there.

Who I Am in Christ

Many of us have seen the booklets that have all the scriptures listed from the Bible that tell us what being a new creature in Christ affords us. It is important that we know some of these verses so we can call upon them when Satan attacks our character and tries to send us spinning back into who we used to be. It is an important part of renewing our minds as Romans 12:1–2 tells us to do.

The cool thing about this is not just that we should do it because the Bible says to (although that should be reason enough), and it's not just so we can war against Satan (also reason enough), but because it works! Renewing our minds is a real thing! Therapists spend their entire careers and clients spend their entire savings learning how to renew minds, and it was all right here in scripture long before therapy was a thing!

Cognitive behavioral therapy is the process of taking distorted or negative thought patterns and changing them to thoughts that are grounded in truth, which in turn hopes to alter behavior.[1] Do you recall the beginning of this week when we said thoughts beget feelings and feelings beget actions or behavior? It turns out psychology has proven this true. Our thoughts about ourselves affect how we feel about ourselves and how we feel affects our actions or behavior.

The other thing that psychology has proven true is that when we *change* our thoughts, we can change our feelings, and our behavior can also be changed. So when God's Word tells us we are His beloved children and we set our thoughts on this truth and meditate on this truth, it begins to change how we feel about ourselves. If every morning for a month we started our day by saying, "I am a beloved child of God," "I am God's child and He loves me," or "I am deeply loved by God because I am His child," how might we begin to feel by the end of the month? How might that affect our behavior?

Sometimes it seems easier to believe what the Bible says than at other times. It is important for us to be certain that everything the Bible says is true. Everything God has ever promised He has already done or *will* do. God *always* keeps His promises. His promises are not based on our feelings or our situations. When a situation seems completely hopeless to us, we can say with assurance that nothing is impossible with God (Matthew 19:26). When it seems there is no purpose in what is happening around us, we can know that God is somehow working the whole situation for our good (Romans 8:28). And when we cannot see how anything that is happening could possibly be used for good, despite God's working, we can trust that our Almighty God is not like us. He sees things from an eternal perspective and does things in ways our minds cannot always comprehend (Isaiah 55:8–9). We *need* the scriptures!

So it is with what God has to say about us. No matter how worthless we may *feel,* when God's Word says we are worth dying for, we can believe it. Because God never changes (Hebrews 13:8), our worth and our place in His family, His heart, and His eternal home are not conditionally based on how we feel about ourselves once we are His. Our shame or guilt or past cannot disqualify us from what He says about us. We are loved, cherished, included, forgiven, protected, and provided for! This is probably the only time that something sounds too good to be true but *is.*

It is important for our transformation into a renewed and healthy person that we know and trust what God's Word says about who we are in Christ. We not only need to know it in our heads, but also in our hearts until we know it in our very being, or we are *being* it. *Then* we are renewing our minds (knowing it in our heads), which leads to feeling it (knowing it in our hearts), which leads to being and acting and behaving differently (knowing it in our being).

Could God transform us miraculously without all this hard work we have to do? Of course He could! And sometimes He changes people instantly, and those miracles are always amazing! But He also knows that when we spend time in His Word searching for His promises to us or when we cry out in desperation, depending on Him to come near and be with us, we are spending time with Him. Without these precious, intimate times with Him, our relationship with Him wouldn't grow. And He longs to show us His power and His love for us.

Below is a list of some of the scriptures that affirm who we are in Christ.[2] Choose several that resonate with you and the issues you are overcoming. Write them down, carry them with you, memorize them, and flood your mind with these truths. Keep a journal of your thought patterns and note how your feelings about yourself and others change. See if you might be surprised how your behavior might change in time.

Use the first list of scriptures to date and highlight verses that resonate with you today. Use the second identical set to tear out or copy and keep as a way to renew your mind throughout your healing journey.

Who I Am in Christ

John 1:12: I am God's child.
John 15:9: I am loved by God as certainly as Jesus is loved by God.
John 15:15: I am Christ's friend.
Romans 5:1: I have been justified.
1 Corinthians 6:17: I am united with the Lord, and I am one spirit with Him.
1 Corinthians 6:19–20: I have been bought with a price. I belong to God.
1 Corinthians 12:27: I am a member of Christ's body.
Ephesians 1:1: I am a saint, a holy one.
Ephesians 1:5: I have been adopted as God's child.
Ephesians 2:18: I have direct access to God through the Holy Spirit.
Colossians 1:14: I have been redeemed and forgiven of all my sins.
Colossians 2:10: I am complete in Christ.

Romans 8:1–2: I am free forever from condemnation.
Romans 8:28: I am assured that all things work together for good.
Romans 8:31–34: I am free from any condemning charges against me.

Romans 8:35–39: I cannot be separated from the love of God.

2 Corinthians 1:21–22: I have been established, anointed, and sealed by God.

Philippians 1:6: I am confident that the good work
God has begun in me will be perfected.

Philippians 3:20: I am a citizen of heaven.

Colossians 3:3: I am hidden with Christ in God.

2 Timothy 1:7: I have not been given a spirit of fear but of power, love, and a sound mind.

Hebrews 4:16: I can find grace and mercy to help me in time of need.

1 John 5:18: I am born of God and the evil one cannot touch me.

Matthew 5:13–14: I am the salt of the earth and the light of the world.

John 15:1, 5: I am a branch of the true vine,
Jesus, and a channel of His life.

John 15:16: I have been chosen and appointed by God to bear fruit.

Acts 1:8: I am a personal, Spirit-empowered witness of Christ.

1 Corinthians 3:16: I am a temple of God.

2 Corinthians 5:17–21: I am a minister of reconciliation for God.

2 Corinthians 6:1: I am God's coworker.

Ephesians 2:6: I am seated with Christ in the heavenly realm.

Ephesians 2:10: I am God's workmanship, created for good works.

Ephesians 3:12: I may approach God with freedom and confidence.

Philippians 4:13: I can do all things through Christ who strengthens me!

Who I Am in Christ

John 1:12 - I am God's child.

John 15:9 - I am loved by God as certainly as Jesus is loved by God.

John 15:15 - I am Christ's friend.

Romans 5:1 - have been justified

1 Corinthians 6:17 - I am united with the Lord and I am one spirit with Him.

1 Corinthians 6:19, 20 - I have been bought with a price, I belong to God.

1 Corinthians 12:27 - I am a member of Christ's Body.

Ephesians 1:1 - I am a saint, a holy one.

Ephesians 1:5 - I have been adopted as God's child.

Ephesians 2:18 - I have direct access to God through the Holy Spirit.

Colossians 1:14 - I have been redeemed and forgiven of all my sins.

Colossians 2:10 - I am complete in Christ.

Romans 8:1,2 - I am free forever from condemnation.

Romans 8:28 - I am assured that all things work together for good.

Romans 8:31-34 - I am free from any condemning charges against me.

Romans 8:35-39 - I cannot be separated from the love of God.

2 Corinthians 1:21, 22 - I have been established, anointed and seaaled by God.

Phillippians 1:6 - I am confident that the good work God has begun in me will be perfected.

Phillippians 3:20 - I am a citizen of heaven.

Colossians 3:3 - I am hidden with Christ in God.

2 Timothy 1:7 - I have not been given a spirit of fear, but of power, love and a sound mind.

Hebrews 4:16 - I can find grace and mercy to help me in time of need.

1 John 5:18 - I am born of God and the evil one cannot touch me.

Matthew 5:13, 14 - am the salt of the earth and the light of the world.

John 15:1,5 - I am a branch of the true vine, Jesus, a channel of His life.

John 15:16 - I have been chosen and appointed by God to bear fruit.

Acts 1:8 - I am a personal, Spirit empowered witness of Christ.

1 Corinthians 3:16 - I am a temple of God.

2 Corinthians 5:17-21 - I am a minister of reconciliation for God.

2 Corinthians 6:1 - I am God's co-worker.

Ephesians 2:6 - I am seated with Christ in the heavenly realm.

Ephesians 2:10 - I am God's workmanship, created for good works.

Ephesians 3:12 - I may approach God with freedom and confidence.

Phillippians 4:13 - I can do all things through Christ who strengthens me!

Day 5

Read: 1 Timothy 4:15

Today's reading is about being diligent and giving our all to something. Paul was instructing a young Timothy about how to live and lead others in the future when different beliefs would be mixed in with the truth. He reminded Timothy he would need to set an example in his speech and conduct. He would need to devote himself to reading scripture and all the things he had learned. It was all about putting into practice the things Paul had taught him. Practice doing these things, Timothy! It's all about practice.

Remember taking piano lessons or learning a sport or another skill? If you were one who took practice seriously, you likely accomplished a great deal of competence. If you practiced, you could play the piano, catch or hit a ball well, make bread, or paint a beautiful picture. And if you shunned your practice or didn't take it seriously, you probably quit piano, warmed the bench, made floppy rolls, or never picked up a paintbrush again. It's all about the practice!

It is difficult these days to give ourselves wholly to one thing. If we are parents, we feel like we are giving ourselves wholly to our kids or our family. But for most of us, that is really giving ourselves wholly to three, five, or more people—and each of their needs and interests. Giving ourselves wholly is exhausting. Giving ourselves wholly to Christ is more than just adding to our calendars church services, Bible studies, and prayer times. It is a posture of the heart and a state of mind that underlies and surrounds everything we do, whether it's work, laundry, or worshipping at church. It happens by spending time with Jesus, praying without ceasing wherever we are, whatever we're doing. And it happens by listening to Him and reading His Word. And even that takes discipline and practice!

Prayer for Today

Dear God, I have spent so much of my life carefully living to the best of *my* ability. But that was based on what others said about me or to me and even what others may have taught me about You. I confess I may not have been living to the best of *Your* ability. I have been lax in my discipline of listening to You and believing what You say *to* me about me and Your plans for me. Help me create a routine of discipline in spending time with You. Help me to practice being in your presence and communicating with You regularly. Amen.

Practice Makes Perfect

Who loves practice? So many hands did not go up. Yet we all know it is true that anyone we admire who has achieved great things has succumbed to the rigors of practice. All of the great swimmers in the Olympics have spent countless hours in the pool. Many of my grandchildren swim on the same swim team, and while none of them are Olympians, they are in the water at 7:30 every morning of their summer break swimming laps, learning the strokes, and practicing, practicing, practicing. And because of that, they are really good swimmers! I have other grandchildren who are gymnasts. They spend three to four hours at a time in the gym going over the same routines again and again to get to the next level or to medal at the next competition. And they are really good gymnasts!

We all know practice is the key to doing anything well. So you won't be surprised to learn we are taking a day to practice what we learned yesterday—who I am in Christ. Even if these are truths we have grown up with, reviewing them will cement them in our hearts for use when we need them.

If you did not highlight the verses that spoke to you yesterday, take a few minutes to pray and ask God to speak directly to your heart and show you which verses your inmost being struggles with believing. Highlight those verses and write down what you hear Him saying to you.

Which of the verses spoke to you? Write the reference and the verses here.

_____

_____

_____

_____

What category would you say your highlighted verses mostly fall into? Explain.

- being loved or feeling significant?
- being forgiven or feeling abandoned or condemned?
- being unacceptable or feeling rejected or ashamed?

_____

_____

_____

_____

What did your heart hear God speaking to you about these issues?

_____

_____

_____

_____

How can you keep the truths God has spoken to you alive and active in your heart?

_____

_____

_____

_____

Where are you in the process of living out these truths? Explain.

- the renewing my mind stage
- the change of feelings stage
- the change of behavior stage
- the completely transformed stage and working daily to maintain these truths in my life

_____

_____

_____

_____

Chapter 8

Making All Things New Ain't Easy

Day 1

Read: Luke 8:16–17

Jesus's analogy of light and the lampstand in Luke 8 comes right after He has explained the parable of the sower and the seed. The light He is referring to is His message or His Word. He is telling His disciples not to hide everything He has just told them. He has given them a good word, and He expects them to share it with anyone who will listen. But it's more than that. Since the first verses of the book of John tell us Jesus *is* the Word (and He refers to Himself as the Light of the world), we can feel sure that Jesus, and everything He says and does, is the light in this passage. And we know the purpose of light is to dispel the darkness. So everything Jesus has just said or ever said, everything Jesus has just done (raised the widow's son and healed the centurion's servant) or ever did, and everything Jesus will ever say or ever do is Light. And its purpose is to blast away darkness.

Furthermore, it doesn't do any good to try to hide anything from this Light. Whatever is hidden will be exposed. That's what happens when light enters a dark room. Whatever is in that room is now seen—out in the open. So it is with our sin and shame. Nothing is hidden. No sin you have ever committed, and no sin that has been committed against you. Exposed. Because Jesus. The Light. And no shame you have carried, yours or someone else's, can be concealed, no matter how many masks you wear. Blasted. Because Jesus. The Light.

But it's not that Jesus is going around exposing all our sin and shame. He knows it. He sees it. Nothing is hidden from Him. But He never forces Himself on anyone. We never see Jesus in the New Testament holding someone down because they need healing. Whatever sin or shame we choose to bring to Jesus loses its power when it's exposed to the Light. Read that again. Whatever sin or shame we *choose* to bring to Jesus loses its power when it's exposed to the Light. Jesus is in the house.

Prayer for Today

Today as we continue on our path toward healing, thank God for His healing power. Thank Him for being able to see all our sin and shame that led Him to the cross so we can be forgiven. Thank Him for being the Light of the World that dispels the darkness, and ask Him to keep shining His light into your life for healing, for guidance, and for blasting away the shame.

Getting Off the Merry-Go-Round

Remember back to grade school when most playgrounds had the big hop-on merry-go-round? They typically had a large flat floor and six or eight strong metal bars to hold onto. They held as many kids as the biggest, strongest ones could make go around. Sometimes, the biggest, strongest kids could make the merry-go-round fly, and that was the goal! Invariably, when it was going the fastest, one kid would scream, "I want off!" Rather than slow it down, the more sinister spinners would keep it going and require the poor kid who wanted off to make a jump for it. Tuck, duck, and roll!

This week we are going to be discussing how to get off the merry-go-round safely. More accurately, we will talk about what the cycles of emotional growth and awareness look like. This will help us better understand where we have been, where we are now, and how we can continue growing to a healthier place.

First, we are going to circle back around to feelings and emotions today, because as we learn to live from a new place of healing, it's important we keep checking in with how we're feeling. Hopefully there has been some practice in renewing our minds and reminding ourselves of who we were created to be in Christ. Remember the next step is to see if our feelings are coming along also. It's not helpful if we allow ourselves to become overwhelmed with emotion, nor is it good whether we are numb or not allowing ourselves to feel anything at all.

Hopefully, by now, you can see some of the stages you have gone through, and steps you have taken, to get to this point. While many of your actions may have been unconscious as you attempted to survive an event or cope with difficult circumstances, the steps you will take from here on out will be done intentionally and courageously. You may find this comes easily for you, or it may require some practice. Each step you take and each stage you go through will bring more healing and new pathways for emotionally healthy living. The chart below is a visual for the work you have done and are doing. It shows the cycle of stages we go through when trauma enters our lives.

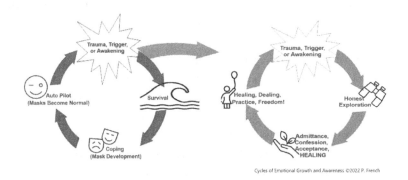

Cycles of Emotional Growth and Awareness ©2022 P. French

In the first cycle, some initial event or experience happens that is traumatic. In chapter 4, trauma was discussed as an event or experience that overwhelms the emotional part of the brain causing the "fight, flight, or freeze" state to remain active, which disallows the brain to return to a normal, calm functioning (seen at the top of the left cycle). This overwhelm throws us into survival mode. We are in crisis and may not be able to function at all for a couple days or longer. If the initial trauma happened to us as children, we may have very few, if any, memories of the time surrounding the event, perhaps months or years. God has designed our brains to repress or hide horrific things that still developing brains cannot understand.

Since the mind is susceptible to suggestion, and our imaginations can run wild, there is rarely a need to try to recover things that are repressed. God, in His healing mercy, allows things to bubble to the surface of your memory as you can handle them if they are important for your healing. Perhaps you have already experienced this in the inner healing section. This means God thinks you are able to handle that memory now and is now entrusting it to you. He may also provide ways to verify the truth of the memory, which is a beautiful gift when that happens. Accept these times as the gifts they are and know God is active in your healing and is there with comfort and help when you need it.

If the trauma happened at an age when you are old enough to remember, you may recall the confusion surrounding the event(s). All of life can seem disrupted. Depending on our age, someone may need to remind us to eat or to get out of bed and get dressed. Our normal daily functions are interrupted, and we lack the ability to concentrate on the simplest things. This is when we put the milk in the pantry and the markers in the freezer. We may have missed homework assignments, days of school, appointments, or forgotten to pick up kids from school.

Eventually we gain some sense of bearing and begin moving through our routines, taking care of the kids, going back to work or school, etc. But it feels heavy and too difficult, and we know something still isn't right. We begin to cope the best way we can, especially when things are stressful. At these times, we may lash out in anger, or turn to food. As children we may begin to act out or withdraw. As adults we may eat or drink or smoke to calm ourselves. We may stay in bed longer than usual or neglect our regular hygiene habits. On the flip side, we may become quite rigid in our routines. We may eat only enough to stay alive, clean the house in an obsessive way, or become a straight-A student. All of these coping mechanisms, and others, are outside ways we try to control a situation we could not control.

While we are searching for a way to cope, we are really looking for a way to soothe the inner turmoil going on, often unconsciously. This is when we realize we must also figure out how and who to be around our friends, family, coworkers, and others. We begin to go out of way to avoid the "How are you doing?" questions. Everything is always fine, or we isolate. Or we work harder to prove we're OK. Perhaps we began to blow off the concerns of others by making jokes, or maybe we shut off our emotions altogether.

All of these are ways we learned to cope. We learned to wear one or more masks to get through without losing it. This stage may have lasted for weeks or months, but eventually we found what worked enough to keep the pain, fear, and confusion pushed down so we could go on with our lives. That brings us to the autopilot stage that can last for years or even decades until something happens that triggers us: a place, a smell, a sound, a comment, a movie, or anything that puts us right back in that trauma place.

If we stay in the unhealthy emotional cycle, we may only make a brief stop in the survival mode—maybe a few minutes to a few hours or days. We may slip back into our coping habits a little heavier than usual for a while, but soon we will be back to our autopilot stage—until the next trigger.

Unless we have an awakening! This catapults us over to the right cycle. An awakening can be an invitation to a study like this one, or it can be a weariness inside you that is ready to deal with the past. It can be a sermon or a conversation, an article, a movie or book, or anything else that moves us to begin looking backward for clues to the inner turmoil we have now become accustomed to.

Then we begin the exploration phase of searching in our family, our past relationships, our upbringing, or a host of other places and ways to put pieces together. If you are a Christian, you can be sure God will guide your search, because His healing is complete and He leaves no necessary stone unturned. Trust Him. If you are not a Christian, you can also be sure God will guide your search, because He is always finding ways to reach you, rescue you, and heal you. Trust Him.

Currently in this study, we are in the 9:00 position of the right cycle. You have nearly completed your exploration (though pieces may pop up here and there for a long time). You have written and shared your story and received healing for the shame, and should any new pieces pop up, you will know exactly where to place them. We still have much to learn about living in this place of healing, and we will be doing that in our final chapters. But before we do, we need to check in again to see how we are feeling.

What impacted you most about seeing the work you've done in diagram form? Explain.

_____

_____

_____

_____

What stages of the left cycle did you relate to? Why?

_____

_____

_____

_____

What caused you to go into the awakening phase that led you to the right cycle?

_____

_____

_____

_____

Do you think it's possible to be doing your work in the right cycle and find yourself back in the left cycle? What will you do if that happens?

_____

_____

_____

_____

Day 2

Read: Luke 2:41–49 and Matthew 9:1–13

The gospels are full of stories about Jesus. They tell of His miracles, His friends, His enemies, and a little about His family. One thing we can see throughout His life was His confidence in who He was and why He had come to earth. He knew His identity and His mission. Both of our readings for today bear witness to this, beginning with a recounting of an occurrence from a twelve-year-old Jesus. Even at this young age, He knows who He is. Luke tells us His parents had been looking for Him for days only to find Him teaching in the temple. When they confront Him, He acts astonished that they wouldn't have known where to look for Him, asking, "Didn't you know I had to be in my father's house?"

Matthew 9 tells of the man, Jesus, healing, forgiving sins, and calling people to follow Him. By now He wasn't so popular with everyone, but He never let that sway Him from His mission. Even when He healed the lame man who was bound to a mat on the ground, they didn't get it. Most of them never did get it and still don't get it today. But what I love about this scripture is that Jesus knows who He is, and He knows why He was sent. He is certain of His identity and His mission. He made it clear He had the authority to heal and forgive sins, and if that wasn't enough, He added that He was not there for the stuffy, arrogant, righteous people but for the sinners. He never once doubted who He was or why He was there.

This is why we have been studying and reviewing the scriptures that tell us who we are in Christ. We must be certain of our identity. Jesus Christ gave us a new identity that is different from the identity we had growing up in dysfunction. Many of us thought our identity was unlovable, worthless, never good enough, or damaged.

That's not who we are! We have been made new! We are beloved, valuable, fully accepted, healed from our brokenness, and called beautiful! We must always be sure of our identity!

We must also be sure of our mission—to become disciples of Christ, learning and growing into His unique plan for each of us. We must live up to our new identity, always seeking to see ourselves as Christ sees us and not allowing anyone or anything to drag us back to our old identity or convince us we are anything other than what God's Word says about us.

Just like Jesus, being sure of our identity may rub some people the wrong way. We may feel resistance from close friends, family, or others just like Jesus did. Jesus had strong, sure boundaries and didn't let people sway Him from who He was and what He came to do.

Don't stop studying about your new identity. Don't stop believing the truth and denouncing the lies. Don't stop growing, trying, praying, and asking God to help you every day. Remember to renew your mind so your feelings about yourself will change, so your behavior and your whole countenance will change. Walk worthy!

Prayer for Today

Meditate on the scripture readings for today. Imagine seeing Jesus heal and hearing Him speak so confidently. Thank Him for coming to heal you and for giving you a new identity. Ask Him to plaster your new identity onto your heart as you read through the verses of "Who I Am in Christ." Ask Him to continue to help you grow and ask for strength as you face obstacles and people who don't want you to change—people who need you to stay dysfunctional so they can maintain their own dysfunction. He knows exactly what that is like.

Hold It Right There!

Wouldn't it be great if we could instantaneously be confident of our identity and our mission and never waiver from that? And wouldn't it be great if once we wake up to our dysfunction and experience healing, we could flow through the healthy cycle we learned about yesterday without any hiccups or bumps in the road? Yay! We made it! We're all better! Everything is great! My relationships are great, my finances are great, my spiritual life is great, my whole life is great!

Unfortunately, life doesn't work that way, does it? I can't think of one single thing in life that goes from start to finish without some kind of hardship or obstacle. Babies fall when they're learning to walk, injuries and surgeries take time to heal and often have setbacks, our bodies give out, wrinkle up, and eventually die, honest, healthy relationships are never free from disagreements, even million-dollar bank accounts will eventually be whittled away by spending and taxes unless they're maintained and replenished. Like the Bible says, the grass withers and the flowers fade and only the Word of God lasts forever (Isaiah 40:8). Thank God for that, at least. That is why we spent so much time on what God's Word says about who we are in Christ—because it's lasting and eternal truth.

We don't yet live in that perfect forever world where God's truth reigns unhindered. And we already know Satan is prowling around waiting to destroy us (1 Peter 5:8), so he will use every opportunity available. Thankfully, God has provided us with practical ways we can continue to grow and avoid some of the pitfalls that await us. We have already discussed using scripture and calling on God for help to dispel the lies we have believed for so long. Another brilliant way to thwart our failure is to learn to set healthy boundaries.

No doubt we have realized the things we learned about how to interact with others, how to express our feelings, and how we are to be treated were not always taught in the healthiest manner. People teach what they know, and often our parents or caregivers weren't taught to set healthy boundaries themselves. Learning to set healthy boundaries is necessary for

- appropriate self-care and self-respect
- learning to communicate your needs and feelings in a family or a relationship
- learning to make time for positive interactions
- learning to manage or eliminate negative interactions
- learning to set healthy limits in a relationship

What exactly are boundaries? Boundaries are invisible lines around each of us or covenants we make with ourselves about what we will or won't allow in our interactions with other people. Toddlers instinctively set boundaries when another child tries to take a toy away. A protest cry or a scream of "Mine!" shows a boundary is being broken and that it's not OK! As the toddler grows up, his or her personal space and covenants with themselves may or may not be respected. If the parent or caregiver respects the toddler's boundary and returns the toy, it teaches the child she and her needs matter while also teaching the grabber that other people's boundaries are to be regarded. If, however, the child is constantly taught to share or always give in to others no matter what, then she may grow up with weak or passive boundaries allowing others to take advantage of her or treat her poorly.

Looking back over our lives, particularly as children, and recalling lessons we learned about our personal property, needs, and desires can alert us to any boundary issues we may have. Were we permitted privacy or personal space and possessions for some of our things? Were we taught to share in a healthy way that was out of our plenty or our own desire to be kind and give to others? Or did we get the impression other people's needs and wants were more important than ours no matter what? Were we taught to have clear boundaries around our bodies, meaning there are private areas no one else should have access to without our consent? Were we appropriately permitted to say, "No, thank you," when there was something we didn't want to have or participate in? And did someone defend us when others were mean, said unkind things to us, or ignored our boundaries?

All of these lessons define where you or I end and others begin. Learning proper personal boundaries helps decide how we want to be treated in conversation and behavior and what interactions are acceptable and not acceptable.[1] Among the lessons learned from healthy boundaries are the following:

- learning to say no
- expecting people to treat us fairly and respectfully
- using our best initial judgment about situations or people's character
- not having to be all things to all people
- adjusting boundaries when people either ignore our boundaries or prove trustworthy
- setting and following through on consequences when necessary

We will be learning more about these boundary lessons tomorrow and learning where in our relationships boundaries might be needed. Hopefully you can see why it is important to know your identity. People who do not have a strong sense of identity and purpose do not see the need for boundaries. By understanding that we are children of God with value and purpose, we will not allow others to define us or control us. We will not be controlled or manipulated by the needs, desires, or words of others.

Did you learn setting and respecting healthy boundaries when you were a child? Explain.

_____

_____

_____

_____

Do you find it easier to set or stick to your boundaries as an adult? Why or why not?

_____

_____

_____

_____

Of the five reasons below that show boundaries are necessary, which are most difficult for you and why?

- appropriate self-care and self-respect
- learning to communicate your needs and feelings in a family or a relationship
- learning to make time for positive interactions
- learning to manage or eliminate negative interactions
- learning to set healthy limits in a relationship

_____

_____

_____

_____

Day 3

Read: Galatians 6:7–8

Throughout the Bible are stories, references, and parables of boundaries. In the very beginning of the Bible, God sets a boundary with Adam that he may eat of any tree in the Garden, except the Tree of the Knowledge and Evil. God, the perfect Father, also laid out the consequence beforehand so there was no mistake what would happen to Adam if he ignored or disobeyed the boundary God set; He would surely die. Sounds so simple. "If you do this, then that will happen." God repeats Himself many other times in the Old Testament, the old "If ... then" boundary.

> If you obey me fully and keep my covenant, then out of all nations you will be my treasured possession. (Exodus 19:5)

> If you do not listen and honor me, I will send a curse on you. (Malachi 2:2)

> If you do not forgive others, I will not forgive you. (Matthew 6:15)

> If anyone destroys God's sacred Temple, God will destroy that person. (1 Corinthians 3:17)

There are hundreds more that show the benefits of respecting a boundary, like the first one above, but there are also many examples of unpleasant consequences. Life is full of boundaries with natural consequences. Don't stand under a tree during a storm or you may be struck by lightning. Don't stick your finger in an outlet or you may be shocked. Don't jump out of a moving car or you may be killed. We don't think anything about respecting these boundaries because we know the consequences are real.

214

The warning in our reading for today is simple. We reap what we sow. We will harvest according to what we plant. Those who ignore boundaries will pay the consequences. It is difficult to watch that in our own families. Many times, we can be manipulated into not setting boundaries or letting them down because when people we love are involved, we want to come to their rescue and prevent their consequences. It's hard to see the people we love hurting. But to get in the way of their natural consequences or refuse to give them consequences ourselves when they make their own bad choices, we are not helping them or loving them well. Our scripture today is clear. God's justice will not be mocked. God is love, and love does not participate in or enable sin.

'No' Is a Complete Sentence (Anne Lamott)

Looking back to the beginning of this book, you were asked to think about how your life was working for you—your relationships, your finances, your job, etc. Now perhaps you can see the connection between needing healthy boundaries and how your life goes. Healthy people who practice healthy boundaries enjoy healthy relationships, healthy finances, etc. That is not to say everything is always perfect and trouble never comes to healthy people. We know that is not the case. But healthy people are better equipped to handle adversity and are less likely to resort to unhealthy coping behaviors. And healthy Christians are even still better equipped to handle adversity. They too make changes or adjustments as they are able and find solutions where they can, and then they trust God for what is out of their control. But often, our Christian ideals get mixed up with what it looks like to set healthy boundaries. In fact, many times, we fail to set boundaries or enforce consequences because we feel it is un-Christian to do so. We get confused with teachings of self-denial and putting others first.

We often think it is either/or. Either I put myself first or I must put the other person first. Either I always enforce a consequence, *or* I always forgive and let people off the hook. Either/or rarely works. Both/and may be a better way to understand these confusions. We *can* be a Christian *and* have healthy boundaries, *and* we can modify our boundaries *and* forgive when it is warranted.

Having healthy boundaries does not mean we think we are better than others or that we value ourselves more highly. We value others as much as we do ourselves, but we value them no more, and we value ourselves no less. Sometimes Christians can misinterpret turning the other cheek and walking the extra mile. Is it right that we are to turn the other cheek or go the extra mile? Yes. We are to do these things purely out of kindness and a desire to give to others for the sake of Christ. However, when we do these things from a heart that believes it is less than, that someone else deserves the treatment more, or we are hoping for acceptance, appreciation, recognition, or reciprocity, then we are simply not capable of giving purely from a kind or giving heart because our motives are distorted.

The kindest thing we can do is give to others from a healthy sense of self-worth. And sometimes that means setting a boundary that says no. It sounds counterintuitive, especially for a Christian. But let's take an example from scripture. In Matthew 25, we read about the ten virgins who were waiting for the bridegroom to come take them to the wedding banquet. (We are assuming the typical Jewish wedding tradition was the reference here, meaning the ten ladies were part of the bridal party whom the groom would escort to the wedding and were not all candidates for the role of the bride. But this is not the point of this example.) Jesus clearly says half of them brought extra oil in case of a long wait. When the other half asked them to share the extra oil (because indeed the wait turned out to be long), the girls with extra oil said no. That sure seems rude, doesn't it?

Jesus indicated it was not rude. He says upfront the half who had extra oil were "wise" and the others were "foolish"! The ones who understood the importance of the event and carefully prepared accordingly were indeed wise. Their boundary was calculated and admirable. They had no idea how much longer they would be waiting for the bridegroom when the lamps began to run out of oil. When asked to share, the girls who were prepared replied, "No, there may not be enough for both us and you. Instead, go to those who sell oil and buy some for yourselves" (verse 9). Their refusal to share was not out of meanness. Rather, they grasped the seriousness of their duty to wait for the bridegroom and came prepared to wait however long it took. And Jesus called them "wise."

Learning to say no appropriately and graciously is part of healthy and mature living. We are stewards of the time, energy, and responsibilities God has given to each of us. Managing these things well in our own life sometimes means saying no to what others want from us. We can always adjust boundaries as we see the outcome. For example, you may not allow your teenage daughter to go with friends on a trip because you don't know the parents well enough. Despite her objections, you are making a judgment call only to find out later the parents are wonderful people with like values to whom you would entrust your daughter. In this case, the boundary is then loosened. If the opposite were the case whereby you allowed your daughter to go with certain conditions and later discovered things happened you didn't approve of, the boundary could then be tightened.

Saying no isn't the only boundary important to our growth and healing. There is a lot to learn in setting healthy boundaries including

- learning to say no, which we've already discussed
- expecting people to treat us fairly and respectfully
- using our best initial judgment about situations or people's character
- not having to be all things to all people
- adjusting boundaries when people either ignore our boundaries or prove trustworthy
- setting and following through on consequences when necessary

There is another example in scripture where Jesus teaches all of these boundary principles. Look at Matthew 10:1–17. Here Jesus has called His disciples together and is sending them out to minister on His behalf. The Bible says He sent them out *with instructions.* Their mission was to drive out evil spirits and to heal every disease and sickness. But not every disease and sickness of every single person—*only* to the lost sheep of Israel (the Jews). Jesus had another plan in mind for reaching the Gentiles.

Verse 5 says, "Do not go among the Gentiles or enter any town of the Samaritans. Go rather to the lost sheep of Israel." They were not to be all things to all people, meeting every need before them. Sometimes we do that, don't we? We will be listening to someone's troubles and within us arises a deep desire to help or to fix their situation. The fact that we have that deep desire isn't a bad thing. It shows we are compassionate. Often, however, we step in before checking our hearts. Is there a need to be a hero, be recognized, or be appreciated here? Does God have another plan for meeting their need, or is there a lesson in this for them we know nothing about?

A few verses later He tells them not to take with them any money, extra clothes, or supplies because they can expect to be taken care of by those they are helping. They can and should expect others to treat them fairly and respectfully. Jesus exact words were "The worker is worth his keep" (verse 10).

In the next verse He tells them to "search there for some worthy person and stay at their house until you leave" (verse 11). They were to make a judgment call on people's character and make their decision on where to stay according to their best judgment. And with that instruction, they were also to act respectfully themselves and then evaluate whether their judgment about the people was correct. "As you enter the home, give it your greeting. If the home is deserving, let your peace rest on it; if it is not, let your peace return to you" (verses 12–13). We can always adjust our boundaries according to how people treat us as we interact with them.

Finally, He tells them what to do if they are not welcomed, respected, or listened to. There may be appropriate consequences when someone ignores or disrespects our boundaries. Verse 14 says, "If anyone will not welcome you or listen to your words, leave that home or town, and shake the dust off your feet. Truly I tell you, it will be more bearable for Sodom and Gomorrah on the day of judgment than for that town." Commentary writer Matthew Henry says, "The apostles [were to have] no fellowship nor communion with them; must not so much as carry away the dust of their city with them." That's a pretty serious consequence. Sadly, in extreme cases, cutting people off is necessary for our own or our family's well-being, when the relationship proves toxic and unyielding. This requires we first treat them with respect as Christ would and requires seeking God's guidance with much prayer.

Jesus knew the hearts of those the disciples would be encountering. And He knows the hearts of those we also encounter. "I am sending you out like sheep among wolves. Therefore, be as shrewd as snakes and as innocent as doves. Be on your guard…" (verse 16). Relationships can be difficult, and our boundaries are often met with resistance and even anger and hostility. When people realize they can no longer control or manipulate you, they will no longer want a relationship with you, particularly if you impose a consequence for their actions.

Proper personal boundaries must be followed up with proper consequences when boundaries are consistently ignored. Without the consequence, the boundary might as well not exist. It is not enough for us to value ourselves enough to simply set a boundary. We show we value ourselves when we care enough to do something about it when the boundary has been broken. But that doesn't mean we won't suffer backlash for doing so.

Consider this example of a couple with middle-school children who were staying with the grandparents. The parents approached the grandparents this way: "Mom and Dad, we have a rule in our house that we do not watch R-rated movies. The last time the kids spent the night with you, the movie you selected was full of bad language and violence. Will you be sure any movies you watch in the future are not R-rated ones? They love sleeping over here, and we'd appreciated your help with this. If you can't go along with this, the kids won't be staying here anymore without us. Thanks."

The rule was explained kindly and stated it was to be followed. The consequence of not following the rule was clearly stated. And when the boundary was ignored? "Mom and Dad, we have asked you not to let the kids watch R-rated movies when they come here. Again, last week you chose another movie that's rated R. This is a rule we have agreed on for our family to keep that stuff out of our home and out of our kids' minds as much as possible. So I'm sorry, but they won't be able to spend the night here anymore."

This couple noticed something that disagreed with their values, and they addressed it kindly and forthrightly by setting a boundary. If this, then that. Please do not let our kids watch R-rated movies here or they can't spend the night anymore. When the boundary was once again broken and ignored, as though they had never had the discussion, the boundary was brought up again, the infraction was pointed out, and the consequence was delivered. Painful for everyone, including the kids.

After several months had passed and there were apologies and discussions where both sides agreed, the boundary was lifted. That was the ideal outcome, but it doesn't always work out that way. Some people are truly wolves in sheep's clothing, and we need to be discerning with setting boundaries and following through with consequences when necessary.

Do you believe a person can follow Christ and also have healthy boundaries? Why or why not?

_____

_____

_____

_____

Which scripture passage resonated the most with you about setting boundaries: the parable of the virgins in Matthew 25 or when Jesus sent His disciples out in Matthew 10? Explain your answer.

_____

_____

_____

_____

Of the list of boundaries below, which are the easiest for you and which are the most difficult? Why?

- learning to say no
- expecting people to treat us fairly and respectfully

- using our best initial judgment about situations or people's character
- not having to be all things to all people
- adjusting boundaries when people either ignore our boundaries or prove trustworthy
- setting and following through on consequences when necessary

_____

_____

_____

_____

As you think about your own relationships, are there any you can identify as needing to either set or strengthen a boundary? Explain what the boundary might be and why.

_____

_____

_____

_____

In the remaining space below, practice writing what you might say to the person(s). State the boundary, the reason for the boundary, and what consequence you are willing to follow through with if the boundary is ignored.

Boundary _____

_____

_____

_____

Reason for the Boundary _____

_____

_____

_____

_____

Consequence for Ignoring Boundary _____

_____

_____

_____

_____

Day 4

Read: Genesis 37

If any of us are feeling badly about the families we grew up in, we need only read the Old Testament story of Jacob's family. We could do an entire study of the different roles played out by the twelve sons of Jacob. Recall the dysfunction in Jacob's family that we may have also seen in our own families. Jacob played favorites. Big time!

Joseph was his father's favorite, and his father, Jacob, didn't try to hide it. In fact, the cloak he made for his favorite son created all manner of jealousy, competition, lying, deceit, and hatred. It would have led to murder, had the elder brother Rueben not stepped in. "Let's don't kill him, let's just throw him in an empty cistern and leave him!" Now the Bible is clear that Rueben's motives were at least protective; he planned to go back and rescue his little brother. Not sure whether Joseph knew that or not. Either way, he never got the chance to rescue him because the other brothers sold Joseph off to some travelers before he could be rescued. Deceit, covering up, lying, and ruining the beautiful robe all ensued as a result of their hatred and jealousy.

In the end of the story, God greatly used Joseph and reunited him with his brothers and his father. While there was reconciliation in this case, and the brothers were shocked and humbled by their punky little brother's rise to power, they were also forgiven by Joseph.

I like to think that while Joseph was young, he probably played the role of the golden child, which we will discuss today. I like to also think he may have also been able to outgrow or overcome his assigned role among his brothers and may have been a role model for them to do the same.

Prayer for Today

Today as we take another look back at our family interactions, ask God to reveal to you any places that still need healing. Ask Him to give you fresh eyes to see patterns of dysfunction that you may have unknowingly been a part of and ask Him to give you the courage and strength to overcome these strongholds.

Role Casting: Don't Get Sucked In

In the early chapters of our study, we looked at our family of origin. We discussed how our parents expressed many different emotions and handled crises, discipline, etc. It may be helpful at this point to take one more look back. Understanding why families develop in the ways they do may make it easier to learn to set boundaries, especially with family members, when necessary.

One of the most widely accepted theories in the field of family therapy was developed by a psychiatrist in the late 1960s named Dr. Murray Bowen. His theory states families are one emotional unit where members are interconnected and interdependent and cannot be fully understood apart from one another. Further, he suggested each family member has an unspoken role to play and that each member is expected to play out their "assigned" role. This ensures a type of balance (even if it's dysfunctional), so everyone can predict and depend on how the others will act and react in family interactions.[2]

The roles in this family system have been named throughout the past five to six decades and have been proven to be fairly accurate. Some theorists have added roles or slightly changed the names, but basically the common roles are the golden child (or hero or saint), the scapegoat (or troublemaker or black sheep), the lost (or invisible) child, the peacemaker or mediator, the mascot (or clown), the caretaker (or enabler), the doer, and the martyr. Defining these roles will help us recognize the unspoken part we played in the functioning of our family unit.

about confrontation and will ignore their own needs and wants to prevent an argument or a relationship divide.

5. **The Mascot** (or family clown) is also intuitive and can read a room for tension but will lighten things up with a wisecrack or divert the controversy with a joke or a funny story. They use their humor to deflect trouble for themselves or others, to minimize real problems, or to keep the denial going. This role is easily carried into adulthood to become the parent who doesn't deal with real problems and frustrates significant relationships by never taking anything seriously.

The truth is sometimes these are deeply sensitive kids, and they can feel so deeply that they are afraid of their own feelings. They may feel if they start to cry, they may never stop. Since other people quickly learn to rely on them to lighten the mood or deflect an uncomfortable situation, it can be difficult to limit this behavior.

6. **The Caretaker** (or enabler) might be mistaken for the Peacemaker, except the Peacemaker works on a prevention model and the Caretaker is the cleanup guy. The Caretaker tries to save siblings or others from facing consequences they may or may not deserve. They will get right in the middle of trouble making excuses for a younger sibling and may even take a blow in their place. They may cover, lie for, or enable an alcoholic or addictive parent or do whatever it takes to protect a younger sibling or parent.

As an adult, the Caretaker has not learned healthy boundaries and can easily become an enabling parent should addiction come calling in their own family as well. This is all done out of "love," of course, and is genuinely well-intentioned but denies the addict or person the chance to deal with their own consequences or learn from their mistakes.

7. **The Doer** is the family member everyone looks to when things need to get done. It is often the mother who is the greatest multitasker. Often it falls to her to coordinate everyone's schedule, make sure everyone has what they need for the day, oversees the

laundry and household chores (even if these are delegated), plans and often prepares, and may work away from home herself. This person can also be a "Doer in training," whom younger siblings look to when Mom isn't around or an older daughter who is called on to take Mom's place in the case of death, long-term illness, or an inability to be emotionally present.

The Doer is often stressed out and exhausted because their own needs are put last or ignored completely, they can't say no, they rarely get sufficient rest, and they must always be busy doing something. They can't seem to relax and enjoy the moment as they are always thinking about the next thing. Sadly, their value comes from needing to be needed, so many times, they resent everything they do.

8. **The Martyr** takes the doer role a step further by making sure everyone knows what a big sacrifice they are always making for the family. While they need to do these things to feel valued, they also want other family members to feel guilty for the Martyr's help. The mom who tells her children they could be joining friends for a day at the zoo if she didn't have to stay home and wash all their clothes tries to make them feel responsible for missing out.

It can be painful to see ourselves in these roles, particularly as we are recognizing the dysfunction that may have been present in our families. It may also be easier to recognize other family members in these roles than it is to recognize ourselves. Asking the Holy Spirit to reveal dysfunctional patterns and roles in ourselves and how to change them may be the first step to more healthy family interactions.

However, don't expect your healthy changes to always be welcomed if there is dysfunction in your family. Recall the premise of this theory is seeking balance where family members can predict and depend on how the other family members will act and react in family interactions. Making changes, even healthy ones, disrupts and threatens the familiar.

Think of it like a mobile over a baby's crib. All the objects hang and move in balance with one another. If one of the objects is cut off, the whole mobile hangs lopsided. No one enjoys hanging lopsided, and no doubt your family members will resent your growth. Not only does it disrupt the familiar family patterns, but it also may cause other family members to make changes as well. Rarely are these changes wanted.

Despite the challenges that may come with making healthier choices for yourself, it will be worth it in the end. You can reassure objecting family members these are changes you feel you must make for yourself and you are not trying to change them, just yourself. You can express your continued love and support for them and your hope that perhaps they might do the same. However, the path you are on is a one-way street with no option to turn back.

Do you agree with this theory of family roles? Why or why not?

_____

_____

_____

_____

Do you recognize your siblings in any of the roles mentioned? Explain.

_____

_____

_____

_____

Do you recognize yourself in any of the roles mentioned? Or which one would your family members say you resemble? Explain.

_____

_____

_____

_____

What are some ways living out these roles affect your life today?

_____

_____

_____

_____

What is one thing you could do to move from the role you grew up in to a healthier, more authentic place?

_____

_____

_____

_____

What do you think the result might be if you made that one change?

_____

_____

_____

_____

Are you willing to make that change? Why or why not?

_____

_____

_____

_____

Day 5

Read: 2 Corinthians 10:5 and Philippians 4:8–9

We have already discussed how important our thought life is to our growth and healing. Our first reading today reminds us to take negative thoughts, sinful thoughts, unproductive thoughts, or rebellious thoughts and bring them before God. We are to expose any lies and confess areas of rebellion or sin, asking God to forgive and strengthen our resolve.

But not only are we to dismiss negative thoughts, we are to replace them with positive thoughts. A much more positive approach! As long as we are filling our minds with truths that are lovely, admirable, or praiseworthy, it will leave little space for ugly thoughts that are harmful to our healing and our spiritual growth.

You may have heard it said that for every negative comment we hear, we need five positive comments to counteract it. Think about what you think about. Make it a point to fill your mind and your heart with positive, pure, excellent thoughts several times a day. Find scriptures or quotes that inspire you or boost your self-worth. Write them on three-by-five cards and carry them with you. Write them on sticky notes and place them where you will see them throughout your day. Take a five-minute break to "think about such things … And the God of peace will be with you."

Prayer for Today

Today ask God to help you with your thought life. Knowing that your thoughts impact your feelings and your feelings impact your behavior, ask Him to fill your mind with things that are pure, lovely, and praiseworthy.

Ask Him for thoughts of His beautiful creation to remind you of His love for you and to help you remember you are chosen. Praise Him for all things praiseworthy, and tell Him you desire a pure, positive, and happy thought life that is honoring to Him.

A Word about Triggers

We have been taking in a lot of information about healthy interactions and relationships. Learning to live from a healthy place is not always easy no matter how perfect your family of origin may have been. We can make healthy choices and act in healthy ways, but invariably there will be those around us who will resent it or not understand. No doubt when you see the need to set a boundary with someone who tries to use you for their own unhealthy motives, you will be viewed as unkind, arrogant, or self-centered. Your own family may resent the changes you try to make and may accuse you of thinking you are better than they are.

Still, in your quest for growth and healing, you press on, putting into practice the things you have learned, determined that the past will not control you. You may be feeling proud of the changes you have made and may not even have to think about them anymore as they become like second nature to you.

Until one day, someone in your family makes a comment, you see an old picture, or a family joke is resurrected, and *boom!* You find yourself right back to that vulnerable place in your childhood where you were powerless over your own circumstances and emotions. Perhaps you immediately feel anxious, sad, or angry. You may feel belittled, criticized, or worthless. The feelings are real, and you can't seem to control them.

This is what happens when we are triggered by something in the present (a sound, a sight, a smell, a comment, etc.) that takes us right back to the past. It is important to recognize we are being triggered, but we are not in the past. The feelings are old, and we don't need to allow them to control us. So what do we do?

1. Recognize the feelings. Name them. "I am anxious." "I am sick to my stomach." "I am feeling angry." "I just want to crawl in a hole because everyone is laughing at me."

2. Recognize the cause. "I am feeling this way because I am back here" (in the location of the trauma). "I can see how my family is playing out their roles and they're trying to drag me back into mine."

3. Claim your progress. "This is not who I am now, and I don't have to let it get to me." Give yourself grace and space. Breathe or remove yourself from the situation until you can collect yourself.

4. Pray! Ask God to go before you into these situations and provide wisdom and discernment in how to handle the triggers. Ask for healing as you work on living from a healthy place in the present.

5. Practice leads to fewer triggers. The more you go through the above steps, the less the triggers may bother you, and eventually you may be able to be in the same room where others are playing out their roles like always, but you will not feel the need to participate. You may be able to be peaceful in certain places you could not be in before without being triggered.

> The more severe the trauma you experienced, the longer this process could take, and the best thing for you might be a firm boundary where you distance yourself permanently from places or relationships that prove too difficult to overcome. Again, give yourself grace and space as it is necessary, and remember to pray!

Can you recall times where you were triggered by people or places that whisked you back to the past? Explain.

_____

_____

_____

_____

✦ BEAUTIFULLY BROKEN ✦

What is the most common feeling you experience when you have been triggered? What is that feeling related to?

_____

_____

_____

_____

What can you tell yourself when you are triggered in the future?

_____

_____

_____

_____

Which of the five steps discussed above is the most difficult for you? Why do you think that is?

_____

_____

_____

_____

Can you foresee a time when you are no longer bothered by being triggered?

_____

_____

_____

235

Paula French ✦

Is there a boundary you may need to set regarding your trigger(s)? Explain.
Do you think this boundary will be short term or long term?

_____

_____

_____

_____

Chapter 9

Forgiveness

Day 1

Read: Matthew 6:14–15 and Luke 6:37

As Christians, we are called to forgive. Dare I say it? We are commanded to forgive. Not always the easiest thing to do, especially if we are sincere. And we should be sincere; otherwise, we haven't really forgiven.

Some commentators point out the word Jesus uses in these verses for the wrongs done against us ("trespasses") is different from the word "debts" He uses a few verses earlier when teaching the disciples how to pray. We could argue that point, asking whether we must forgive *all* wrongs done to us or just the unintentional ones. If that were the case, it would be easier to measure up to the forgiveness command. I could quickly forgive the lady who bumps into my cart at the supermarket or backs into my car in the parking lot. But if she were drunk and ran over my dear one, that would be a much more difficult matter of forgiveness.

Regardless of the words Jesus used, it is clear He takes forgiveness seriously. The underlying message here is when a person comes before God asking to be forgiven, if that person is living in a way that refuses to extend mercy to his fellow man, how could he possibly expect to receive mercy for himself?

Jesus takes forgiveness seriously because He knows the cost of forgiveness. To leave the heavenly realms where angels do His bidding and come down, joining the human race with all the trials, and suffering here is something we will never fully understand in this life. Then to suffer ridicule, hatred, and beatings and go willingly, silently, to die on a cross—all so that we might be forgiven our sins and find reconciliation with an Almighty, Holy God is a cost none of us would ever be able to pay. Yes, He takes forgiveness seriously. It cost Him His life.

Prayer for Today

As we look at forgiveness, begin the week by asking God to search your heart for areas that need forgiveness—things you need forgiveness for and others whom you need to forgive. Thank Him for His incomprehensible sacrifice, and ask Him to give you the spirit of forgiveness toward people He may bring to your mind this week.

Forgiveness Is ... and Forgiveness Is Not ...

One of the most *difficult* relational tasks in life is forgiveness. Also, one of the most often *overlooked* relational tasks in life is forgiveness. Also, one of the most *critical* relational tasks in life is forgiveness! Research shows refusing to forgive can cause us to harbor anger and resentment and often leads to bitterness. Carrying these emotions causes our bodies to release the stress hormones cortisol and adrenaline. These chemicals can cause us to be unproductive and full of anxiety and can affect memory and creativity. Over time, high levels and continuous release of these stress hormones (associated with harboring unforgiveness) can even result in raised blood pressure, increased risk of heart attack, depression, and other physical ailments.[1]

On the other hand, the benefits of forgiveness are many. Lowered blood pressure, less anxiety and depression, along with general feelings of happiness, calm, and relief have been attributed to forgiveness. It seems by God's design we have more reasons to forgive than just His command, as if that weren't enough.

So what exactly is forgiveness? Forgiveness is the willful act of deciding to let go of the heavy burdens of negative feelings, anger, and resentment associated with an event and/or the person or persons who have hurt you.[2] It also means letting go of hatred toward that person along with any thoughts of ill will toward them. We can choose to forgive even if the offender isn't sorry, doesn't apologize or ask for forgiveness, or doesn't deserve our forgiveness.

In short, forgiveness can be a godly act that may show compassion to an offender, but forgiveness is really for us. It says the other person's words or actions no longer control us or hold our thoughts and emotions hostage. It releases us from the pent-up anger and resentment that cannot change what has happened anyway. It can relieve the weight of all the negative thoughts, feelings, and energy and give us back our lives. And it brings us into a right relationship with God.

Don't misunderstand forgiveness, however. It doesn't mean we are not holding the person accountable for their actions. There well may be consequences the person must face. You can choose to forgive the robber who broke into your home, stealing your possessions and peace of mind, but you will still press charges, sending him to serve time for his actions. We are not side-stepping the law. We didn't make the laws, and the laws are clear; if you break the law, you pay the consequence.

Forgiveness also does not necessarily mean a reconciliation of the relationship. If the person who has harmed you is someone you had a relationship with, it may not be in your best interest to reconcile with that person. The person may not be repentant or may not be safe for you emotionally or physically. Certainly, God desires reconciliation between people in conflict, but not at any cost. Romans 12:18 says, "If it is possible, as far as it depends on you, live at peace with everyone." Our hearts are to be at peace in all our relationships and sometimes returning to a toxic or dangerous relationship would be anything but peaceful for us. Still, forgiveness would increase our peace!

While forgiveness for the Christian is necessary, and for the non-Christian it is wise, forgiveness is not easy. Depending on the offense, it may take time to forgive. Forgiveness given too quickly simply because we are following scriptural commands may lead to cheap and insincere forgiveness. God knows we are human and knows we will feel the full weight of the offense and that may take time. The important thing is the acknowledgment that forgiveness is something you are committed to in due time.

You may have to forgive in stages, relinquishing a little more of the pain each time you remember and then bring the issue before God. You may have to remind yourself you have forgiven whenever the person or the memory comes to your mind or crosses your path. Just because you make the choice to forgive does not mean the person or event will be struck from your memory. For that reason, we often say forgiveness can be a process. Simply telling God you want to be obedient to His Word in the area of forgiveness and asking for His help to begin the process is the first step. You can be sure His Holy Spirit will guide you as you choose to forgive. Forgiveness is an act of your will. Bad feelings may still exist, or good feelings may follow. What is important is that you make the decision to forgive.

How do you feel about the issue of forgiveness being a requirement for Christians?

_____

_____

_____

_____

What has been your experience with forgiveness in the past?

_____

_____

_____

_____

How has forgiving (or not forgiving) affected you emotionally or physically?

_____

_____

_____

_____

How do you explain forgiving someone but still expecting them to serve consequences?

_____

_____

_____

_____

Is forgiveness generally easy or difficult for you? Explain.

_____

_____

_____

Day 2

Read: Mark 11:20–25

Our passage today takes place right after Jesus rides through the palm-covered streets of Jerusalem on a donkey with all the people shouting, "Hosanna! Blessed is he who comes in the Name of the Lord!" For a few brief moments, the masses praise Him even while the authorities still seek to kill Him.

Jesus then spends the night in Bethany and returns to the temple the next morning, evidently before eating breakfast. At first reading, it seems Jesus is "hangry" when He curses the fig tree for not having any figs on it that He was hoping to eat for breakfast. But of course, Jesus doesn't do anything out of sheer impulse without a meaning and a teaching behind it. Even throwing the moneychangers out of the temple described in this same chapter appears to be uncontrolled anger, but He is very much teaching a lesson to those who would hear.

So here again we have a dead fig tree Jesus cursed the day before. His curse was that it would no longer bear fruit, but the effect was complete death from the roots upward. This is symbolic of the death of the Jews' faith and influence in the world—their intended purpose but resulting failure. Also, a reminder for us today that if we are not bearing fruit, we will eventually die spiritually.

Tying into this "miracle" Jesus had just performed and the disciples had just witnessed, Jesus begins to teach the disciples what their faith in Him could produce. He alone knows the extent of His power and authority, but He is eager for them to understand what power and authority they also could possess simply by having a strong faith in Him! They could move mountains! We can move mountains!

Then in the same teaching about faith, Jesus includes something very interesting about what faith requires. Faith isn't just hanging onto Jesus's coattails to get power for miracles. Faith requires adopting and developing the very character of Jesus. And that includes forgiveness.

Yep, there it is. Forgiveness. Remember we talked about how seriously Jesus takes forgiveness? Not only will we not be forgiven without forgiveness, but our faith will be worthless. We understand we must forgive to be forgiven and for our faith to be activated. But who should we forgive? Aren't there some circumstances and some people we would be excused from forgiving? Read verse 25 again and let's discuss this.

Prayer for Today

Ask the Holy Spirit to bring to your mind and heart people you need to forgive. Ask Him to deal with your heart regarding people who don't deserve forgiveness and who it will seem impossible to forgive—people who have ruined lives and stolen from you deeply personal and sacred things and relationships. Ask Him to help you see these people and yourself through His eyes and do a work in your heart.

Exactly Whom Must I Forgive?

We have all been wounded by *someone*. From being bullied on the playground to being abandoned by a parent or spouse, being physically or sexually abused, being rejected or humiliated publicly or privately, or something worse, we have all experienced a deep hurt caused by another person. Perhaps we were victim of a crime or we lost someone we cared about to a crime. Some of us here or across the world have lived through a genocide or been victims of the horrors of war. Regardless of the cause, pain is pain.

While we seem to collectively rank these and other experiences as greater or lesser than another, the truth is it may be just as difficult for someone to heal from being bullied or abandoned as a child as it is for the person who has suffered severe loss in war. Many factors affect the depth of our woundedness and our willingness to forgive. The other truth is none of us can say how another person should or shouldn't feel about the experiences they have been through. No one can tell you your pain isn't as great as their pain or that your ability to forgive should be easier than theirs. Life is hard and pain is pain.

The Bible tells us that Jesus is not only able to empathize with our pain and struggles, but He was also tempted in every way that we have been tempted (Hebrews 4:15). This must mean that Christ was also tempted at some point toward an unforgiving spirit. Could that be true? When Jesus was in the Garden of Gethsemane before His crucifixion, we don't know everything He prayed to His Father, but we know His agony was so intense He sweat like drops of blood falling from His brow. (Whether He actually bled or not, scholars have differing opinions, but none refute the anguish He suffered.)

We do know, however, He was in agony over facing the horrors of being nailed to a cross and hung there until He died. Three times He begged the Father for any other possible way to achieve forgiveness for us—or forgiveness toward us. This doesn't mean that He didn't want to forgive us, but it is possible that, in His humanness, for even a moment, He contemplated what the consequence might be if He called legions of angels to rescue Him and take Him back to His rightful place in the heavens. After all, He had done nothing wrong; He was without sin! He was completely unjustly accused and abused and in no way deserved to die. Thankfully, He obeyed His Father's will. He *chose* forgiveness on our behalf.

Jesus *knows* how hard it is to forgive. He knows! And He is tender and compassionate and empathizes with our weaknesses when forgiveness is difficult for us. Imagine Jesus saying, "I get it. I too would have been justified if I didn't forgive, but I chose forgiveness, and you can too. And I will give you grace and help you in your time of need."

So let's go back to our first reading for today to see exactly whom we are to forgive. It's simple really. Verse 25 says, "And when you stand praying, if you hold anything against anyone, forgive them, so that your father in heaven may forgive you your sins." If we hold a*nything* against *anyone,* we are to forgive them, no matter who it is or what they may have done. "*Anything* against *anyone.*"

Is there someone in your life you have struggled to forgive? Explain.

_____

_____

_____

_____

What have been the effects on you for harboring unforgiveness? Physical? Mental? Relational? Spiritual? Explain.

_____

_____

_____

_____

What do you feel is standing in the way of you forgiving?

_____

_____

_____

_____

What do you feel would be a first step you could take toward forgiveness?

_____

_____

_____

_____

What difference might it make in your life if you could forgive that person or persons? Explain.

_____

_____

_____

_____

Day 3

Read: Matthew 18:23–35

The Bible is full of stories about forgiveness. One story that grabs our attention and elicits emotional response is our reading for today, the parable of the unforgiving servant. This parable touches our compassion but also our self-righteousness. We like it when this mighty king who has the power to annihilate people is touched by the pleadings of one of his subjects and shows mercy by forgiving this outlandish debt. He saves this guy's family and his entire existence. He shows kindness and uses his power and authority for good. We like stories like that because we like to think those who are high and mighty have feelings like us and can be sensitive. It makes us think that's how we would be if we had all that power and authority.

But then there's the other side of the story where the guy who has just been forgiven this huge debt runs out and gets all mean and bossy with someone who owed him money. The amount wasn't anything near what he had just been forgiven, yet he would not forgive the person who owed him. That's where our self-righteousness activates. How dare he! He was just let off the hook for what he owed, but did he pay it forward? No! That guy deserves to be put away for the rest of his life!

Sadly, the truth is while we would like to see ourselves as the king who forgave, we may actually be more like the servant who refused to forgive. We sit in our victim seats and judge who is and isn't worthy of forgiveness, when all along the king has already forgiven us the hugest debt. We hold grudges, withhold love and relationship, avoid contact, spread stories, or simply harbor secret resentment in our hearts toward those who have wounded us.

We feel justified in this because we miss the point of the first part of the parable. We forget, or we fail to realize, just how much we have been forgiven. We weren't forgiven a lot. We weren't even forgiven a huge amount. We were completely exonerated for something we could never in a million years repay. We weren't pardoned for a debt we could never repay because we were somehow above the law or knew somebody that knew somebody. At that point we were a nobody, and we had no connections and we deserved death. We were forgiven, cleared of all wrongdoing, vindicated, and completely acquitted of dripping with sin for one reason only: love. Not because we in any way deserved that love but because of *His* character. Because God is love. And because He so loved us that He gave His only Son to suffer the death that I deserved.

Love. It was because of love. And we are called to that kind of love. We're supposed to love like that. We are supposed to love people who don't deserve it. We are supposed to love people who can never pay it back and will never even try. We are supposed to love like that.

Prayer for Today

Spend some time today before God thinking about the love, forgiveness, and pardon He lavished on you, without you doing anything to deserve it or without any way to repay Him. Tell Him how you feel about that. Ask Him to make His holiness real to you. Thank Him for His Son, Jesus, who paid your sin penalty and the freedom you have because of it. Ask Him to help you extend that same love and forgiveness to those who have hurt you, who are also undeserving of His love and forgiveness. Talk to Him about those you need to forgive.

One More Look at Why

Lest we think forgiveness will be easy, just because Jesus commanded it and we want to follow Jesus, it very well may not be. Sometimes we can say with our words that we forgive, but still, there seethes inside us a root of unforgiveness whenever that person's name is mentioned or the event is brought to mind. We can't help it; we are human. Which is exactly the point. True forgiveness for some offenses requires help from the Holy Spirit. It may not be something we can accomplish on our own.

There are circumstances where going from a simmering, eye-squinting, wish-they-would-die feeling to a love-like-Jesus feeling—as if it never happened—just isn't possible as a human. And what about when the offender isn't sorry or continues to hurt us over and over again? What if they are in your life twenty-four/seven and their narcissistic ways don't even get that there is a problem? Or what if they think *you* are the problem?

Many of you live every day picking up the pieces a divorce left behind. Finding a job, affording child care, caring for kids' emotional and spiritual needs, meals, bedtimes, homework, and illnesses leave zero time for yourself, and thinking about forgiveness either never happens or seems like a sickening impossibility.

Others of you have been violated and used in unthinkable ways and have no idea what it's like to truly be cherished and loved for who you are. You may not even know who you are aside from feeling damaged and different. Still others have experienced other losses too many or too unfair to forgive.

These are the reasons we need to grasp the meaning and importance of forgiveness. We need to take some time to get out of our own circumstances, like you are doing now in this study, and think what it means to forgive. You see, it's not really about you or your pain, as awful as that might be. And it's not about the person or persons or event that hurt you so deeply and wrecked your life. It's about what it means to stand before a Holy God. It's about catching a glimpse of how Holy He is and understanding that He has created and owns everything in this life, on this planet, and in all the universe.

The Bible refers to our lives as a mist or a vapor that is here today and gone tomorrow (James 4:14), and we know from stacks of history books and acres of cemeteries that is true. Psalm 144:4 compares our lives to a passing shadow and as fleeting as a breath. As hard and long and complicated as our lives here are, all of it will be over one day. And all that will matter is being called into the presence of the most humbling, awe-inspiring, majestic, and mind-blowing Presence and Person we could never imagine.

Until we grasp how Holy God is, how sovereign and completely in charge He is, we will never fully understand the need for forgiveness. This is a God so holy, so righteous, and perfect that it is impossible for Him to be anywhere near sin. It's like trying to push two same-charged magnets together. Can't be done. Sin cannot come near this Holy God without exploding into shards. Which means neither you nor I can come near this Holy God without exploding into shards.

I don't know about you, but I am certainly not perfect, spotless, or sinless. Try as I might, thoughts pass through my mind that are critical, vengeful, judgmental, impure, and downright mean. Have you ever told the tiniest lie? We are liars. Have you ever taken *anything* from *anywhere* that did not belong to you? We are thieves.

Sinners we are, and we cannot approach this Holy God as we are, on our own, dripping in our sin. We need a mediator. We need a way to approach this Holy God who cannot be near sin. We need an insider, someone who *can* come near this Holy God and present us as sinless before Him. So there are two problems there: one, who can be the mediator and be allowed in God's presence without sin, and two, how can we become sinless so we can go in with the one who has this access? The first problem is answered in 1 Timothy 2:5. "For there is one God and one mediator between God and mankind, the man Christ Jesus." So Jesus is the One—the One without sin—who is allowed into God's presence. But how do we get in with Him if we are dripping in our sin?

Hebrews 9:22 tells us that there can be no forgiveness of sins unless blood is shed, which is why the people offered animal sacrifices before the priests in the Old Testament. But when God sent Jesus into the world, He did so to put an end to the imperfect practice of animal sacrifices and to offer once and for all the only perfect, sinless, spotless lamb, Jesus. Jesus's sacrifice, death, and shed blood would be the forgiveness of sins that allows us to go with Him into the presence of His Father, this Holy God, where we can stand in His presence sinless, having the same righteousness as His Son, Jesus. *What would we do without Jesus?*

And so, we're back to the great cost of forgiveness on Jesus's part. But equally as important is that we see our own impossible ability, our own impossibility, to stand before a Holy God on our own. Who do we think we are that we could declare someone else unforgiveable when here we stand dripping in our own unforgiveable sin—were it not for Jesus.

Believe me: I understand the unfairness. I understand the difficulty. Jesus understands the unfairness. Jesus understands the difficulty. But no matter how unfair or how difficult, refusing to forgive or holding onto unforgiveness isn't worth losing your soul. Whoever it is isn't worth your anxiety, headaches, high blood pressure, overeating, drinking, or keeping you out of God's presence. Your life is but a vapor, a reed blowing in the wind, here today and gone tomorrow whereby you will either be welcomed into God's presence or be turned away. Forgiveness is an act of the will, not necessarily whether you are feeling it.

Choose forgiveness. Your own healing is not complete without it.

Write how you are feeling about forgiveness after reading today's lesson.

_____

_____

_____

_____

What is the hardest part of your circumstance about forgiving?

_____

_____

_____

_____

Will you make the choice to forgive, even if it is difficult? Why or why not?

_____

_____

_____

_____

Day 4

Read: Ephesians 4:20–32

These scriptures are good reminders for us about the life we have been called to live. We are to emulate Christ in everything we think, say, and do. They don't say we should be like Christ only when things are going great and everyone is kind toward us. We have been called to a higher standard of conduct when it is easy and when it is not. That is what we have been saved to: a new life, a new way of living. Being a Christ-follower is not for wimps.

It has always been a challenge to know how much of this new standard is up to us and how much of it the Holy Spirit will do through us. The answer is both. We are to make every effort. We are to renew our minds. We are to work out our salvation. We are to do all of this *as* the Holy Spirit helps us, disciplines us, trains us, convicts us, and shows us new ways of acting toward others. Still, these verses are full of imperatives: "Put off ... Do not ... Get rid of ... Be kind ..." There is nothing in those imperative statements that suggests someone is going to do any of those things for us. Those are efforts we must make if we want to be followers Christ.

The way of the cross is not easy. It is full of untold blessings, help, joy, and love that the Father lavishes on us every day. But it is not easy. It means taking a stand in the midst of opposition, but it also means turning the other cheek. It means self-denial and trusting God for what you need. It means being ridiculed, criticized, and ostracized. And it means forgiving all of that—even when it's not fair, when it's not asked for, and when it doesn't stop.

Verse 32 says, "Be kind and compassionate to one another, forgiving each other, just as in Christ God forgave you." And there it is. "Just as in Christ God ..."

We love because God loved us. We forgive because God forgave us. It's that higher standard of conduct, that new life, that new way of living. And sometimes, it will be hard.

Prayer for Today

Today when you pray, tell God how you are feeling about forgiving those who have hurt you. Then tell Him you want to be obedient with His help because of the forgiveness you have received from Him. Remember He already knows your heart, your desires, your hurts, and where you need strength and help. Thank Him for that.

Launching into the Deep

Whether you feel ready to forgive or not, it is important to begin the process by at least having the conversation with God that expresses your desire to be obedient, and with the help of the Holy Spirit, begin the process of forgiveness. Our "Prayer for Today" was a good start toward that. You may need to pray that prayer several times in the coming weeks.

Today's session will be a step-by-step guided journey into forgiveness. Think of it as having been moored to the dock but now you are ready to untie the lines and push off, launching into the waters of forgiveness. When you reach the other side, the waters will be calmer and your heart will be lighter.

As with our inner healing prayer in chapter 6, try to set aside extra time for this part. Spend more than one day here if you feel the need. There is a separate page outlining the steps for you to copy and take with you, should you want to get away somewhere to work on forgiveness or if you find you need to return to this process later for other matters. Listen to God's direction. He will lead you exactly where you need to go for complete healing.

Before we begin our forgiveness journey, find a quiet place to spend the next hour or two. Use the spaces below to record your thoughts and feelings and any words God may say to you.

1. Begin with prayer. Spend a few moments inviting God into the process with you. Ask the Holy Spirit to bring to your mind people and events either whom you have wounded or who have wounded you. Ask Him to work in your heart, giving you the desire to be obedient to His leading. Write your prayer here if you wish.

_____

_____

_____

_____

2. Recall the offender. As people or events come to your mind, write the person's name or initials. You will be separating those you need to forgive from those you may need to ask forgiveness.

People I Need to Forgive   People I Have Hurt

_____   _____

_____   _____

_____   _____

_____   _____

3. Recall the offense. As specifically as you can, write again each person's name, and write the offense they committed that you want to forgive. Then write how what they did made you feel and how it impacts you today. This is your opportunity to let your true feelings be known and to speak as if they were in front of you now without any of the uncomfortable emotion of them being

physically present. Take as long as you need to with this step, and use additional paper if necessary. Finally, if there is someone you have hurt, also write that person's name or initials and the offense you committed that you need to ask forgiveness for. Include your feelings about your actions and how what you did may have made them feel.

Name	Offense	Feelings/Impact
_____	_____	_____
_____	_____	_____
_____	_____	_____
_____	_____	_____
_____	_____	_____
_____	_____	_____
_____	_____	_____
_____	_____	_____
_____	_____	_____
_____	_____	_____
_____	_____	_____
_____	_____	_____
_____	_____	_____
_____	_____	_____
_____	_____	_____

4. Humble concession. Next, try to write a message called "Your Humble Concession." This is a message that expresses empathy toward the person despite their actions. (If there is any understanding on your part for why they may have done what they did, including brokenness in their own past. This in no way excuses their behavior or the choices they made. It simply acknowledges there is a broken human being behind the hurtful action. Some of you may not be able to feel any empathy whatsoever or have any understanding how or why someone could do what they did. That's OK. Instead, write to them explaining how you also are a sinner and are capable of sinful behavior. Take this opportunity to convey your own humble posture before a Holy God who has forgiven you.

My humble concession toward _____.

_____

_____

_____

My humble concession toward _____.

_____

_____

_____

5. Commit to forgive. This next step is a commitment step. This is your intention to forgive and your commitment to follow through. You will write out your commitment to forgive, but you may also feel the need to declare your forgiveness in some way (perhaps symbolically) or use this as the basis for a letter to the person you are forgiving, even if you never share it.

Sometimes, letting the person know you have forgiven them may prove to derail your own progress with forgiveness, especially if the person isn't sorry, hasn't asked for forgiveness, or doesn't think they have done anything wrong to hurt you or need your forgiveness. There is nothing in this step that *requires* you to share this step with the person who hurt you. If the person is aware of their offense and feels remorseful or has asked for forgiveness, or if offering your forgiveness will repair the relationship, it can be a powerful healing moment, but it is not necessary for you to be able to forgive.

Remember, however, that having wise boundaries is always important in dealing with hurtful people and that forgiveness is for your own healing, not theirs. Before sharing your commitment to forgive with the person or persons who hurt you, pray about it, get wise counsel from someone you trust, and use your best judgment. Your commitment to forgive and the benefits of forgiveness to you physically, spiritually, and emotionally are not dependent on the other person's acceptance of your forgiveness.

Today I hereby commit to forgive _____

_____ for_____

_____. I understand this is for my own healing and I have examined my feelings toward this person and the hurt they caused me. I am choosing to forgive out of obedience to Christ, and because I also am a sinner who did not deserve forgiveness. I ask God this day to help me let go of any anger, resentment, bitterness, or other negative feelings toward

_____ and to turn any and all vengeance and punishment over to God or any authorities involved. I further understand this may be a process for me and I may have to refer to this commitment again in the future or may have to repeat this process if other hurts are brought to my mind.

Committed on this date: _____

Signed: _____.

_____

Today I hereby commit to forgive _____
_____ for_____
_____. I understand this is for my
own healing, and I have examined my feelings toward this person
and the hurt they caused me. I am choosing to forgive out of
obedience to Christ and because I also am a sinner who did not
deserve forgiveness. I ask God this day to help me let go of any
anger, resentment, bitterness, or other negative feelings toward
_____ and to turn any and all vengeance
and punishment over to God or any authorities involved. I further
understand this may be a process for me and I may have to refer
to this commitment again in the future or may have to repeat this
process if other hurts are brought to my mind.

Committed on this date: _____

Signed: _____.

_____

Today I hereby commit to forgive _____
_____ for_____
_____. I understand this is for my
own healing and I have examined my feelings toward this person
and the hurt they caused me. I am choosing to forgive out of
obedience to Christ and because I also am a sinner who did not
deserve forgiveness. I ask God this day to help me let go of any
anger, resentment, bitterness, or other negative feelings toward
_____ and to turn any and all vengeance
and punishment over to God or any authorities involved. I further
understand this may be a process for me and I may have to refer
to this commitment again in the future or may have to repeat this
process if other hurts are brought to my mind.

Committed on this date: _____

Signed: _____.

_____

Consider the obstacles. As we have said several times, and you are
perhaps now seeing for yourself, forgiveness is both a choice and a
process. You have done a lot of work in recalling the offense and
how it has affected your life and you have committed to forgive.

Good for you! For many of you, that is no small thing. We also are aware that neuropathways have memory and the thoughts and emotions you may have had toward that person or the event will likely not disappear just because you signed the commitment. That is precisely why you signed the commitment, however. The purpose of having you sign the commitment was to remind yourself that you made the choice to forgive your offender(s) even when you don't feel so forgiving, even when those old feelings of anger or resentment or injustice creep back in, and even when you find yourself face-to-face with that person at a family gathering or someone brings up their name in normal conversation.

Each circumstance of forgiveness is different, and only you know whether you will have a difficult time sticking to your decision to forgive. It's wise to prepare for the obstacles that may hinder your complete healing and your process of forgiveness. Take a few minutes to think about your own circumstances and complete the following exercise to give yourself every advantage of being successful in becoming a person of forgiveness.

As you look ahead, what are three of the biggest obstacles to maintaining a forgiving spirit?

_____

_____

_____

When any of the above obstacles happen, what actions could you take to prevent being triggered back into unforgiveness or negative attitudes?

_____

_____

_____

One of the obstacles some people face is the inability to forgive themselves. While there are a lot of differing viewpoints on whether we can technically forgive ourselves, there is often the real need to accept forgiveness from God. There is a point where we need to begin thinking and acting like we are forgiven instead of continuing to beat ourselves up, which in effect declares God's forgiveness null and void or insufficient.

Is there anything you have a difficult time forgiving yourself for? What can you do to let yourself off the hook and accept God's forgiveness? Explain.

_____

_____

_____

_____

Most Christian therapists recognize many people harbor anger toward God. People sometimes feel God has allowed things to happen in their lives that He could have prevented. There is, in a sense, an unforgiveness toward God. We know God does not need forgiving because He is perfect. And we don't know everything He knows. We just have to trust. Accepting God's sovereign will and His purposes does not mean we will always understand His ways or that we will see any resulting good in this lifetime, but it does mean reconciling ourselves to His sovereignty and coming to the place where though we may not understand, we choose to trust.

Is there anything in your life for which you have harbored anger, resentment, or unforgiveness toward God? Explain.

_____

_____

_____

_____

What can you do to accept His sovereign will instead of harboring anger or resentment?

_____

_____

_____

_____

Let the healing begin! Congratulations! You have walked through a difficult process of forgiveness and have been obedient to Christ in His command that we forgive those who have hurt us. This is not an easy thing to do, but God will reward you for your obedience.

What are some things in your life (physically, spiritually, emotionally, or relationally) you are hoping will be benefits to this forgiveness process?

_____

_____

_____

_____

Day 5

Read: 2 Corinthians 2:5–11

This is an interesting chapter that we need some context for. Paul is referring to someone in their congregation who has committed a serious grievance. Some scholars think this person is the man from 1 Corinthians 5:1, while others believe it is someone else. While we cannot be certain, we do know that Paul is encouraging the believers to forgive him and show him love since it is clear he is repentant to the point of despair.

There are three principles that stand out in these scriptures that we should pay attention to. One refers to the charge that not only should they forgive this man, but since he is so sorrowful for his actions, they should actually comfort him and reaffirm their love for him. In other words, welcome him back into fellowship. Recall in the previous chapter of 1 Corinthians Paul tells them God comforts us in our troubles so that we can comfort others with that same comfort (1:3–4). Now Paul is telling them to use that same principle (that they have been comforted by God in their own troubles) to comfort this one who is now suffering from his own remorse. There are times when those who need our forgiveness also need to be shown they are still loved and accepted.

The second principle is found in verse 9 where Paul tells them he wanted to see whether they would be obedient in everything. Earlier in 1 Corinthians, Paul is firm in his teaching that we should have nothing to do with sexual immorality. He urges these believers to set a strong boundary and remove the offender from their congregation. Now he is saying they should forgive, love, and comfort him! What gives?

Whether this is the same person or not, the difference is the repentant heart of the man. We are to be obedient in forgiveness always but remember that does not always mean reconciliation. However, when someone is truly remorseful and repentant as the man in our reading today was, we need to not only forgive but also mend the relationship (at least to the point of kindness). Here reconciliation may not mean to fully or immediately restore a personal relationship if it is not wise but to reconcile to the point of being able to be in the same room if necessary. Get counsel if needed, but be obedient in whatever the spirit is telling you to do.

The third principle is in verse 11 where Paul reminds us that Satan is waiting to take any opportunity to derail our forgiveness and our spiritual growth. We talked about this in our session yesterday, that we should be aware of situations that could make us react in our old ways of unforgiveness, anger, resentment, bitterness, etc. Do not let Satan rob you of the healing God has for you. And if you falter here and he does outwit you with one of his schemes, get right back up, confess it, apologize to whomever it is necessary, and continue on with your forgiveness journey. Every time we defeat Satan in one arena, he typically won't bother us there again. But he is still on the prowl cooking up another scheme, so be aware and be resolute in your commitment to forgive.

Prayer for Today

Thank God for His Holy Word that has so much help in it for us. Thank Him for the examples of how we are to behave and for the warnings against Satan's tricks. Most of all, thank Him for His forgiveness and constant presence and for the Holy Spirit who teaches us how to treat others and softens our hearts so we can forgive as we have been forgiven.

Moving to a New State

If you've ever moved to a new state, you know all the weird feelings that go with that, even if you love moving. You have to get a new license and memorize a new address and area code. No one knows you and you have to meet all new people and learn new schools, churches, restaurants, or what the new people think is cool or funny. The worst is after already having a bad day, getting yelled at for doing the carpool pickup line incorrectly. "Give me a break! It's my first time!"

Just as all those things are strange and can be difficult, so can the living in the new state of forgiveness—especially if you've lived in the previous state for a long time. Just because you've said the forgiveness words with all sincerity doesn't mean you will magically be able to live it out. Some of those feelings of bitterness or the snide remarks like to hang around and emerge out of habit. At least now you may be feeling bad about it. Remember we said forgiveness can be a process and you may not do it perfectly right away—on this side of heaven. Be forgiving with yourself and persevere.

You may have to go back and read your forgiveness process more than once. Pick a time when you can get quiet and pray over it, asking God to bring you back to that place of obedience as you reread your commitment to forgive. Every time the hurt or the unfairness comes to your mind, stop right then and pray. Satan does not want you to forgive, and he uses surprising things to remind you why you couldn't forgive before.

You may have gotten the short end of the bank account in a divorce or a business deal gone bad. Every time you come up short for a bill or have to say no to something you want to buy, you feel that anger rising up. Stop! Tell God you meant business and you will not allow Satan to steal your progress. Then thank God for helping you meet all your needs. Ask Him to bless you and help you find ways to stretch your money.

Perhaps you have been plagued with low self-worth because of childhood abuses. Living in the new state of forgiveness now means you are allowing God to deal with those offenses, and you are extending mercy and grace to yourself and to any bystanders from your past who did nothing to stop the abuse. Going to family functions now may mean showing a kinder, gentler side of you. But when you get there and hear the same old comments or catch the same old looks from people, you want to snub them or run away. Stop! Ask God to give you courage to face them and speak with words He would use toward those He had forgiven. Evaluate your boundaries and tread carefully as you see how relationships may or may not change.

Maybe the hurt has been a more recent one in your social circles, at church or the office, or among your friends. Facing those people now that you are living in this new state of forgiveness has you petrified. What does it mean to forgive in actions? Do you keep the relationships? What about the people who have sided with you against them? What about the people who have sided with them against you? Instead of business as usual, stop! Ask God for guidance in navigating these new roads. Should you have a conversation with them as a peace offering? Should you go about your business determined to be cordial and kind from here on? How can you live or work among them and show them Christ? Is there apologizing you need to do?

The three principles in our reading for today are not just to make us feel better. They are for our application, and they are not easy. Now that you have stepped over the line into the state of forgiveness, determine to live a life of forgiveness. Be a forgiving person. Know that your worth does not depend on what others think of you or how they treat you. Your Heavenly Father saw fit to forgive you of what you could never repay. Go and do likewise.

In what ways is living in this new state of forgiveness different for you? Explain.

_____

_____

_____

_____

Describe a specific scenario that you think may bring back the old unforgiveness feelings you just processed through this week.

_____

_____

_____

_____

Write a short prayer asking God to help you maintain your forgiving spirit the next time you face that scenario.

_____

_____

_____

_____

What are the main reasons you committed to forgive this week? Explain each reason you give. (For example, obedience, health reasons, peace of mind, personal growth, or possible reconciliation)

_____

_____

_____

_____

What are two or three thoughts you will take with you from this week of Forgiveness?

_____

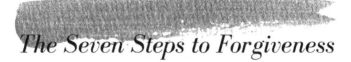

The Seven Steps to Forgiveness

1. **Begin with Prayer.** Spend a few moments inviting God into the process with you. Ask the Holy Spirit to bring to your mind people and events either whom you have wounded, or who have wounded you. Ask him to work in your heart, giving you the desire to be obedient to His leading.

2. **Recall the Offender** - As people or events come to your mind, write the person's name or initials. You will be separating those you need to forgive from those from whom you may need to ask forgiveness.

3. **Recall the Offense** - Write each person's name or initials and the offense they committed that you want to forgive. Write how what they did made you feel and how it impacts you today. If there is someone you have hurt, also write that person's name or initials and the offense you committed that you need to ask forgiveness for. Include your feelings about your actions and how what you did may have made them feel.

4. **Humble Concession** - Write a message that expresses empathy toward the person despite their actions (if there is any understanding on your part for why they may have done what they did, including brokenness in their own past). This is not to excuse their behavior but acknowledges there is a broken human being behind the hurtful action. If you have no empathy for the person, that's OK. Instead, write to them explaining how you also are a sinner and are capable of sinful behavior. Take this opportunity to convey your own humble posture before a Holy God who has forgiven you.

5. **Commit to Forgive** - Write out your commitment to forgive in the paragraph below. You do not need to share this with the person who hurt you. Your commitment to forgive and the benefits of forgiveness to you physically, spiritually, and emotionally are not dependent on the other person's acceptance of your forgiveness.

   > Today, I hereby commit to forgive _____
   > for_____. I understand this is for my own
   > healing and I have examined my feelings toward this person and the hurt they caused me. I am
   > choosing to forgive out of obedience to Christ, and because I also am a sinner who did not
   > deserve forgiveness. I ask God this day to help me let go of any anger, resentment, bitterness, or
   > other negative feelings toward _____, and to turn any and all vengeance
   > and punishment over to God or any authorities involved. I further understand this may be a
   > process for me and I may have to refer to this commitment again in the future or may have to
   > repeat this process if other hurts are brought to my mind.
   > Committed on this day, _____ (date)
   > Signed_____.

6. **Consider the Obstacles-** Make a list of the possible obstacles that may hinder you forgiving.

7. **Let the healing Begin!** Congratulations! You have walked through a difficult process of forgiveness and have been obedient to Christ in His command that we forgive those who have hurt us. This is not an easy thing to do but God will reward you for your obedience.

Chapter 10

Finding Purpose

Day 1

Read: Acts 9:1–22

Our reading for today tells the story of the most amazing conversion in the Bible. In a single instance, God changed Saul from a terror to the Jewish Christians to one of the most influential believers in all Christianity. Don't you wish God would make all the changes we pray for happen that way?

I don't know why God chose to do that for Saul. Perhaps it was the only way to get him to make that kind of career move. No doubt, it was the quickest! The purpose of choosing this reading for today was for us to look at the meaning in Saul's life before his conversion and the meaning in his life afterward.

Before his conversion, Saul got something out of persecuting the new Christ followers. Maybe it made him feel important, feared, or powerful. Maybe he needed that feeling of power to feel like he mattered. Even if his tactics had been of a purer intent, such as holding a deep belief he was doing the right thing, he would still have had to deal with the power thing. He was still feared, and he was still important. His relationships probably weren't caring, supportive, and vulnerable.

After his conversion, however, he is completely different. Even his name is different! His life before may have held meaning or purpose for him, but it was for man's praise, for the Jewish authorities, and for his own personal power. Now his life held eternal purpose. Purpose exploded out of him without him even thinking about it. He had seen the Messiah, and it changed him! And it's a good thing that he was certain it was real because he would suffer greatly for his transformation and newfound belief.

Some of you may also suffer for changes you will be making. Your family relationships may change as you set boundaries. Your marriages may shake as you practice healthier ways of communicating. Your friendships may change as you no longer use old ways of relating.

You will survive the changes or suffering or persecution when you know the healing is authentic. When you know what you have learned is sound and practical and that God has healed your past, you will do things differently going forward. Saul knew without a doubt He had been touched by the One the Jews had been waiting for, and it made all the difference for his future. He had a new meaning for life and a new purpose.

Prayer for Today

As you begin the final week of this study, ask God to settle all the things you have learned deep into your heart. Thank Him again for His healing and for His eternal appointment for you in this study. Ask Him to begin speaking to your heart how He wants to use your experience and what new meaning He might bring into your life because of it.

Making Meaning

Psychologists and social scientists have long explored and theorized about the meaning of life and have encouraged and taught others how to find meaning in their lives. Victor Frankl, the Austrian-born psychiatrist and philosopher who lived throughout the 1900s, believed meaning is the driving force for man's existence.[1] Without a meaning to our lives, life is not worth living. We can take that in many different directions in both the spiritual and the secular worlds, but we may understand it better when we learn more about Frankl.

Frankl was a Holocaust survivor who lost family members to the horrors of the concentration camps. He also spent several years in four different camps, including Auschwitz. To maintain his sanity and keep himself alive, he decided he needed to stay positive about living, and the only way to do that was to identify a purpose in life and constantly think about that purpose coming true.

Hopefully, none of us will ever know the despair of trying to stay alive in a concentration camp. But perhaps some of us have known times where we felt we had no purpose. It's interesting to note that while the Bible lays out for all of us a collective purpose (to know and glorify God and to spread the good news of salvation through Christ), even we as Christians have spent a lot of time thinking about and searching for our individual purpose. We have already been given a hugely important purpose. And that hugely important purpose naturally comes with other purposes: developing our own spiritual disciplines to know God, discovering our gifts and talents to glorify God, and spreading the good news of salvation by living it in our families, raising up our children, and being witnesses to those around us.

Still, often there remains this tugging inside us, this wondering in our minds that says, "What was *I* created for? If God was aware of me and knew me and set me apart before I was conceived (Psalm 139:16), then clearly I'm here on purpose. But for what purpose? What is it I am supposed to accomplish with my life?"

Because we are self-absorbed creatures, many of us think that purpose must be grandiose, public, or heroic. And for some of us, it turns out that way. I don't know if Victor Frankl had those aspirations. I rather think he was more concerned with survival, but it turned out his life served a very public, even famous, purpose. At some point, however, in those concentration camps, figuring out how he was going to stay alive and sane until he could be freed and find out the fate of his family members, his purpose became intensely personal. Yes, he wrote books, he lectured and taught, and he made great contributions to the social sciences, but those were not his goals. Those were not his driving passion. His driving passion was intensely personal between only him and his Creator (consciously or not), and only he could know if his purpose had been fulfilled in the twilight of his life.

When we have had profound experiences that cause us to stop and take stock of our lives, as perhaps you have had in this process, our minds seem to automatically turn to doing something with what we have discovered. That may mean sharing it with other people. It may simply mean living in a different way from this point on. Or it could mean using the knowledge you have gained and the experience you have been through in another larger way. Your purpose in life may have changed directions or come more clearly into view. And this is different for every person. Like many of the other things we have discussed in these sessions, finding purpose in your healing and growth won't happen overnight. It is part of the process of growing and learning to live a healthier life spiritually, emotionally, and relationally.

In the weeks ahead, pay attention to the stirrings inside you that hint at a purpose for the things you have learned. How will you use what you've learned? What changes will you make in your life and your relationships? How might God want to use what you have learned? What changes might He want you to make? Don't be afraid of these questions. You might be the kind of person who already has a plan all figured out and can't wait to get to it. Or you might be a slower processor open to changes and a new purpose, but you will take time figuring all that out. And there may be those who do nothing and stay the way they have always been.

Whatever you do, take some time to process what you've been through. Talk about it with others you can trust who support you and understand you. Spend time journaling and praying about all of it. Continue to grow when God shows you more healing is needed. God's healing is complete. He doesn't do anything halfway. That includes healing you.

How are you feeling about the things you have learned and the healing you have been through in these sessions? Write a few sentences about it here.

_____

_____

_____

_____

Have you had any thoughts about linking your healing to a purpose in your life? Explain.

_____

_____

_____

_____

What meaning are you beginning to make about what you have been through? Think about a spiritual, emotional, or relational meaning?

_____

_____

_____

_____

Some of you may have felt like Frankl, and you too have been in a season of survival. What is one thing you have learned or experienced that will help you move from survival to a purposeful life?

_____

_____

_____

_____

Day 2

Read: Jude 1:17–25

Our reading for today is all about remembering and taking stock of where we have been. Clearly Jude is warning believers about people who are trying to undermine and destroy what the believers have been learning and cautioning them to contend for the faith. All of us should read this book and understand it for the intended meaning. But like much of the scriptures, we can apply the principles laid out here to other areas of our lives as well.

Jude tells his listeners to look back and remember the things the apostles told them would happen in the last days. He told them to go back and remember, to take time to recall and review the teachings of Christ's apostles.

He also cautions them there will be people who will try to derail their efforts and divide them. We might learn from this admonition as well. Jude lays out for these believers a fourfold plan for contending for their faith. Jude's recommendation for them as they pressed on was to build themselves up, to pray, to stay in God's love, and to wait until God's mercy ushers them into eternity. And we likewise should hold fast to what we have learned and to have the same steadfastness and determination to continue to be our new improved selves until we are perfected in eternity.

Jude's emphasis on prayer is key for us too! It is important to constantly be in prayer for God to affirm who you are in Christ, to guide you through tough transitions and relationship changes. Pray that those relationships might be strengthened and you might have discernment concerning them.

Jude's ending instruction is "Be merciful to those who doubt; save others by snatching them from the fire; to others show mercy, mixed with fear—hating even the clothing stained by corrupted flesh" (verses 22–23). What a challenge it will be to show mercy to those who doubt the changes we are making or the healing we have received. We may have the opportunity to break cycles and "snatch from the fire" to teach those who might otherwise continue the dysfunction we grew up with. And finally, for others, there may need to be strict boundaries set when they refuse to accept our changes and want to continue in dysfunctional ways that corrupt our relationships.

I love how Jude ends the chapter. "Finally, to Him who is able to keep us from stumbling, to Him belongs all the glory for" what we have learned and for our transformation and healing for now and forevermore!

Prayer for Today

Today praise God, and give Him thanks for His transforming power. Thank Him for this group, for this study, and for His ability and kindness to change you, heal you, and keep you from stumbling along the way. Tell Him how you feel about being ushered into eternity whole and lacking nothing, all because of His perfect Son.

Remember!

Ten weeks ago, you began this study hoping for healing and working on growth. You have done a lot of thinking, praying, and discussing. You have been through amazing changes, and you have dealt with some very difficult things. When we spend so much time intentionally working toward improving ourselves and experiencing new ways to look at things, it is good to stop and evaluate where we have been. It is helpful to review what we have learned in these weeks. An effective review includes highlighting principles that stood out to you, noting what changes you want to make, and taking inventory of how you feel about what you learned and how it has changed you.

Besides holding onto to things we have learned about ourselves, our past, and the changes we are determined to make, an effective review also includes building on those things and continually making progress by practicing what we have learned. The best way to do that is to make a plan for keeping ourselves accountable. Without this step, everything you have done becomes nothing more than a few moments of inspiration that result in zero change. And all the work you have poured into this study has been wasted and amounts to nothing.

We are going to make sure that doesn't happen. We are also going to allow for grace. For some of you, the changes you want to make seem overwhelming. It seems you still have so much work to do, so many boundaries to set, so many losses to grieve, and so many relationships to repair. It's OK. Remember almost everything we have done is a process. Do not allow yourself to become overwhelmed thinking you will never be able to change everything you need to. Take time to be grateful for the healing you have received and choose just one thing to work on first. Work on that one thing until you have accomplished what you wanted, then work on the next thing. God will show you what is most important and will guide you along, because remember once more He does not heal halfway.

In this session, we will review some of the lessons and objectives you have already worked on to see how far you have come and to help you prioritize your next steps. Most of this session will be a journaling exercise to keep track of these things for yourself. You will have them to look back over as you continue to grow and change. There is no end to the timeline you can create to do this work. We are never finished working on ourselves until we arrive in heaven in our perfected states. *Won't that be awesome?* Until then, we press on!

In chapter 1 you assessed what coping behaviors you used when life gets tough. Go back and review what behaviors you listed and write them below.

_____

_____

_____

_____

During the course of this study, have there been any changes in your coping behaviors? Are you using those behaviors more? Less? The same? Explain your answer and tell why or why not.

_____

_____

_____

_____

In chapter 2 we discussed childhood unmet needs and healthy and dysfunctional family traits. From the lists below that are taken from chapter 2, check the traits you still see at play in your life today. Look back to chapter 2 for any definitions you may need.

Dysfunctional Family Traits

- _ lack of empathy
- _ poor communication
- _ abuse (all kinds)
- _ addictions
- _ perfectionism
- _ fear or unpredictability
- _ denial
- _ enmeshment / lack of boundaries

Healthy Family Traits

-    clear roles and boundaries
-    effective communication
-    mutual respect and accountability
-    family resilience
-    promoting healthy growth

Which of the traits you checked have you seen growth in since beginning this study? Explain.

_____

_____

_____

_____

Also in chapter 2, we discussed feelings and emotions. Which of the following circumstances do you believe you manage better since this study began? Which do you believe you may need to do more work on? Mark each one B for better or M for more work.

_ Conflict _ Loss or Sadness _ Anger _ Failure _ Success _ Fear

Of the ones you marked M for needing more work, what is one thing you could do to better manage your feelings in those circumstances?

_____

_____

_____

_____

Chapter 3 included a session on your God attachment. After reviewing your thoughts at that time, do you think your God attachment has changed? Why or why not?

_____

_____

_____

_____

In chapter 4, we covered shame and the shame messages you took from events in your past. How much does shame still affect you? In what circumstances does shame still affect you?

_____

_____

_____

_____

Chapter 5 was all about trust, current struggles, and grieving losses. What losses were you able to grieve, and what losses are you still grieving? Explain.

_____

_____

_____

_____

In chapter 6, we talked about healing and being willing to make changes that healing may include. How committed are you to making changes your healing may include? Explain.

_____

_____

_____

_____

Describe your experience in the inner healing exercises.

_____

_____

_____

_____

Chapter 7 explained eliminating the victim mentality from our lives by accepting and fully knowing "who I am in Christ." We discussed the stages of that process of knowing "who I am in Christ." Which stage are you currently in? Explain your answer.

- renewing stage
- change of feelings stage
- change of behavior stage
- completely transformed stage

_____

_____

_____

_____

Briefly review chapter 8, where you learned about the cycles of growth and awareness. This process helped you move from the left cycle to the right cycle as you worked through the study. On your own, however, where are you on which cycle? What do you need to do to either move to the right cycle or stay on the right cycle?

_____

_____

_____

_____

The ninth chapter was all about forgiveness. Describe your experience with the content in that chapter and the forgiveness exercises.

_____

_____

_____

_____

Of all the chapters you have covered in this study and all the work you have done, which section (or sections) was (or were) the most difficult for you and why?

_____

_____

_____

_____

Which chapters were the most beneficial or healing for you and why?

_____

_____

_____

_____

As you look back over your answers in this section, you may see the areas in which you have grown, but you will also see the areas in which you may need more healing. In the remaining space, write a plan for moving forward in your healing and growth. List the areas or topics you want to grow in or need more healing in and what changes you want to make in your life. Finally, write what you will do to accomplish that growth, healing, or change. (Suggestions may include continuing to meet with your group or members of your group for accountability, setting boundaries, healing relationships, working on forgiveness, going through this study again in six months to a year, talking to a counselor or pastor, reading other material on the subject, etc.) Be specific in stating your action to accomplish.

Area/Topic	Growth? Healing? Change?	Action to Accomplish
Ex.: Shame	Healing	Write letter to Uncle Ray. Refuse lies I believed about myself.

Day 3

Review: Genesis 37
Read: Genesis 38–46:30 and Genesis 50:15–21

The scriptures today are lengthy, perhaps more than you may have time for in one sitting. I encourage you to take the time to read these chapters telling the story of Joseph, Jacob's favored son. There is so much in this story that speaks to everything we have been learning. The family dysfunction, beginning with Jacob favoring one son over the others, and the deceit and unhealthy relationships between the brothers showing us family dysfunction have been a part of humankind from the beginning. The events that transpire in these relationships, however, also show us God has been healing family dysfunction from the beginning, as long as there is at least one person willing to listen to God's leading and be obedient to His direction.

I love Joseph's attitude throughout his story. He remains committed to feelings and behaviors that honor God, even in the midst of responding to his brothers' harsh and evil treatment. It may be easy for us to skim over his story, viewing it as an interesting story or even entertainment (especially as some of the songs go through your head from the musical!), but to really stop and imagine what Joseph went through puts everything in a more solemn perspective.

First of all, growing up knowing you were your father's favorite might sound pretty cool, but Genesis 37:4 tells us it may not have been so fun for Joseph. His brothers hated him because he was the favorite. It probably didn't help that their seventeen-year-old brother tattled on whatever they were up to when they were supposed to be tending the flocks or that he told them about his dream of them bowing down to him, so we can't say they didn't have reasons for their feelings. But hate is a strong word, and judging from Joseph's attitude in later chapters, while he may not have been close to his brothers, it doesn't seem he hated them.

Later we see how far their hatred goes when they plot to kill him. He finds himself thrown into a dry cistern and left to die. Plans change when they see travelers coming whom they decide to sell Joseph to as a slave. Now separated from his family and his homeland, Joseph's life becomes a roller coaster of experiences and emotions as he is sold into the house of Potiphar, captain of Pharaoh's guard. There he is wrongly accused and sent to prison where he is amazingly put in charge of the other prisoners and meets the king's cupbearer. Because of His gift of interpreting dreams and his connection with the king's cupbearer, he is called to the king's or Pharaoh's aid where he successfully interprets Pharaoh's dream and endears himself to the king.

After thirteen years of separation from home, Joseph is freed from prison and made powerful in a position of great authority in Pharaoh's service, second in command over Egypt! Here he is responsible for preparing the country of Egypt for a great famine and successfully leading them through such a difficult time. Not only did every Egyptian have enough food during the famine, but there was surplus to feed others outside Egypt as well. And this is where the story comes full circle. We finally see Joseph reunited with his brothers, and eventually his father when they come to buy grain during the famine.

God took Joseph through some circumstances most of us will never experience. He kept His hand on Joseph, honored Joseph's integrity and faithfulness, and favored Joseph with His presence, blessings, and the healing of at least some of the dysfunction in his family relationships.

Prayer for Today

As you pray, thank God for His Holy Word that has survived the generations and allowed us to know this story and so many others of God's faithfulness. Thank Him for the many reminders He gives us that He is faithful and He not only stays with us during trials but uses those trials for our benefit, even when it is hard to see Him working. Ask Him for strength to continue your healing journey so you may carry out the changes He has in store for your healing.

God Wastes Nothing

Did you think through the story in our scripture reading for today to see how God used all of the trials and sufferings Joseph went through? Did you read the verses in chapter 50 where Joseph speaks to his brothers after their father has died and tells them he knows they meant evil against him but that God had greater purposes in all of their actions? It's amazing Joseph had such insight about God's greater plan. Joseph wouldn't have been able to have that perspective if he had been always thinking about all of his brothers' evil actions toward him and their actions landed him in prison and put him through years of separation and suffering. Maybe we sometimes miss what God is doing because we are so caught up with our victimizations and holding grudges.

Whatever you have been through in your life, God will not waste those experiences. They will not be without lessons learned, stories to help comfort or teach others, opportunities for healing, or to put things in place so His will can be accomplished. We may not see those redemptions come quickly. We may not see them in our lifetime. We may not understand why we had to suffer what we did, but we can be sure there either was a purpose in them happening or God used them or is using them to accomplish His purposes.

We are not saying it was God's will that someone sinned against you, hurt you, and caused your life to be turned upside down. We are saying God is not bound by every single thing in life working perfectly according to how He would choose it to in a world without sin. We saw that in the garden. God is not bound by sin. His plans and purposes are not thwarted just because someone sins and causes chaos here on earth. He simply comforts, heals, and takes those experiences into His plans and uses them to His advantage and our benefit.

Since God is omniscient, of course, He knows what things are going to happen. He is never surprised by sin or its results. And the deeper theological questions of why He then allows such things or why doesn't He prevent suffering is beyond the scope of our quest here, but we do know He is a good God with good purposes, and whether He allows or wills things to happen, He has all authority to use them for our good and His purposes. He wastes nothing!

When my girls were young, sometimes they would feel slighted when one got to do something the others didn't or one didn't make a team or something they tried out for. As siblings sometimes do, they would compare their gifts and abilities to each other, thinking the others had it so easy while their life was unfair and unbearable. I would tell them to imagine God had a big, beautiful kitchen filled with colorful recipe cards with each of their names on one. The pictures represented the perfect cake He envisioned when He created them. One might be the most delectable strawberry shortcake, one a decadent chocolate layer cake, and one a colorful confetti cake. God put into each one the exact ingredients and amounts for that perfect cake. Then as they went through life, the variable factors like what temperature they were baked at or how long they stayed in the oven could affect how the cake would turn out. But even if they were baked too hot or burned from being in too long, God always has His ways of stepping in to be sure the finished product is exactly what He purposed all along. All He asks is for our trust in Him and our willingness to go through the fire.

This is a silly little comparison and no doubt has some questionable theology, but there is truth in God's amazing ability to waste nothing we go through in life. We can see in our example of Joseph that God used his own suffering and mistreatment to enable him to have empathy for those who were suffering in the famine. He used a wrongful accusation and prison sentence as lessons when Joseph was put in charge of other prisoners. He used Potiphar's wife to test his moral purity and integrity. He used the two additional years in prison after the cupbearer forgot about him to teach him patience. He used Joseph's willingness to forgive to lead his brothers to humility and repentance. He used the gift of dream interpretation to place Joseph in the right place at the right time, and as a result, Joseph was able to tell Pharaoh about the mighty God he served. God wastes nothing!

Whatever you have been through in your life can be used for God's glory and for the advancement of His purposes. You may not see it now or know about it for years to come, or you may only hear of it on the other side of this life. All God asks is that you accept your story, allow Him to heal and change you, repent, forgive where you need to, and trust He is working it all for a good purpose.

Permit me to tell you the end of the personal story I started in the introduction. It was at a time when I was faced with the most devastating disappointment of my life: the ending of my marriage after thirty-nine years. I sat in my red chair in my office crying out in confusion to God. "How could You let this happen? I have tried to serve You and do all the right things in my life!" My confusion turned to anger and frustration. "You *knew* this was going to happen! You *knew* this all along! You *knew* it years ago and every day since! *How could You let this happen?*"

Now for the rest of that story. Several months ago, I was sitting in that same red chair thanking God for His protection and provision in my life when my words from that day of ranting and crying out to God came back to me. I repeated those words, but with a completely different attitude in my heart. With praise and deep, *deep* gratitude, I said, "You *knew* this was going to happen. You knew it all along. You knew it years ago, and You have prepared me and provided for my every need in every single instance since that day, and You have walked so close beside me, loving me and protecting me every step of the way. Thank You, God, that You knew this all along." I wept tears again, but they were not tears of bitterness or anger. They were tears of joy and gratitude over His faithfulness to me and over the healing that had taken place in me, though my circumstances had not changed.

I still don't know God's purpose or plan in everything, and there are things that have happened in my life that I have to honestly say I don't see anything good coming from. Yet. But I trust Him. I know He is a good God, and He has good purposes. His plans and purposes aren't just good; they're *perfect!* And because I am sure of those things, I don't need to see the outcome. I know He wastes nothing.

What is it in your life you are waiting for God to make something good out of?

_____

_____

_____

_____

We saw where Joseph was slave, prisoner, prosperous, and powerful yet patient, faithful, and forgiving. What parts of Joseph's story do you relate to and why?

_____

_____

_____

_____

What parts of Joseph's story can you not relate to and why?

_____

_____

_____

_____

Do you believe God wastes nothing that happens in our lives? Why or why not, and give examples.

_____

_____

_____

_____

Tell about a time when there was a trial and later you saw how God used it for good.

_____

_____

_____

_____

How do you feel about God knowing ahead of time the trials you would go through? Why do you feel that way?

_____

_____

_____

_____

What would you have to do for you to completely trust God with your future, even those trials He already knows you will face?

_____

_____

_____

_____

What would help you take that next step of trust?

_____

_____

_____

_____

Day 4

Read: John 8:31–36 and Galatians 5:1, 16–26

These verses in John 8 are beautiful reminders of the freedom we have in Christ. Christ is truth. His Word is truth, and it is indeed what sets us free. Notice there is an assumption here to being set free. Verse 1 says, "If you hold to my teaching [then], you are really my disciples." This freedom is pronounced to Jesus's followers, those who hold to His teaching. Once we accept Christ, our freedom is at least fourfold. We are immediately free from the curse of death and the penalty of sin. We are free from the condemnation sin brings. Third, we are free from all the sacrifices, laws, and rituals the old covenant required. And finally, we are free from the bondage of sin as long as we live in this life. We do not have to remain sin's slave. All the powers of sin don't have to own us and enslave us. We are free!

The second reading we had today is a good read for encouragement on what being free looks like. Not so that we might imitate these behaviors, thereby hoping to be free. They are outcomes, results of being free. But there are warnings here to hold steadfastly to the things we have learned and not to turn back to old ways that were in essence bondage for us.

The fifth chapter of Galatians also clues us in to what we can already feel: the tension between flesh and spirit. Always, as long as we live on this earth, we will wrestle with our human side that wants the easy way out, the selfish way, or the path of pleasure or of least resistance. This is part of our fallen nature since the days in the Garden of Eden. We will wrestle with this as long as we are alive and Satan is present to tempt and trick us.

This passage tells us five things we can do to be sure we stay on the right path.

1. Stand firm (verse 1).
2. Don't go backward into the bondage of old ways (verse 1).
3. Walk in the Spirit (verse 16; that's a decision).
4. Keep in step with the Spirit (verse 25; that's the discipline of the decision).
5. Watch your attitude, stay humble, and avoid provocation and jealousy (verse 26).

Thankfully, we have the gift of the Holy Spirit who is here to help us. He is our helper, our counselor, and our guide. He will help us implement the good plans we have made in this study, and He will encourage us to keep going. He will comfort us when people don't respond like we had hoped or when our plans don't work out.

Prayer for Today

Today is all about praise! Thank God for the freedom from sin and the freedom from the bondage of the past. Find as many ways as you can to praise Him today for the blessings of healing and the promise of a new and healthy future!

Freedom from the Past

Freedom! What a wonderful thing! Ever since we have been old enough to crawl or walk, most of us have longed to be free. Free from mother's grasp, free from food we didn't like, free from chores, free from homework and school, free from rules and laws, and … But wait a minute! Our lives are still full of rules, laws, and restrictions! Are we really free?

This uncovers a truth that only the mature know. We have rules and laws to protect us from people in the world who want to be free of all rules and laws. There are people in the world who are selfish and evil and would take every opportunity at every intersection to go first or not stop at all (because they are "free" from that law). So now we have stop signs and laws that require us to stop. If everyone were kind and loving and had the "You go first," "No, you go first!" mentality, we might not need all the laws we have. But there are sin and evil in the world; therefore, there are rules and laws.

The flip side to that scenario is the question of whether those who refuse to be bound by rules and laws are truly free. These people who refuse to obey laws, thinking they are free, pursue the selfish, evil lifestyles, looking out for only themselves, and wind up burdened with chains of debt, broken relationships, jail sentences, addictions, and other bondages. Is that freedom? Of course not! The bondage of sin and unhealthy living is real, and guess what. We are all slaves to it. Not all of us live without restraint or regard for anyone else. But every single one of us has a sinful nature that tries to come out at every turn. That is why we all need a Savior!

The freedom Christ brings us as our Savior is freedom from the death our sins deserve. That freedom is worth more than a million diamond mines, and the best part is that it is free! It costs us nothing, but cost Jesus His life. We can be free from sin by accepting God's free gift of salvation because of Christ's death on the cross that canceled our sin debt. That is an incredible healing from the power of sin!

But remember how we have said, "God desires complete healing"? We can be healed and set free from that sinful past and still be in bondage in other ways. Now these other ways won't keep us out of heaven. Once we have accepted Christ as our Savior, we are sealed by the Holy Spirit and separated as a son or daughter of God and an heir with Christ of all God's blessings and benefits.

Once we are saved, however, the Holy Spirit continues to refine us as Christ's followers. He continues His healing work in us to mold us and make us more like Christ. And this includes freeing us of other "bondages" in our lives. For some, it may be an addiction. For others, it may be cleaning up our language or our attitudes. There are many things that can have hold of us keeping us from enjoying our freedom in Christ through healthy, happy living. That is what this entire study has been about.

Sadly, many of these bondages have been passed down to us through dysfunctional families. The bondage of abuse, addiction, or unhealthy ways of communicating and relating have all been in many of our families. Some of us have suffered as a slave to shame because of events that happened in our lives. The bondage of shame is one the enemy would love to see us continue in.

You have worked hard to define and identify these things and to learn new ways of coping and relating. You have prayed for healing for some of the wounded places that held you captive. You have acknowledged the truth of your past and how it affected you years later, and you have been set free from the past!

For some of you, this freedom feels like you are looking at your life with a new pair of glasses. You are seeing pain more easily in others and can more easily overlook when someone wrongs you. You may be feeling lighter because the shame you carried for so long without knowing it is gone. You might want to tell everyone you know what has happened to you. You might be eager to make some changes in your life now that you are no longer bound by someone else's opinion or some unhealthy identity they placed on you. You are free from the past!

What does it mean to you to be free from the past?

_____

_____

_____

_____

Explain the difference in this study between being set free from the bondage of sin and free from the bondage of the past.

_____

_____

_____

_____

Have you ever been set free from the bondage of sin? If so, share your experience here.

_____

_____

_____

_____

Day 5

Read: John 4:1–42

I have always loved the story of the woman at the well. Although she doesn't typically come up in the list of those Jesus healed, I believe she had a profound healing through their meeting at the well.

The first thing to notice is that verse 4 says Jesus "needed" to go through Samaria. Knowing what we know about the Jews and their avoidance of Samaritans, we might at first assume Jesus was going through Samaria just to show the disciples He didn't approve of discriminating against people and they shouldn't either. And that assumption might be true. But I believe it to be more a result than the reason.

The reason Jesus had to go through Samaria was for this encounter. It was no accident Jesus happened to be there when the woman came for water, especially knowing she wasn't coming at the usual time for drawing water. He knew where she would be and when she would be there.

Once there, their interaction shows her woundedness and His responses. When she arrives to draw water, Jesus asks her for a drink. She acknowledges their cultural differences and the unique and puzzling position in which she finds herself. Imagine the King of glory coming to speak with a woman, and not just a woman but a poor woman, and not just a poor woman but a Samaritan woman—a woman whose entire nation was excommunicated from the Jewish temples and traditions. Their discussion continues as Jesus answers each of her questions gently, sharing more and more about who He is. She is stunned when Jesus tells her things about herself that she evidently had been denying publicly.

Finally, He reveals for the first time that He is the long-awaited Messiah. The result is this woman essentially becomes the first evangelist, since she told everyone she encountered about meeting the Christ and many Samaritans believed in Jesus after that.

As we look at her questions and comments from a counselor's point of view, let's look deeper into the possible meanings behind her questions and comments.

She Says ...	She Means ...
1. "How can *you* ask *me* for a drink?"	1. "I am not good enough to give you a drink."
2. "Where can you get this living water? You have nothing to draw with and the well is deep."	2. "Even if what you say is true, you can't help me."
3. "Are you greater than our father, Jacob, who gave us the well and drank from it himself, as did also his sons and his flocks and herds?"	3. "You don't know my circumstances or my background."
4. "Sir, I can see that you are a prophet. Our fathers worshiped on this mountain but you Jews claim that the place where we must worship is in Jerusalem."	4. "I could never live up to what you require."
5. "I know that Messiah is coming. When He comes, He will explain everything to us."	5. "I might believe the things you are saying but I'll figure it out someday."

After Jesus tells her about her own past with many men and that He is the Messiah, she is so shocked and elated she runs off forgetting her water jar. She is obviously not quiet when she tells people in the town (the same people she typically tries to avoid by fetching water in the heat of the day) because the whole town is running out to see the Messiah she is yelling about. She is changed. Verse

39 tells us many Samaritans first believed because of her testimony, and later after they saw for themselves.

Here is a woman who lived in shame because of her past and current life. She didn't feel good enough about herself to join the other women or even their servant girls in the mornings when they went to get water for their families. Perhaps she had gone before but was ridiculed or shunned because of her immoral lifestyle. Her life was a mess and her relationships a disaster.

We can only imagine the levels of dysfunction she lived in. Yet here was Jesus, the long-awaited Messiah, the Creator of heaven and earth, coming on purpose to talk to her, to heal her, to set her on a new path, and to give her a new life. And although she previously had a reputation that people would avoid and criticize, Jesus chose her to reveal Himself to as the Messiah. Her reputation had changed as she led those around her to the Christ. And although she had before discounted herself as worthy of Jesus's help, she now found herself healed and whole. And she was telling anyone and everyone!

Prayer for Today

Thank God for His presence throughout these past weeks and for His help and healing. Ask Him to continue to be present with His help as you learn to walk as this new person. Ask Him to help you press on and not quit and to be kind and loving toward each other even when others are not kind toward you. Tell Him your desire to serve Him and be more like Him every day.

Expressing the New You!

Congratulations on completing this study. It took a lot of courage to face some of the things you faced. It will take courage to continue to be what you have become in the past ten weeks. You have shared with your group much of your journey and hopefully learned the value of a supportive and vulnerable group experience. One of the greatest values of a group is accountability. It is helpful and biblical to walk alongside each other, knowing standards and goals we have each set for ourselves. It is also helpful and biblical to remind each other of those standards and goals when we perceive someone may be slipping back from them or veering off course.

In this last day of the final week, it will be important to set for yourself a new image or a new vision of this new you. Like the woman at the well, you are changed. You have a new identity. You may have been living in shame before but now are living in freedom from shame. You may have seen yourself as unworthy or less than but are now claiming your identity as worthy and valuable. Perhaps you were untrustworthy and vow to be trustworthy from now on, or maybe you were harsh and critical and by God's grace you will be gentler and accepting. Whatever God has healed you from, whatever He is teaching you and growing you through, it is important to name it and share it.

On day 2 of this week, you were asked to complete a goal chart of things you intend to work on. That chart can be refined. Each task can be broken down into specific steps and more manageable actions. You can use that chart to check in with others in your group, reviewing it periodically together and writing new goals and steps to take as you complete ones above.

Expect there may be some stress as you try on the new you. Remember not everyone will be happy about your changes. Read back through what you will do when you hit those obstacles. You won't do things perfectly every time. Give yourself grace; give others around you grace. When you mess up, own it. Clean up whatever mess you might make. Apologize and get right back on the horse. This is a process, not typically an instant miracle.

Stay determined and keep track of positive changes. Celebrate little victories. Pray constantly. Pray for those whom you have difficulty loving or being kind to. Stay connected to supportive people and support them when they need it. Take time to sit before God asking Him for direction. And focus on who you are in Christ—not who others have said or say you are but who God's Word says you are. Memorize the scriptures that give you inspiration and calm about who you are in Christ, and repeat them until they become reality to you.

You are worthy. Christ has made you worthy. You are enough. Christ has declared you are enough. Nothing you have done or that has been done to you is outside where the grace and salvation of Christ can reach. Nothing in your past is beyond redemption. Nothing. He wastes nothing. In the weeks and months ahead, you will likely begin to see how God used people or experiences in your past to prepare you for difficulties in your life. You may also begin to feel differently about yourself because of God's healing and the work you continue to do in setting boundaries and evaluating relationships. This is the new you emerging, your new identity. And Christ will continue to heal and mold you into His likeness. You will be better able to see others with eyes of truth, yes, but also with eyes of grace. Jesus was both truth and grace. That is also His goal for you.

Looking at your life past this study, are there fears or concerns you have moving forward? Explain.

_____

_____

_____

_____

What are some ways you can lessen the fears and address the concerns?

_____

_____

_____

_____

What do you think will be your biggest challenge? Be specific.

_____

_____

_____

_____

How satisfied are you with the work you have accomplished in this study, the healing you have received, and the new _you_ emerging? Explain.

_____

_____

_____

_____

As you look back when you started this study, describe who you were inside at that time.

_____

_____

_____

_____

If you had to choose three words that sum up who you were, what would they be?

_____

_____

_____

_____

Now that you have completed the study, describe who you are inside.

_____

_____

_____

_____

If you had to choose three words that sum up who you are now, what would they be?

_____

_____

_____

_____

Often when there are programs or experiences of great change, groups have decided to symbolically display their changes individually for the group to celebrate the changes together. Some groups choose an object to represent themselves before and an object to represent themselves after, and some groups make it area specific—only using objects from the forest, the ocean, etc. Your group may choose this type of activity also.

Today so you can have your change recorded, we will use words to describe the changes we have been through. You might know this as cardboard testimonies or flip-up testimonies.

From the three words you wrote above to describe yourself before the study, choose one that best describes you before. Write it in the space below. Be as creative as you want.

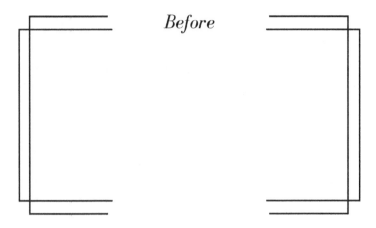

Before

From the three words you wrote above to describe yourself after the study, choose one that best describes you now. Write it in the space below. Be as creative as you want.

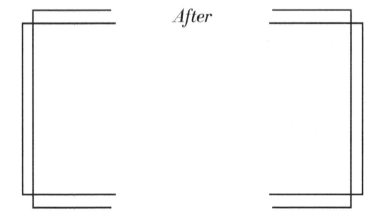

After

Conclusion

Ten weeks can feel like a long time. But ten weeks can also feel like a short amount of time to spend on things you have been wrestling with for a lifetime. Is it possible to be healed and changed of so much brokenness in such a short amount of time? The answer is both yes and no.

It is possible to be healed of the shame and pain of the brokenness in ten weeks. That answer is yes. Many of you have been. That healing is real, and don't allow the enemy to confuse you or cause you to doubt that. It may not be possible, however, to completely change in ten weeks those patterns of thinking, feeling, or behaving that the dysfunction of the past has caused. It may take months to recognize triggers or believe you are who God says you are, instead of who others continue to believe you are.

You have worked hard, reaching deep within yourself and facing difficult and painful memories. You have dared to be vulnerable, acknowledging things were not always as perfect as they might have seemed. Your hard work will pay off in the weeks ahead as you practice managing your feelings as we talked about in chapter 2, as you grow your attachment to God, discussed in chapter 3, or as you recognize and refuse to allow the shame messages to control you, which was the essence of chapter 4.

This will be your first evidence that change is occurring and you are becoming a more emotionally healthy person. Of course, it won't happen perfectly. At times, you may experience a few days of a familiar funk before you realize you have been allowing that old shame to drive your feelings. The fact that you recognize it and evict the shame that no longer belongs is huge growth. The time it takes to recognize what the funk is all about will diminish until you no longer own one bit of the shame that used to consume you.

In the next few weeks, I hope you will begin to see your true worth. You may not feel like you own the world just yet, and for sure your life will not be without problems. But look back to chapter 6 and don't let Satan tell you God didn't heal you. Healing and being set free from shame were immediate yet different from learning to live shame free. For some, the changing will take longer than others. However, two things are certain. One is that your salvation will always be the greatest healing. When you are tempted to doubt your emotional healing, you can always be grateful for being healed from the sentence of death and permanent separation from God. And the second less-positive certainty is there will always be struggles and hard times in this world.

When difficulties come again, the key to not slipping back into old shame messages and ineffective ways of coping was covered in chapter 7 where we emphasized knowing who you are in Christ. And knowing who you are in Christ becomes more natural as you believe He really loves you! Learning to feel secure in who Christ says you are will keep you grounded when you are triggered and feel forced into a family role you are trying to grow out of, as we talked about in chapter 8.

As time goes on and you become more emotionally healthy, I hope you will see some purpose in your past. Often our own changes are solidified when we help others change. The purpose and new you we discussed in chapters 9 and 10 may slowly be seen as relationships improve and are mended. I hope you will see the broken pieces put back together and realize God uses every chip to mold and repair perfectly for your good and His glory. You will be stronger, more useful, and more beautiful. Where there were cracks and brokenness, there will be valuable and beautiful gold, restored as only the Master Potter can.

As I have prayed for you, dear reader, throughout the writing of this book, I will be praying for you in the days ahead. May you find gold in every part of your story.

Appendix A

Group Leader Notes

Welcome, group leaders, and thank you for agreeing to lead this study for the next ten weeks. It is wise for you to look through the material ahead of time and see if there are any topics that might raise questions for you before leading a session. Please do not attempt to lead a group without sufficient personal healing and growth. Rather, check with your pastor, ministry leader, or professional counselor before leading a group.

You may choose to add two weeks to this study to make a twelve-week study. You may add a week to the beginning to pass out books, assign the first chapter, familiarize the group on the weekly assignments of reading and completing each day's questions, and allow members to discuss how they are feeling about doing such a study. The first week is also important to read and discuss the group agreements and pray together as you begin this study.

After the final chapter, another week may be beneficial for the group to discuss how they have grown overall, what healing they received, and how they hope it will impact their lives. A final prayer for healing to continue and for the courage to continue growth.

You will find listed below some things to consider for each chapter. Prayer is the most important preparation for each session of this study. I have prayed much over the topics, the questions, the scriptures, and also those who will lead and who will participate. God is a great healer. He can use any one and any circumstance to bring healing. May He do so in your groups.

Meeting Structure Notes

Each week when you meet you will go through the discussion questions for each day. Some discussion questions will take up more time than others, especially as your group becomes more comfortable with sharing. As the leader, it is helpful to know ahead of time which days you feel may require more time. It is also helpful to get to know your members and encourage the nontalkers to participate, as well as move the discussion away from anyone who seems to take up most of the discussion.

A typical group meeting would be two hours long and be structured something like this: Allow ten minutes for opening and ten minutes for closing (prayer, announcements, reminders of topics to be discussed, conclusion, etc.). That will leave a little over an hour and a half for the discussion questions. Each chapter has five days, which allows about twenty minutes for each day's questions. Plan each week according to the weight of the material. For example, some of the days in chapter 6 may require more time. Feel free to gauge the responses and skip over some of the questions to allow more time for sharing the heavier topics. As mentioned earlier, you can always make the study longer than ten or twelve weeks to spend more than one week on some topics. Survey your group ahead of time for their availability and interest.

The following prompts may be helpful in facilitating different aspects of discussion issues:

- Thank you. Now let's hear from someone else.
- What were some other responses to that question?
- Let's give someone else a chance to share.
- You each will have about two to three minutes to share.
- Excuse me. You have about one more minute.
- We seem to be getting offtrack. Let's go to the next discussion question.
- Lynn and Tricia, we haven't heard from you. Would one of you care to share?
- This seems to be a difficult subject matter to open up about. Let's stop and ask the Holy Spirit to help us.
- We are running out of time and I want to be sure everyone has time to share, so let's try to keep our comments brief.

Chapter 1 Leader Notes

Main concepts: assessment, self-honesty, and vulnerability.

Here we begin to assess our lives and our current life circumstances. We will also begin to assess our family of origin. For some, this may feel like a betrayal. Saying what is true is not the same thing as betrayal. It is possible for families to have unhealthy traits and still love each other. It is also possible to be honest about our families without judging. Sometimes acknowledging the truth is the most loving thing to do. It can be the beginning of change and healing.

Tips for Discussion

This chapter sets the stage for group members to be open and honest with themselves and others and therefore requires both courage and trust. Reminding the group of their agreements and the importance of confidentiality within the group will create trust and build it as the weeks go on.

Chapter 2 Leader Notes

Main concepts: deeper assessment and learning.

This week we are asked to be more specific about how our families handled certain circumstances as we also learn about feelings and emotions and how healthy families behave. Some families place high importance on image management, meaning they are to appear as though everything is OK all the time even though it may not be. Family members can become very loyal to such unspoken family rules and will often repeat them in their own families in adulthood.

Tips for Discussion

Remind group members that staying loyal to unspoken family rules that are unhealthy or untrue is living in denial. It is simply denying the truth and does not benefit anyone. Encourage the group to simply speak what is true in this safe space.

Chapter 3 Leader Notes

Main concepts: introspection and spiritual self-awareness.

As we continue to delve into our early memories of family, we begin to turn our focus more inward. Instead of looking at family dynamics where we can be bystanders or onlookers who simply observe what is going on, we are pressing in to realize how any dysfunction affected *me*. What messages did I receive from those interactions or lack of? Then we turn again to discover how we may have projected those messages as coming from God. This can be a powerful week, but also one that can be easily ignored. Encourage the group to dig deep and invite the Holy Spirit into the process.

Tips for Discussion

As part of your discussion this week, talk about how God designed the family to operate as a mirror of our relationship with Him. His design was for children to learn obedience from wise, loving parents so that as adults, we would practice obedience to our Heavenly Father. Within His character, God possesses both the gentle, nurturing traits of a mother as well as the authoritative and firm traits of a father. However, because we live in a sinful and fallen world, no earthly mother or father will ever fulfill their roles as perfectly as our Heavenly Father does. But He is able to heal and restore our wounded places and distorted messages.

Chapter 4 Leader Notes

Main concepts: shame and shame messages.

This week group members may begin to make connections they have never made before. They may begin to recognize that beliefs they have about themselves originated from trauma or significant events in their past. For some, this may be great news they will be able to grow from, while for others, it may be confusing and require longer processing. It is important for group members to be patient as these connections are made. No doubt, they have lived many years believing these distorted messages, so taking time to examine them and pray over them is wise and practical.

Tips for Discussion

Help group members recognize that the sins that birth shame in our lives are among the best tools in spiritual warfare. The enemy considers it a huge victory if he can get any of us to believe we are mistakes or failures and that God has either forgotten us or abandoned us or cares for everyone else except us. Many group members have worn these beliefs and shame like a second skin. It has become who they are. The goal is to begin to see the shame not as a part of them but as something that does not belong to them, placed there by someone else, and something God's grace can cover and take away.

Chapter 5 Leader Notes

Main concepts: trust and suffering.

The concepts of trust and how we experience suffering come down to whether we believe God is loving and sovereign. His purpose for everything that happens on this earth has little to do with our fleeting time on earth and everything to do with His kingdom and His glory. If we can move toward that perspective, we will begin to view suffering differently and our trust will grow. He has already provided a glorious and perfect eternity for us that will erase all memories of our suffering here. And He has already made it possible that nothing on this earth, not even death, can stop us from getting to that glorious eternity. As referred to earlier, Satan wants to destroy our trust in people here because it destroys our trust in God.

Tips for Discussion

This chapter could easily take two weeks to discuss. When it comes to suffering and recognizing all of the losses that can result from suffering, it can take some time to process. Your group members may want to spend extra time in examining the losses they have experienced so they may be grieved properly. That is not to say they will be forgotten or never felt again but acknowledged and grieved to the point of acceptance.

Chapter 6 Leader Notes

Main concepts: honesty, courage, and trust.

This week we may not see the words *honesty, courage,* or *trust* mentioned much in these sessions, but they are each critical to the experience. Being honest with ourselves is crucial throughout this study, but God's promise to restore brokenness and bring healing requires trust in Him. And He is trustworthy. We can trust Him to keep His promises. ("He heals the brokenhearted and binds up their wounds" (Psalm 147:3 ESV)).

Tips for Discussion

The discussion this week needs an extra dose of gentleness and grace as the group members will be sharing their stories as well as asking for healing. A reminder of confidentiality is important. Encourage the members to use the talking points cards, and depending on how many group members you have, suggest a time limit so everyone has a chance to share. You may want to decide ahead of time how much time to allow for each day's discussion and allow extra time for days 1, 4, and 5, if possible. Refer to the "Meeting Structure Notes" above for more tips.

Chapter 7 Leader Notes

Main concepts: be alert and practice!

We have turned a corner in our study, and this week begins living in the newness of healing and restoration. We have lived in our old shame messages and used our old coping skills for so long that it will take time and practice to think and act differently. We are human, and old habits die hard. Asking the Holy Spirit to quicken our minds and paying attention to His promptings will hasten the changes His healing has set in motion. Practice makes perfect!

Tips for Discussion

Two things will be helpful in this week's discussion. First, there may be some confusion as to why we need to act differently if God has healed us. Wouldn't that naturally come with it? It is true God's grace and healing immediately cover all of the shame we have carried. It has always been there. He has always been there. God has not changed. It was our inability to see the dysfunction, the shame, and our inability to recognize God as He really is, instead of our distorted view of Him. He has done His part, and now we retrain our thinking to see Him as He is and see ourselves as He sees us.

Second, it will be helpful and interesting to have different members share the ways they are putting this into practice. Some may wear an elastic band and snap their wrist when they catch themselves believing an old shame message. Some may put a quarter in a jar each time. Some may post a note on their bathroom mirror to remember who God is or who they are in Christ. There are many different ways to practice and get the most from our healing. Sharing these ideas can be fun.

Chapter 8 Leader Notes

Main concepts: relapse, triggers, and roles.

We don't actually use the term *relapse* in this chapter, but the concept is throughout. Like we talked about last week, it will take practice to begin seeing ourselves as God sees us, and none of us will do it perfectly in this life. It will be important to grasp the idea that we can catch ourselves and the Holy Spirit will be faithful to nudge us when we return to our "stinkin' thinkin'." Knowing we can exit the cycle of awareness and live free of shame is what our healing is all about.

Tips for Discussion

This week may prove to be a lively discussion, especially if the concept of family roles is new to people. It can be very eye-opening to see how family members have portrayed a particular role without knowing it. But it can also be frustrating to recognize it, not want to portray that role any longer, only to be sucked back into it when we are around family. Spend time discussing how members intend to approach this dilemma, what has worked and what has not, and maybe even role-play some of the more common roles in the group.

Chapter 9 Leader Notes

Main concept: forgiveness.

It is true we need more than a week on almost all of these topics, but none more than forgiveness. We are all called to do it, none of us deserves it, yet many of us rarely think about it much less practice it intentionally. When we really stop to think about it or meditate on forgiveness, we see the vertical barriers between ourselves and those who have hurt us completely disintegrate. Immediately the barrier becomes a horizontal one and we are all together below the line with Jesus Christ being the only person above the line. It is only by His grace and the sacrifice of His life that any of us can come across the line. And we should be trying to bring as many people with us as possible, even those who have hurt us. I'm not saying we bring our rapists or murderers to church. But in time, as we forgive and God's spirit of forgiveness and reconciliation grows within us, our hearts will become concerned for the salvation of people we would never have thought of before. Because none of us is worthy.

Tips for Discussion

This may be another challenging session. Encourage the group to be patient and allow others to express their thoughts and feelings without judging them. How we view forgiveness can change over time as we heal and grow. What we say and how we feel today may not be the same weeks, months, or years from now. Remind the group forgiveness is a process but the decision to forgive can be immediate. "God, I know You call me to forgive, and I want to be obedient to that. Right now, I am struggling with that, and I need Your help. I am still angry and hurting. Help me to grieve the losses and prepare my heart to forgive. I will continue to work on this as You help me."

Chapter 10 Leader Notes

Main concepts: assessment, purpose, and freedom.

Coming to the end of a study like this can feel overwhelming. Group members have shared with each other things they may have never shared before. A lot of hard emotional work has been done. There may be a fear of going back to old ways or of feeling alone trying to live in freedom without the group. All of these feelings are normal. Hopefully there is also an excitement for the future and praise for what God has done. It will be good to go back through the workbook yearly or so to measure growth and see the changes made. Group members can also go back and spend more time on any topic where they need more healing or further work.

Tips for Discussion

Allow members time to express how they feel about the study ending. The last exercise of sharing their before and after words can be very powerful, and sufficient time should be allowed for these expressions. Encourage the group to continue their growth and healing journey by going back through the study and doing further work wherever and whenever they feel the need.

Appendix B

Agreements

Agreements with Myself

1. I agree to *pray* and ask God to lead me through this healing process.
2. I agree to be *patient* with myself throughout this journey, allowing God's grace to cover any setbacks or places where healing takes time.
3. I agree to *courageously* allow God to shed light on things in my past Satan is fighting to keep in the dark.
4. I agree to be *honest* with myself and others.

Signed _____ Date _____

Group Agreements

1. I agree to *attend* all sessions and to be on time. If I miss a session, I will complete the assignment and tell the leader ahead of time that I must miss. If I must miss more than two sessions in a row, I will wait and join a later group.
2. I agree I will do the *weekly work* (even if I must miss) and will participate in group discussions for the benefit of everyone.
3. I agree to *pray* for this group as God brings people to my mind.
4. I agree to strict group *confidentiality*. I will not talk about things that are shared in group outside the group sessions.

5. I agree to give and receive *feedback,* as appropriate, in a compassionate manner, speaking and receiving the truth in love.
6. I agree *not to isolate,* shut down, or quit if my feelings become overwhelming. Rather, I will speak up in group or talk to the group leader privately.
7. By keeping all these agreements, I agree to be a *trustworthy* group member for others on their journey.

Signed _____ Date _____

Notes

Introduction

[1] Robert G. Morgan, *The Red Sea Rules*. Nashville, Tennessee, Thomas Nelson Publishing, 2014.

[2] Kelly Richman-Abdou, "Kintsugi: The Centuries-Old Art of Repairing Broken Pottery with Gold," My Modern Met, March 5, 2022. https://mymodernmet.com/kintsugi-kintsukuroi/.

Chapter 1

[1] C. R. Snyder, *Coping: The Psychology of What Works*. Oxford, UK: Oxford University Press, 1999.

[2] Monica McGoldrick, *The Genogram Casebook: A Clinical Companion to Genograms: Assessment and Intervention*. New York: W. W. Norton & Company, 2016.

[3] John Ortberg, "Life in the Kingdom." Plenary Session, American Association of Christian Counselors, Nashville, Tennessee, October 11, 2019.

[4] Ortberg, 2019.

Chapter 2

[1] Joseph C. Segen, MD. The *McGraw-Hill Concise Dictionary of Modern Medicine*. 1st ed. New York: McGraw-Hill Medical, 2005.

[2] "Can You Break the Cycle of Dysfunctional Families?" Greg Thomas, *The Good News* 12, no. 6, (Nov/Dec 2007): 14–17.

[3] Vanessa Sacks, MPP, et al. "The Family Environment and Adolescent Well-Being." Child Trends. November 2014. https://www.childtrends.org/wp-content/uploads/2015/08/2014-52FamilyEnvironmentRB.pdf.

Chapter 3

1   Susan M. Johnson and Valerie E. Whiffen, *Attachment Processes in Couple and Family Therapy*. New York: the Guilford Press, 2003.

2   Silvia M. Bell and Mary D. Salter Ainsworth. "Infant Crying and Maternal Responsiveness." *Child Development* 43, no. 4 (1972): 1171–90. https://doi.org/10.2307/1127506.

3   Mark Wolynn. *It Didn't Start with You: How Inherited Family Trauma Shapes Who We Are and How to End the Cycle*. New York: Penguin Books, 2016.

4   Tim Clinton, EdD, and Gary Sibcy, PhD. *Attachments: Why You Love, Feel, and Act the Way You Do*. Nashville, Tennessee: Thomas Nelson, 2009.

5   Tim Clinton, EdD, and Joshua Straub, PhD. *God Attachment: Why You Believe, Act, and Feel the Way You Do about God*. New York: Howard Books, 2010.

Chapter 4

1   Lewis B. Smedes. *Shame and Grace: Healing the Shame We Don't Deserve*. San Francisco: Harper One, 2009.

2   H. Norman Wright, MRE. *The Complete Guide to Crisis & Trauma Counseling: What to Do and Say When It Matters Most*. Bloomington, Minnesota: Bethany House Publishers, 2011.

3   Wright, *Crisis & Trauma Counseling*, 192–211.

Chapter 5

1   Carolyn Custis James, *The Gospel of Ruth: Loving God Enough to Break the Rules*. Grand Rapids, Michigan: Zondervan, 2008. 132.

2   Bob Sorge, *The Fire of Delayed Answers: Are You Waiting for Your Prayers to Be Answered?* Kansas City, Missouri: Oasis House, 1996.

3   Timothy Keller @timkellernyc. Twitter, April 2020. https://twitter.com/timkellernyc/status/1251911027031183360?lang=en.

4   Elisabeth Kübler-Ross and David Kessler. *On Grief and Grieving: Finding the Meaning of Grief through the Five Stages of Loss*. New York: Scribner, 2014.

Chapter 7

[1] Judith S. Beck. *Cognitive Behavior Therapy: Basics and Beyond.* 3rd ed. New York: Guilford Press, 2020, 4–5.

[2] *Who I Am in Christ, KJV.* http://delivertheword.com/whoiaminchrist/. Used with permission. http://delivertheword.com/about/.

Chapter 8

[1] Henry Cloud, PhD, and John Townsend, PhD. *Boundaries: When to Say Yes, How to Say No to Take Control of Your Life.* Grand Rapids, Michigan: Zondervan, 2017.

[2] Michael P. Nichols and Richard C. Schwartz. *Family Therapy: Concepts and Methods.* 4th ed. Needham Heights, Massachusetts: Allyn and Bacon, 1984, 44.

Chapter 9

[1] Fred Luskin, PhD. *Forgive for Good: A Proven Prescription for Health and Happiness.* New York: Harper Collins Publishers, 2002, 80.

[2] Everett L. Worthington. *Dimensions of Forgiveness: Psychological Research and Theological Perspectives.* Radnor, Pennsylvania: Templeton Foundation Press, 1998.

Chapter 10

[1] Victor E. Frankl. *Man's Search for Meaning.* Boston, Massachusetts: Beacon Press, 2006.

Printed in the United States
by Baker & Taylor Publisher Services